# AMERICAN SOCIAL PROBLEMS

# AMERICAN SOCIAL SCIENCE SERIES

## AMERICAN ECONOMIC LIFE
By HENRY REED BURCH

A study of our economic problems from the civic and social point of view.

## AMERICAN SOCIAL PROBLEMS
By HENRY REED BURCH and S. HOWARD PATTERSON

An introductory sociological study of American civilization.

## PROBLEMS OF AMERICAN DEMOCRACY
By HENRY REED BURCH and S. HOWARD PATTERSON

A combined treatment of the political, economic, and social questions of the day.

# AMERICAN SOCIAL PROBLEMS

## AN INTRODUCTION TO THE STUDY OF SOCIETY

BY

## HENRY REED BURCH, Ph.D.

SOMETIME FELLOW IN ECONOMICS, UNIVERSITY OF PENNSYLVANIA
HEAD OF DEPARTMENT OF HISTORY AND COMMERCE
WEST PHILADELPHIA HIGH SCHOOL FOR BOYS
PHILADELPHIA

AND

## S. HOWARD PATTERSON, A.M.

DEPARTMENT OF HISTORY AND COMMERCE
WEST PHILADELPHIA HIGH SCHOOL FOR BOYS
PHILADELPHIA

New York

## THE MACMILLAN COMPANY

1925

*All rights reserved*

HN
64
.8944

Norwood Press
Set up and electrotyped by J. S. Cushing Co.
Norwood, Mass., U. S. A.

302

To

SIMON N. PATTEN

9254

# PREFACE

THE stress of modern education upon the social sciences has become increasingly evident during the present decade to all students of secondary education. Whether it be the historical, the political or the economic side that is emphasized, the tendency of such study is always to bring to light the outstanding features of American civilization. In fact, it is now everywhere recognized that the very existence and permanency of our institutions is conditioned upon a sound understanding of present American problems.

This book has grown out of the attempt to socialize one phase of secondary education and to bring it into harmony with present day demands. It is designed to meet the needs of an elementary course in the study of society — especially of American society. A conscious attempt has been made to emphasize the social aspect of American life, rather than the political or the economic. Although the three phases naturally overlap and are in many cases inseparably interwoven, the main stress has always been placed upon the social point of view. This has been consistently emphasized and logically developed in the discussion of the problems presented.

The method of treatment has been evolutionary and historical, because growth and development is the very essence of social institutions. It is also hoped that this

vii

method of approach and the material presented will help to meet the demand for what has been termed "socialized history." The aim has always been to guide and suggest, while the language employed is easily within the beginner's comprehension.

Philadelphia, May 1, 1918.

# TABLE OF CONTENTS

# AMERICAN SOCIAL PROBLEMS

## CHAPTER I

### INTRODUCTION

**The Social Ideal**. — The ideal of society in the twentieth century is that of social betterment, and he is greatest among his fellows who best serves their truest *The older* interests. But such an attitude was not always *attitude.* openly accepted. The modern ideal, already rooted in the past, was overshadowed for several centuries by the apparently conflicting principle of individualism. That is, the advance of the individual, rather than the betterment of society, was the direct and conscious aim of most of man's activities. This individualistic spirit was the natural reaction against the principle of authority that slowly grew up during the Middle Ages. With the rebirth of learning, known as the Renaissance, the minds of men began to acquire a new freedom, to cast off the bonds of authority and the shackles of superstition. Thus the individualistic attitude, fostered by intellectual development, found its way through reformation into religion, through revolution into government and through economic reorganization into industry. Its development was therefore logical, and it is not difficult to understand how the interest of the individual grew in importance while that of the group to which he belonged correspondingly declined.

However, after centuries of experiment, individualism has been tried in the balance and found wanting. The The period world is now in a period of transition toward anof transition. other stage of development which we may call that of socialization. Under the *laissez faire* or " let alone " system of politics the women of England toiled under an industrial day of twelve and fourteen hours, while " the bitter cry of the children " made government regulation imperative. In our own day groups of individuals have monopolized and exploited for their personal gain the free gifts of nature so that the voice of the socialist and single taxer is heard throughout the land. Antitrust laws, interstate commerce acts, and industrial and price-fixing regulations begin to give us the dawning shock of paternalism. Regulation has become necessary because the life of mankind is a group life; no man is a law unto himself. It is right for men to exercise the rights of life, liberty and the pursuit of happiness only when such action does not interfere with the corresponding rights of others. Thus, intemperance is no longer a matter of individual concern but of social regulation, because the families of such unfortunates are not only deprived of their rights to life and the pursuit of happiness, but also because they become an additional charge on the public expense. Again, the tipsy engineer holds the lives of hundreds of others in his unsteady hand. The frontiersman of yesterday slaughtered his own cattle and baked his own bread but, to-day, the city consumer serves upon his table articles of food prepared in many distant places, by many different hands. Hence pure food laws become necessary to social welfare. Society must protect itself against the extreme individualist whether he be monopolist, spendthrift or food adulterator.

Democracy and liberty for all are not assured until every individual in society realizes his duty toward other members of his group. The individual and the group are reciprocal. Each exists for the benefit The new ideal. of the other and their interests must harmonize if social welfare is to be attained. The monk of the Middle Ages, immured in his hermit cell, might work out his own individual salvation while the social group — the world around him — went perhaps to perdition. The twentieth century ideal, however, is that of rendering social service, and he is greatest in society who best serves his fellows. This modern ideal is the antithesis of medieval isolation. It is the ideal of socialization — the twentieth century spirit of Christianity.

**The Study of Society.** — Since the dawn of civilization man has sought an explanation of the world about him.

Early writers.
The early literature of each race, such as the mythologies of the Chaldeans and of the Greeks, has its own national and characteristic explanation. Existing institutions and codes of law are explained in terms of some mythical lawgiver like the Spartan Lycurgus. From the days of ancient Israel is heard the story of oppression, and prophets of old from Moses to Amos lift up their voices in protest against the social evils of the day. Each age has dreamed its own Utopia which the march of centuries has not yet brought to pass. Among the early Greeks, Plato imagined an ideal " Republic " in which the just man could live in happy security, while the drones worked, the soldiers policed and the philosophers ruled. He was followed by the more practical and less idealistic Aristotle who, as tutor of Alexander the Great, had an opportunity to visit the ancient world and make a comparative study of the constitutions of the various city-states existing at that time. In his book called " Politics " appears the oft-quoted statement that " man is a political animal," — a being to whom political association is natural.

It will be observed that these early views are interesting, but that many of them lack proof and conviction.

The rise of science.
There is a great mass of writing in all ages and in many lands upon social problems and conditions. Much is fragmentary and imaginative, but some of the material is sufficiently orderly and complete to be called an embryotic science of society. It is only within the last century, however, that a true science of society has come into being. Let us then inquire into the nature of a

Nevertheless, in spite of these handicaps, the science of society has progressed wonderfully during the last half century. / The modern science of society aims to study social conditions as they exist, to understand the principles at work and to formulate laws accordingly. ( Before the engineer builds his bridge across the river he must understand thoroughly the theory of the strength of materials, otherwise his structure will collapse and result in great loss of life and property. Similarly, before we seek to solve the problems of the feeble-minded, the criminal and the poor, we must understand the laws of heredity and of environment. Otherwise our social structure will be unsteady. Behind individual fluctuations the great law of averages holds good. The modern science of society, therefore, enables us to understand the true significance of such vital problems as immigration, poverty, divorce, prison reform and other social phenomena of everyday life.

*The progress attained.*

A society is a group of individuals enjoying conscious relations with each other. Mere habitation of a common economic environment is not sufficient to cause a people to constitute a society. They must perceive their mutual relation and their common lot. Furthermore, a society is not synonymous with a nation; although a nation may constitute a society. There may be many associations within a nation, such as political parties, industrial organizations and religious associations. A society is an association. The realization of the similarity of the members of a group to each other is called " consciousness of kind " and constitutes the tie which binds the society together. Thus, a religious association is a society bound together by the principle of " consciousness of kind."

**Meaning of society:** *Definition.*

science and observe how it differs from mere speculat
In the first place, science is really a method of investiga
rather than a body of subject matter. Its essential
ments are the careful observation of data, the accu
classification of phenomena and the observance of
quence, that is, the repetition of the same phenom
under the same conditions. In the development o
science an hypothesis or unproved theory is formula
which is tested by repeated experiments and conti
observation. After many such confirmations a scien
law arises. Thus the science of astronomy emerged fi
the superstitions of medieval astrology, just as the scie
of modern chemistry emerged from alchemy when Ba
insisted upon the experimental method of study rat
than the deductive logic of antiquity.

The study of human society was slow to develop int
science because of the complex and human character
the subject matter. The physical and natural *The mo*
sciences deal with matter, while the science of so- *science*
ciety deals with man. Matter may be dissected *society:*
*How ha*
and analyzed, but man is ofttimes a creature of *capped.*
whims and fancies. It is easy to predict how matter
react under given conditions, but it is often hazardous
foretell man's conduct. Furthermore, the student of so
problems is handicapped by the element of personal f
ing and preconceived notions. Prejudice and perso
bias retard the development of social science beca
science is impersonal. The aim of science is the discov
of truth which must be accepted regardless of perso
opinion. Many social reforms have therefore failed
cause they represented individual ideals rather than sci
tific knowledge.

On the other hand, mere possession of a common religion is not in itself, under all circumstances, sufficient to constitute a unified society, because Christendom is *Examples.* composed of many societies. Again, allegiance to one sovereign and one flag is not in itself sufficient to constitute one society because the great British Empire, with its numerous and loyal colonial possessions, is a union of many societies, — not one organic whole. In the world of nature, a forest of pine trees is not a society because there is no mentality or intelligence capable of realizing similarity. There is no consciousness of relationship. On the other hand, a colony of ants and a swarm of bees do constitute societies because they enjoy conscious relationships.

The study of society is generally called sociology. From what has been said it is easy to see that this subject is a study of the process of association; that is, a study **The field** of group life in any form in which it may con- **of study:** sciously exist either in the past or in the present. *Social evolution.* It therefore comprises a study both of the past evolution and of the present organization of societies. In the first place, the study of society seeks to understand the origin and development of our great social institutions such as the state, the church and the family. How, for example, has the family become what it is to-day? It did not always exist in its present form. Or, how has American society of to-day developed such undesirable phenomena as divorce, illiteracy and criminality? Certainly these were not characteristic of our early Puritan ancestors. The present can only be understood by a knowledge of the past. Many of the causes and social forces of the past are operating to-day or have left an indelible impress upon modern social life.

The other side of our study is to investigate the present day organization of society in order clearly to comprehend *Social or-* the structure and functions of existing institu-*ganization.* tions. How is American society organized at the present moment? What are the relations between the different parts of our social system, such as the family, the church, the state and the school? What is the internal organization of each of these institutions? A study of social organization attempts to answer these questions, and thus to throw light upon present day social problems. Such a study will enable us, for example, not only to understand the relation between the family and the school with the resulting overlapping of functions, but also to comprehend the internal structure of each and the task to which each is peculiarly adapted. Armed with a knowledge of principles, the student of sociology will approach the study of modern social problems with the scientific spirit and with the ability to offer effective remedies for social evils and abuses.

**Kindred Subjects.** — Allied to the study of society are the subjects of history, economics and politics. We may *Other social* thus speak of sociology and her " allies." His-*studies.* tory is the study of the development of the past and is one of the laboratories of the sociologist. Again, while history aims at a complete record of events and a true picture of past conditions, sociology seeks to formulate general laws and principles. Indeed sociology may be said to have begun as a philosophy of history. Two distinct social sciences, dealing especially with modern problems and social conditions, are economics and political science. Economics studies the twin problems of wealth and welfare and investigates man's activities relating thereto. Since the whole modern world is wealth-producing, this subject occupies a vital position among the social sciences. Political science deals only with one form of human association, namely the state, which is perhaps the most imposing of all social institutions. Politics is the science of government, while civics deals with concrete political questions.

The foundation stones of the science of society are (1) the science of life and (2) the science of mind. Biology is the science of the world of life, of which the human species is merely a part. A study of biology will show that much of the body-structure of man, like many of his mental reactions, can be traced back to the lower animals. The science of mind is called psychology. A study of this subject will enable the student of society to understand how men feel and act in groups. Of course, the psychologist is interested particularly in the mind of the individual, while the sociologist is chiefly concerned with the mind of the whole group. The social mind, illustrated by public opinion, fashion and the mob spirit, comes within the range of social psychology. Psychology will also help the student of society to understand the origin and development of instincts which find social expression in family life, war and patriotism.

The foundation stones.

Accordingly, in the following pages, we shall proceed to investigate the origin of man both in his physical structure and in his mental development. In the light of the principles thus ascertained, we shall then examine the more important social problems of American civilization.

## QUESTIONS FOR DISCUSSION

1. Show how early institutions were communistic.
2. Show how the period introduced by the Renaissance was individualistic.
3. What do we call the third stage of development?
4. What is the social ideal?
5. How should it mold our idea of the good citizen?
6. Give some actual illustrations of how the interests of the individual and of society could conflict.
7. Was the ascetic life of the Middle Ages a good life?
8. Name some social services of the monks.
9. In what book did Plato formulate his ideas on government?
10. What is the name of Aristotle's work?
11. Name other social philosophers.
12. What is the scientific method?
13. How does a science differ from philosophy?
14. How does a social science differ from a physical science?
15. What does the "law of averages" mean?
16. What is necessary to make a science out of philanthropy?
17. Define a society.
18. What makes it a society?
19. Give some faulty conceptions of society.
20. Give some illustrations of animal societies.
21. What are the two problems in a study of society?
22. Why is a knowledge of the past important?
23. How is the range of sociology wider and how narrower than that of history?
24. Name the social sciences.
25. Define and show the relation of each of the others to sociology.
26. Name, define and show the importance of the two foundation sciences of sociology.
27. What does social psychology emphasize?

## TOPICS FOR SPECIAL REPORT

1. Plato's ideal republic.
2. The social studies of Aristotle.

3. Langland's "Piers Ploughman" and More's "Utopia."
4. The ascetic ideal of the Middle Ages.
5. The rise of the scientific method (*e.g.* under Bacon).
6. The use and misuse of statistics.
7. Animal societies (*e.g.* bees and ants).

### REFERENCES

Ross, E. A. "Sin and Society."

Giddings, F. H. "Elements of Sociology."

Ross, E. A. "Foundations of Sociology."

Hayes, E. C. "Introduction to a Study of Sociology."

Wright, C. D. "Practical Sociology." Chapter I.

Fairbanks, A. "Introduction to Sociology."

Ross, E. A. "Social Psychology."

Dealey, J. Q. "Sociology." Chapter I.

Ellwood, C. A. "Sociology in its Psychological Aspects." Chapters I to VI.

# CHAPTER II

## A Great Discovery

I. The theory
   1. A comparison
   2. The discoverer
   3. A brief statement
II. The proofs
   1. Resemblance to lower animals
   2. Rudimentary organs
   3. The embryo child
   4. Fossil remains
   5. Experiments of breeders
III. The method
   1. Nature's extravagance
   2. The struggle for existence
   3. Importance of variation
   4. Natural selection
   5. Influence of heredity
   6. A later element — altruism

**The Theory of Evolution.** — The discovery of the theory of evolution in the last century by Charles Darwin was A comparison. almost as epoch making as the discovery of America by Columbus. The latter widened the geographical horizon of the Middle Ages and the former the intellectual horizon of our own times. Both men died disappointed and misunderstood. Before the days of Darwin, thinkers as far back as the ancient Greeks had hinted at what we now call evolution, just as they had also

12

guessed that the world might be round and that the East might be reached by sailing westward. But the predecessors of Darwin had no more permanent results than the Viking explorers who caught glimpses of America before Columbus. Let us remember in concluding our comparison that neither of the two discoverers was right in every respect. Later discoveries proved that Columbus had not reached the Indies and that the world was larger than he had imagined. Later researches have changed some of Darwin's theories and we have found that the theory of evolution reaches out into fields beyond biology. Both men were pioneers blazing the trail for others to follow; both ushered in a new era of thought.

Charles Darwin, the great English biologist, was born in 1809, the birth year of so many illustrious men. He spent four years upon a voyage of exploration around the world in which he succeeded in col- **The discoverer.** lecting many valuable specimens and much important scientific data. About the middle of the last century, appeared his first book on the "Origin of Species" and later a second work entitled "The Descent of Man." These books are important because they contain a full statement of the theory of biological evolution with numerous examples drawn from different fields of nature. Their publication aroused a storm of protest which continued long after his death in 1882.

In order clearly to understand the nature of Darwin's discovery let us see what evolution is and what it is not. The popular idea of this theory is far from being **A brief** exact. In the first place the existence of God is **statement.** not denied nor is it stated that man is descended from the ape. In brief, Darwin's theory of descent is that all existing species have sprung from a few simple, primitive types. It asserts the relationship of all forms of life and traces the story of how, from a few simple unicellular forms, have arisen the numerous complex and multicellular organisms now in existence. Man and many of the lower animals have come from the same biological stock.

**The Proofs of Evolution**. — Since Darwin's death new evidence has been discovered in support of his theory of descent. At present we have five main arguments in its favor.

Comparative anatomy shows very striking similarities of structure in man and the higher animals. In comparing

Resemblances to lower animals. man with the other primates, the ape for example, we find similar structures bone for bone and muscle for muscle. The similarities of the skeletons are apparent to the most casual observer in a museum of natural history. While we think of the hairy covering as distinguishing the ape from man, the difference is merely one of quantity due to the fact that man's environment no longer calls for such protection. A close inspection under a magnifying glass will show that almost the whole human body is covered with hair and its slant, noticeably in the arms, is the same as may be observed in the ape.

There are in the human body, as in other higher animals, numerous rudimentary or, more properly, vestigial organs.

Rudimentary organs. The horse at one time had four toes which he has since lost in the long process of evolution. A close examination of the hoof will reveal vestiges of what were once fully developed toes. In human beings the pineal gland and the vermiform appendix are examples of what we call vestigial organs. Many organs, which are now functionless in man, are found active and useful in some of the lower animals. The conclusion drawn from these facts is that there must have been a time in man's earlier history when these organs did function and were of use. For example, we have traces of muscles behind the ears which formerly served to move them. The coccyx of the human spine is a reduced relic of what once functioned as a tail. At the inner angle of the human eye is a fold of tissue which has no meaning unless it be explained as a remnant of that third eyelid which in many lower vertebrates, like the birds, is greatly developed so that it may be drawn over the whole eyeball inside the lids.

The human infant before and shortly after birth resembles some lower forms of life. Pictures of the human embryo at different stages of development seem *The embryo child.* (3) to show that it passes through the same successive stages of development as the species has gone through in the process of evolution. This is known as the recapitulation theory. The human embryo at an early stage resembles a fish and, later on, some of the higher vertebrates. At one stage of development it is impossible to distinguish between the human embryo and that of one of the higher apes. After birth the human infant has a remarkably strong finger grip and an ability to sustain its own weight by hanging with its hands.

If the above reasoning is correct, there must have existed at one time or other primitive ancestral types from which man has evolved. Therefore, search has been *Fossil remains.* (4) made for the so-called missing links, that is for types midway between man and the higher apes. This has resulted in the discovery of a number of very important fossil remains. For example, it is now possible by a series of actual skeleton remains to trace the evolution of the horse back to a creature, not much larger than a dog, which possessed four toes instead of the present hoof. It is likewise possible by means of fossil human remains to trace man back to the time when he was just emerging from a more primitive and apelike form. The first discovery of any importance was made in a cave in Düsseldorf, Germany. On the island of Java, there have also been discovered fossil remains of a creature which must have walked erect but whose brain capacity was midway between man and the ape. Numerous later discoveries in England and upon the continent of Europe have filled the gaps in man's past history. The geological deposits in which they are found and the rock strata above them tell us approximately when each type lived and we marvel at the humble beginnings of our species and at its great antiquity.

From a few primitive types have arisen our various breeds of domestic animals. Breeders have learned that, **Experiments of breeders.** by carefully selecting the type of animal desired, they are able to breed approximately that type. Thus are produced race horses and draft horses by the process of artificial selection made use of by animal breeders. Likewise, nature exercised a natural selection by weeding out those organisms not adapted to their particular environment. Only those plants and animals survived that were best fitted to their locality. Hugo de Vries, a Dutch botanist, has shown how sudden variations of a permanent character called mutations may also produce new types, just as Darwin's slower method of natural selection was shown to produce the survival of the fittest by preserving favorable variations and eliminating the unfavorable. If new types can be produced before our very eyes, how can

AN ARTIST'S CONCEPTION OF NEANDERTHAL MAN.

we doubt that the process of selection took place in the past? Species are not fixed definitely for all time. They change slowly with changes of environment or else they perish.

**The Method of Evolution**. — Having examined the proofs back of this theory, let us inquire into the method of evolution. Here, again, there are five links in our chain of reasoning.

Nature is so very fertile in the number of offspring created as to appear almost wasteful to the casual observer. As we go down the scale of life the number of offspring increases. A single shad in the spawning season produces millions of eggs. Darwin *Nature's extravagance.* showed, for illustration, that if every elephant, which is the slowest breeding animal, lived its normal length of life and if to every pair were born the average of six offspring, there would be, at the end of seven hundred and fifty years, nineteen million living elephants descended from a single pair.

Obviously, not all the numerous offspring ever reached maturity. If every acorn grew to be an oak, the dry land of this world, in the course of a few hundred years, would not be sufficient space for the growth of all the oak trees. If every egg of a shad were *The struggle for existence.* permitted to reach maturity, the rivers would be full of fish. Millions perish and every year countless numbers must be born in order to insure the perpetuity of the species. The world of nature is only apparently calm and peaceful. Underneath the supposed contentment there rages a ceaseless struggle due to competition for food, air, sunshine and space. Throughout the scale of life, larger animals feed upon smaller ones. Two young trees growing side by side

C

are rivals for the sunshine. The one sapling that obtains it may grow to maturity, but at the expense of the other, which soon perishes. For every starfish living, nearly half a million die each year. The fact that the struggle for existence is keenest in the lower forms of life explains their greater productivity. It is necessary for survival.

No two individuals, though born of the same parents, are exactly alike. Children of the same parents, although **Importance** possessing a family resemblance, are quite dif- **of variation.** ferent from each other. In lower forms of life the amount of variation is less, but nevertheless it exists. If we measure the length of oak leaves taken from the same tree, we find that some are longer than others, and birds of the same parents vary not only in size and strength but also in color. Through variation new species are developed.

In the struggle for existence, in which the great majority of organisms perish, the stronger and those better adapted **Natural** to their environment survive, while the weaker **selection.** and unfit are eliminated. This process is called natural selection or survival of the fittest. Out of the numerous variations or types, nature selects the qualities most favorable to survival in that environment. Let us illustrate. In a meadow were placed a number of chickens. Those conspicuous by their white color fell a prey to hawks, but those of a speckled hue resembled the background. Hence the latter survived because of a color variation which was favorable to their existence in that locality. The process of natural selection, going on for numerous generations, tends to eliminate in that locality all types of chickens except those that are speckled. Again, natural selection can be seen working among colonists in a strange land of rigorous climate in which only the hardiest can survive. The function of natural selection is to weed out the unfit or unadapted and thus constantly to raise the type or adapt it to the environment. The old mastodons, whose skeletons we find in museums, were adapted to the marshy environment of thousands of years ago. Failing to adapt themselves to the new environment, they perished. In his early history man won out in the fierce struggle for existence because of his superior intelligence, which enabled him to trap and slay the larger animals among which he lived. ,To-day natural selection exists in the form of conflict and competition between individuals and between groups of individuals.ı Although in civilized communities, few perish from starvation or are ruthlessly killed by their stronger fellows, yet they are forced into the lower or poorer classes in society. Artificial restrictions, like laws of property and inheritance, often prevent many individuals from actually facing a fierce struggle for existence in modern society.

It is a common fact that like begets like, or that the off-spring resemble the parents in spite of individual variations. This is the factor in evolution which in- Influence of sures the persistence of the species. In the heredity. struggle for existence, heredity tends to preserve those variations which have been shown to be favorable to a particular environment. The unfavorable variations tend to be eliminated, and thus are not perpetuated. In the course of many centuries, the favorable variations tend to become the only surviving types. Not all traits, however, are transmissible. Acquired characteristics are those achieved in the lifetime of the individual and, since they are not inherent, they are not usually transmissible. Just as the son of a one-armed man will be born with two arms, so the strong biceps of the blacksmith will not necessarily be inherited. Weak eyes may be inherited, but not the blindness caused by some explosion. Tuberculosis is a disease caused by a bacillus and is not inherited, as are the weak lungs which make possible the attacks of the disease. This distinction between acquired and inherent traits applies to mental as well as to physical characteristics. For example, the problem of the feeble-minded in society is a grave one because feeble-mindedness is an inherent mental trait and will be passed on from generation to generation so long as feeble-minded people propagate, in spite of all the education we may give these unfortunates.

In answer to the controversy opened by the publication of Darwin's "Descent of Man," Henry Drummond put

**A later element — Altruism.** out a volume which he called the "Ascent of Man." Admitting the evidence of Darwin's theory of descent, he objected to the cold-hearted struggle for existence in society and in its place substituted the principle of altruism or the struggle for the life of others. As we ascend the scale of life, the period of infancy becomes longer and maternal care more necessary. Fish merely deposit their eggs and leave them to their fate, but the mother bird not only hatches her eggs but also watches over her young fledgelings. The period of human infancy lasts for many years, and the increased maternal care is the source of altruism and of much that is spiritual and sympathetic in the human breast. Thus the source of altruism arises from the rearing of offspring, and the family group is the generator of coöperation. But the struggle for existence is not eliminated by coöperation. It makes competition a group struggle rather than an individual one. It is a device which enables one group to struggle more successfully against another. Wild horses live in herds and thus protect themselves against wolves. In human society the group having the strongest national life will triumph in war over its more poorly organized rivals. In primitive society, the weakling was eliminated because he was of no value to the group, but in civilized society the sick and unfit are cared for. Thus arise the modern social problems of defectives, delinquents and dependents.

## QUESTIONS FOR DISCUSSION

1. What was the great contribution of Charles Darwin?
2. Show how a belief in evolution need not destroy one's religious convictions.
3. How was Darwin's theory received by the public?
4. State the five proofs of the Darwinian theory of descent.
5. Name the factors in the process of evolution.
6. Show the part each played.
7. Which is the most important to the student of sociology?
8. What traits are transmissible by heredity and which are not?
9. Give some practical examples.
10. How does the non-transmissible character of acquired traits prevent the children of those living in slums from sinking into physical degeneracy?
11. Show how the struggle for existence and natural selection operate to-day.
12. What is altruism?
13. What is the danger of exaggerating this principle?

## TOPICS FOR SPECIAL REPORT

1. The life and work of Charles Darwin.
2. The theory of evolution before Darwin.
3. Later changes in the theory of Darwin.
4. Weismann's theory of germ plasm in the study of heredity.

5. How malnutrition or poisoning of the body cells may indirectly affect the germ cells.

6. Mutations or permanent variations (Theory of De Vries).

7. The culture epoch theory.

8. The evolution of the horse.

## REFERENCES

DARWIN, C. "Descent of Man."

CHAPIN, F. S. "Social Evolution." Chapter I. Variation and Heredity. Chapter II. Struggle for Existence. Chapter III. Origin and Antiquity of Man.

DRUMMOND, H. "Ascent of Man." Chapter II. Scaffolding Left in the Body. Chapter VII. Struggle for Life of Others.

SCHUMUCKER, S. C. "Meaning of Evolution."

CONN, H. W. "Methods of Evolution." Chapters I to V.

CONKLIN, E. G. "Heredity and Environment."

# CHAPTER III

## The Life of the Past

**Universal Evolution.** — We have seen how Darwin worked out the theory of evolution in biology. It was left for another great Englishman, Herbert Spen- **The work of** cer, to show that not only have animal species **Spencer.** come to be what they are by a slow, gradual development. but that nearly everything else in nature has, for centuries, been undergoing a slow but persistent change. Thus,

23

the process of evolution applies to inanimate objects such as the rocks in the earth's crust which have not always been as we know them to-day. Again, that which is intangible, like our human intelligence, our moral code or our great social institution of the state, has not suddenly come into being but has slowly developed from most humble beginnings. Nothing is fixed or final, however permanent it may seem. The slowness of the change makes the development difficult to perceive. This conception of universal evolution Spencer developed in his " Synthetic Philosophy," a monumental work consisting of volumes on various related subjects. Those on sociology marked the beginning of a modern, scientific study of society.

There are four phases of universal evolution, — (1) world, (2) biological, (3) mental and (4) social.

Cosmic or world evolution deals with the development of our solar system and of our earth. It embraces the sciences of astronomy and geology. The nebular hypothesis explains how, centuries ago, out of chaos planets were developed by a process of condensation due to the attraction of particles of matter for each other. Geology goes on to explain how the earth condensed as it cooled. With the formation of the earth's crust, we can read in the various strata of rocks the record of millions of years of geological development.

The evolution of worlds.

A hundred million years ago, as soon as the waters of the sea became sufficiently cool, life appeared on the earth. Science is no more capable of explaining how life originated than is the finite mind capable of grasping the enormity of time required for the evolution of worlds. If we let the width of a man's thumb represent

Biological evolution.

the time that has elapsed between the present time and the gray dawn of history told by the pyramids of Egypt, the length of a walking stick would represent the age of the human species. In other words, man's prehistoric life is many times the length of the historic. A line to represent proportionally the age of the earth's crust, which is roughly the period of biological evolution, would stretch over a distance of several city blocks. The period required by world evolution is so many times the span of biological evolution that a unit of comparison is difficult to formulate. Biological evolution is the story of the development of living forms from the lower to the higher, and from the simple to the complex. Darwin was the pioneer who discovered the theory of biological evolution and we have discussed both his proofs and his method.

As we ascend the scale of life we see a gradual increase of mental power. Lower forms of life have feelings and react according to sensations of pain and pleasure, but do not seem to reason. That intelligence, however, **Mental** is not entirely a human characteristic may be **evolution.** seen by a close observation of dogs and horses. Mental evolution began before biological evolution was over and natural selection worked in favor of the keen intelligence which could see danger and escape it. Thus, primitive man, because of his intelligence, won out in the struggle for existence against the strong and fierce animals about him. But instinct as well as intelligence played a part in man's mental evolution. An instinct may be defined as an inborn tendency possessed by individuals of the same species. Man's instincts are more general and more modifiable than are those of the lower animals. In other words, as mental evolution progresses, instincts become less important and intelligence more important. Mention of some human instincts should be made because they lie at the basis of our social institutions. Thus the family rests upon the reproductive and parental instincts. The instinct of association has been responsible for man's social evolution and upon it rest great institutions like the state and other forms of social organization. Among other human instincts is that of self-defense, because it was usually necessary to fight in the early struggle for existence. Under the strain of modern warfare, when the bitterness of conflict scrapes off the veneer of civilization, we see this primitive instinct showing itself almost as clearly as in savage peoples. However, with the evolution of mind, the instincts play by far a relatively less important part than the reason in the development of mankind.

As we ascend the scale of civilization we see a greater degree of group life or coöperation. Lower forms of life **Social** possess the social instinct and live in groups. **evolution** Witness the schools of fish, flocks of birds and herds of animals. Excellent examples of group life are found among the ants and bees. Thus social evolution, like mental evolution, began before biological evolution was completed. This is shown by the existence of group life among the lower animals. Just as natural selection worked in favor of those possessing keen intelligence, so it placed a premium upon group life or coöperation. Consciously or unconsciously, it was seen that in union there lay strength. Association or group life is a device by which animal species have been enabled to survive, and man's social instinct, like his bodily structure and mental life, can be traced back to the lower animals. Like intelligence, the social instinct has been constantly on the increase and civilized man is distinguished from primitive man by a greater degree of organization. Man's dominant position is due almost as much to his superior power of association as to his superior intelligence.

**Life of Primitive Man**. — Fossil remains of primitive man afford good evidence of his appearance. Likewise, a knowledge of his early environment furnishes additional evidence of the life and activity of primitive man. Finally, primitive races of to-day reveal to us what our own ancestors were like centuries ago. From these three lines of reasoning, we are able to re-create primitive man in our imagination. *Sources of knowledge.*

Let us take, for illustration, the primitive type of Neanderthal man, so named from the valley in Germany where his remains were first discovered. Similar discoveries have since been made in caves from France to Hungary and we infer that Neanderthal man was a common type centuries ago in Europe. Skeletons of the mammoth and woolly rhinoceros found with him seem to show that he lived in the great Ice Age. There have been discovered sufficient of his own bones to give a fairly good description of this early man. Neanderthal man was short and massive in structure and of powerful frame. The thick bones show large muscle attachments and we infer that he was therefore strong and muscular. He must have been a thick-necked individual carrying his head tilted slightly backward. The joints show that he walked upright with a slight bend at the knees. Neanderthal man was just becoming accustomed to a permanent upright posture and walked with a shuffling gait. Such was the ancestor of a large number of present European peoples. *Neanderthal man.*

Fossil remains like those on the island of Java show a more primitive type. On the other hand skeletons like the Essex woman or the Galley Hill man approach more and more closely our own type. The massive jaws and teeth of primitive man indicate that before the discovery of fire his diet must have been a tough one. The large and powerful arms were adapted for climbing to escape the beasts of prey. Huge digestive organs were necessary since primitive man gorged himself after the successful hunt because it might be a long time before more food could be obtained. Tough and hardy, the survivors were able to endure the pain and exposure which killed off the weaklings. Although possessing great natural powers of observation, primitive man's reasoning power was limited like that of the modern savage. He was a good imitator, however, and many of his earliest inventions were copied from the animal world. His interpretation of the phenomena of nature was the simplest and most direct. The running brook in which he saw his own shadow or other self and the whistling wind were to him indications of the numerous spirits always hovering about him for good or ill.

**Achievements of the Past.** — The accomplishments of primitive man in the long prehistoric period are often referred to as social origins. They are good illustrations of both mental and social evolution since they show the increasing power of human intelligence and an increasing degree of coöperation in group activities.

Such a strenuous environment as that in which primitive man lived was fraught with constant danger and calculated to stimulate the development of mentality. Man finally triumphed over his fierce animal rivals by the crude inven-

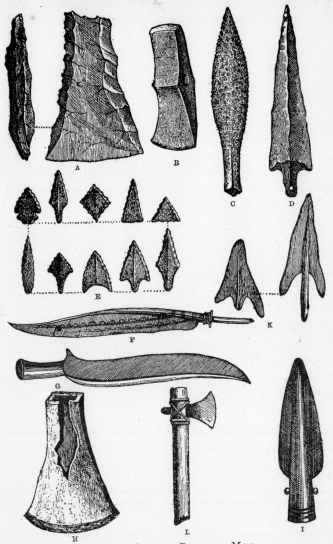

RUDE WEAPONS OF PRIMITIVE MAN.

A Palæolithic Flint Hatchet from Denmark; B Neolithic Danish Axe-Hammer, drilled for handle; C Spear-head from Denmark; D Flint Arrow-head from *Civita Nuova*, Italy; E Various Flint Arrow-heads from the Swiss Lake Dwellings; F Knife with tang to fit into handle from the Swiss Lake Dwellings; G Socketed Knife from the Swiss Lake Dwellings; H Square Socketed Iron Hatchet from the Swiss Lake Dwellings; I Bronze Spear-head from the Swiss Lake Dwellings; K Bronze Arrow-heads from the Swiss Lake Dwellings; L Mode of fixing handle to a Scandinavian hatchet.

tions of his dawning intelligence. These were at first more accidental than conscious, although a useful device was remembered and imitated. Finding that a tree *The process* which had fallen over a stream was an excellent *of invention.* means of crossing, primitive man imitated in other places by dragging a log in position and by this operation invented the first bridge. However, the achievements of man were more or less conscious as compared with those of the lower animals, like the nest-building of birds. As we have said, man relies more upon intelligence than upon instinct. Again, the process of invention is accelerated and becomes more conscious as the history of civilization unfolds. But the great purposive inventions of to-day rest upon the accidental discoveries of prehistoric times. Thus, the modern steam engine would have been impossible without the discovery of fire, somewhere back in the long-forgotten past. The twentieth century " sky-scraper " is but the latest stage in the evolution of housing which began long ages ago when a half-naked savage built a rude shelter for protection from the wind and rain. The child of to-day is the heir of the ages, but primitive man had to learn everything from the beginning.

Let us, then, trace a few of the most notable examples of man's achievements. The earliest implements in use were the club and pointed stick. The bow and arrow *Examples:* constituted as great a discovery for primitive *Tools and* man as gunpowder for the men of the modern *implements.* world. Man learned to work in stone and to chip it down to form a cutting edge. Thus we speak of the rough stone age and of the age of polished stone which covered long years of prehistoric time. It is only within a comparatively recent period that we reach the age of bronze, and finally that of iron and steel.

The discovery of fire made cooking possible, for primitive man like many savages to-day was accustomed to raw
*Discovery of fire.* food. The Fuegians, for example, often eat their fish raw as they take them from the water. How fire was discovered is unknown, but many legends, like that of Prometheus, seek to explain its origin. It made possible the campfire for the center of tribal life, and the hearth-fire for family gatherings.

Primitive man slowly learned that it was poor policy to kill more game than was actually necessary. By keeping
*Domestication of animals.* ing some animals alive in captivity, there was created a constant source of food and man was no longer dependent merely upon the chances of the hunt. The domestication of the dog resulted probably from man's desire for company and amusement. A pastoral life necessitated wandering from place to place in search of new fields. Hence, for the safety of the migratory group, there was developed a closer organization as illustrated by the patriarch Abraham of the Old Testament. As we pass from the hunting and fishing to the pastoral stage, a higher civilization prevails.

Agriculture was accidentally discovered by seeds falling upon the ground of the camping places. The agricultural
*Agriculture.* stage represents an advance over the pastoral. It calls for a more settled life, while a given area is capable of supporting a larger population. This means a greater degree of association, resulting in greater division of labor and greater mental stimulus. Hence the thickly settled river valleys of the Nile, and of the Tigris and Euphrates, were the birthplaces of civilization.

Clothing did not originate so much from the feeling of modesty or the need of climatic protection, as from the desire for personal adornment and visible distinction. At first skins of animals served as a covering, but later came the utilization of the native fibers of the various localities. Weaving and the art of pottery *Clothing.* are good illustrations of woman's share in primitive culture.

Although speech is regarded as a purely human acquisition, the lower animals have certain sounds and cries familiar to their fellows. The origin of human *Language.* speech has been explained by a number of different and fanciful theories. Whatever the origin, its progress has been wonderful. The increasing ideas and needs of civilization have resulted in a corresponding increase in the vocabulary. There are some savage tribes of to-day whose language embraces but a few hundred words. In comparatively recent times, the device of writing was invented. The first attempts are known as picture writing. This was succeeded by the use of characters to represent words or syllables as is shown in the development of Egyptian hieroglyphics. Finally, an alphabet was invented, later carried to Europe by Phœnician mariners, and thence spread all over the western civilized world.

## QUESTIONS FOR DISCUSSION

1. Explain the meaning of universal evolution.
2. Give its four phases.
3. Compare the work of Darwin with that of Spencer.
4. How did natural selection work in mental evolution?
5. How in social evolution?
6. What was the appearance of Neanderthal man?
7. Describe the life of primitive man.
8. What is an instinct?
9. Name the most important human instincts.

10. Show how man's social and mental life can be traced back to the lower animals.

11. Discuss the process of primitive invention.

12. Name five examples of social evolution.

13. Describe each.

14. Compare the length of prehistoric with that of historic time.

## TOPICS FOR SPECIAL REPORT

1. The life and contemporaries of Herbert Spencer.

2. Geological evolution and the nebular hypothesis.

3. Some prehistoric creatures (*e.g.* the mastodons) and their extinction in the struggle for existence.

4. The fossil remains of prehistoric man in Europe.

5. Theories of the origin of language.

6. The discovery of fire and its effect upon the development of civilization.

## REFERENCES

Spencer, H.  "Principles of Sociology."  Chapters V to VIII.

Thomas, W. I.  "Source Book of Social Origins."  (Reference book for any topic.)

Hayes, E. C.  "Introduction to a Study of Sociology."  Chapter XXVII and Chapter XXVIII.

Sollas, W. J.  "Ancient Hunters and Their Modern Representatives."

Keith.  "Ancient Races of Men."

London, Jack.  "Before Adam" (fiction).

Myers.  "Dawn of History."

Chapin, F. S.  "Social Evolution."  Chapter III.  Origin and Antiquity of Man.

Dealey, J. Q.  "Sociology."  Chapter II.  Early Social Development.  Chapter III.  Achievement and Civilization.

# CHAPTER IV

## THE PAST IN THE PRESENT

I. The burden of tradition
  1. A twofold story:
    *a.* The advantage
    *b.* The disadvantage
  2. The origin of folkways:
    *a.* Examples
    *b.* Some survivals
  3. Varying customs:
    *a.* Examples
    *b.* Social heredity
  4. The widening circle:
    *a.* Through conquest
    *b.* Through revolution
II. Other social forces
  1. Imitation
  2. Fashion
III. How the crowd acts
  1. Influence of suggestion
  2. Characteristics of the crowd
  3. Importance of social control

**The Burden of Tradition.** — Social evolution is the story of how men organized into groups, that is, the story of human association. We have seen two good results of this process. In the first place, social organization was a valuable asset to society because thereby the chances of obtaining food and protection were increased; and secondly, in the compara-

A twofold story:

*The advantage and disadvantage.*

D      33

tive safety of group life, the great achievements of prehistoric times were accomplished. Through association,
the invention and gain of one member of the group became
the common property of all. But progress was not so
rapid as might at first be supposed, because there is another
effect of association on group life not so favorable to social
advancement. After the process of social evolution has
been going on for some time, the group tends to develop
certain customary ways of doing things which become
fixed and binding upon all the individuals associated in
that particular group. Patriotism or loyalty to the group
is judged by conformity to its traditions and customs.
Innovations are frowned upon, further progress is hampered,
and the group civilization becomes either stagnant or
static. Even to-day, in every society, we may see both the
static and the dynamic forces at work. The dynamic
forces are those of change and look to the future, while the
static forces oppose change as dangerous and look back
to the traditional past. Thus, we speak of the radicals
in politics who would make constitutional changes, and of
the conservatives who cling to the unaltered constitution of
the fathers. Some nations reach a static condition at an
early stage of their civilization, while other nations and
cultures forge ahead. Western or European civilization
may be spoken of as dynamic in comparison with the static
Oriental cultures of China and India.

After long and crude experimentation, primitive man
arrived at a useful invention or a successful method of

Origin of     doing a thing. The successful method was imi-
folkways:    tated by the rest of the group and unconsciously
*Examples.*    became the customary method or folkway.
After numerous generations, the constant repetition of

this particular method made it as binding upon the group as habit upon an individual. For illustration, a way of building a canoe was hit upon by some individual and followed by the rest of the group. This satisfied a social want and, for a long time, no further discoveries in boat building were made. That particular type of canoe became the model for the group and other types of craft were regarded with suspicion. Again, folkways often originated from false inferences. An Eskimo who happened to have the bone of a dog with him upon the hunt was successful in his undertaking. Primitive man does not reason logically, but draws a conclusion by the most direct inference. Hence in his mind the hunt was successful because the hunter carried with him upon his journey the dog's bone. Others imitated and the custom grew up and became a folkway among those people.

This is comparable to the ignorant man of to-day who ascribes luck to a horseshoe or to a rabbit's foot. Indeed, the source of most of our modern superstition *Some* goes back to a belief in spirits and to the folkways *survivals.* of our untutored ancestors. Hallowe'en is a night of frolic and pleasure, but the origin of this holiday was the serious business of appeasing the evil spirits according to the charms and rituals prescribed in the folkways of the group. If asked the reason for any particular ceremony or procedure, the answer was: " Our fathers did this before us." Fear of the displeasure of dead ancestors prevented any change or innovation. The scope of folkways ranges from the regulation way of making a fire to the tribal laws of royal succession. Indeed, many of our laws and institutions may be traced back to these tribal customs which have grown up slowly and unconsciously. No study of society would be complete without some mention of them because they reflect the life and thought of the group as well as the influence of environment. Tradition is an important and significant phase of the social or group mind as well as an aspect of association.

Each group thinks its own folkways right and laughs at the customs of the foreigner. We think it impolite to **Varying** make a noise while eating, but the Indian would **customs:** deem it a slight to his host not to smack his lips as **Examples.** a sign that the meal has been enjoyed. The Christian gentleman takes off his hat in church, but the Mohammedan his shoes. Our moral ideas are, strictly speaking, not our own but rather those of the group in which we live. We look with horror upon the Eskimos who kill their aged parents, but they regard such action as a serious moral duty when old and infirm people become a burden to the group. We have been taught toleration and sympathy, but had we lived some centuries ago, we should have rejoiced at the burning of heretics and thought that such sacrifices pleased God.

The atmosphere of custom into which every child is born is called social heredity. It is fully as important **Social** as the physical heredity of which we spoke in a **heredity.** preceding chapter. The social environment envelops us as a cloud and unconsciously determines for us almost everything we do from the language we speak to the dress we wear. Individuality represents but a slight variation of the social heredity. We take almost everything as we find it and accept the group traditions from democracy to the dinner hour. We regard other moral systems as undesirable or unworthy just as their followers look upon ours in the same light. Thus, the Japanese who place the duty of the son to the father on a higher plane than his duty to his wife regard their moral codes as superior to our moral and religious systems. As the child learns the mother tongue, so he imbibes the customs and moral ideas of the group, claiming them in time as his own. The individual mind is but a part of the social mind.

Each group, as we have seen, has its own collection of folkways and moral ideas which it believes to be the best and the truest. Thus the " cake of custom " is hard to break. It may be done, however, by forces from within or by forces from without, — by internal revolution or by foreign conquest. In other words, tradition may be broken by changes in the social and physical environment. In the past the method of conquest has been the more common. Each group cherishes its own folkways so highly as to be willing to fight for them. It will resist to the last ditch the invading " barbarians " or will seek to spread by force of arms its own civilization. Thus, Alexander the Great spread Grecian civilization in the East, and the patient Roman soldier carried the Latin tongue and culture from the Tiber to the Thames. So, to-day, our own generation witnessed the titanic struggle between the advocates of Teutonic " kultur " and the proponents of Anglo Saxon liberalism. Often the civilizations of invader and invaded fuse and a resulting culture is imposed upon each. Internally, revolutions are violent changes in the folkways which are shattered in favor of more liberal ideas. It is difficult, however, to force such a change. Peter the Great found trouble in westernizing Russia, and the French Revolution resulted in frightful carnage and vandalism. By the bloody path of war and revolution, history has

*The widening circle: Through conquest and revolution.*

progressed and modern man has become heir to the culture
of all ages and civilizations. Knowledge of other cultures
should rid him of group provincialism, while liberal education should free mankind from the bonds of superstition
and ignorant worship of tradition.

**Other Social Forces**. — We have seen how imitation
has worked as a conservative force to preserve the folk-

**Imitation.** ways of the fathers. It may also work as a progressive force to spread inventions and new ideas
when once originated. The laws of imitation were first
studied by a Frenchman named Gabriel Tarde who was
puzzled by the repetition of certain crimes. Among other
laws he found that imitation is greater in a densely populated region where means of communication are good.
Thus, a new Parisian style of hat or a new English novel
may be found almost immediately in American homes.
News of war with Japan, however, took a long time to
spread throughout the thinly populated and remote parts
of Siberia.

Fashion represents the changing or transient aspect of
the social mind, just as folkways or custom represent its

**Fashion.** more permanent side. Fashion does not show a
steady progress, but rather a series of cycles.
Thus the short sleeve succeeds the long sleeve, and the
furniture of our grandfather once relegated to the attic
has again become fashionable. The origin of style seems
to lie in the instinctive desire for personal adornment and
the wish to be distinguished from the common crowd.
Thus, Occidental ladies pierce their ears, and Orientals
their noses. Another law of imitation is that the masses
tend to copy after the classes. Therefore, fashions represent
the leisure class ideals rather than those of work and service.

MODES OF DRESSING THE HAIR PRACTICED BY THE INHABITANTS OF NEW GUINEA.

The Chinese ladies bind their feet and thereby become incapacitated for degrading physical labor. A style spreads rapidly until it becomes common. Then it is abandoned by its sponsors because of numerous imitations. It is necessary for the safety of democracy to suppress the extravagant fashions of the wealthy and to stimulate the development of practical folkways and social customs among the masses.

**How the Crowd Acts**. — Suggestion is a phase of the social mind associated with imitation. It is the result of one mind acting upon another. Like imitation, it Influence of increases with the degree of association, so that it suggestion. is greater in crowds than among a few individuals. Suggestion is the secret of hypnotism and of many supposed miracles like those of the Hindoo fakirs. It is heightened by abnormal states of mind, such as hysteria or the fatigue brought on by continuous fasting. It is stronger where there is a lack of scientific knowledge. The prophet Mohammed, the dreamer of dreams, saw a vision which he communicated to the ignorant and emotional Arabs among whom he lived. As the story spread, it gained credence from an increasing number of believers, so that Islam finally spread from Persia to the Pyrenees. Children are more susceptible to suggestion than adults and the skillful teacher realizes the power and danger of this device. It is the secret of hero worship and often the source of power wielded by the leader over the credulous multitude.

It is in the crowd that the power of suggestion is greatest. Thus, during the Great Plague in London, when heaps of dead bodies lay in the street accentuating the terror and imagination of the crowd, heightening its power of suggestion, Defoe tells us how one individual pointed to a white cloud in the sky, calling it an angel and declaring that it was robed in white and armed with a sword. Immediately, by suggestion, the apparition spread and all believed and were afraid. The credulity of a crowd is incredible. History furnishes numerous examples, such as the preaching of Peter the Hermit, when thousands followed the example of those around them and shouted for the sign of the Cross. Like a contagion the crusading movement spread. Another characteristic of the crowd is the loss of a sense of individual responsibility. In a mob the individual can be led on to undreamed of deeds of violence, such as the lynching or burning of innocent or untried victims. The excitement and emotionalism of the crowd may be seen in war times as well as in great religious revivals. The crowd feels and acts but it cannot deliberate and reason. When it does so, it ceases to be a crowd and becomes a deliberative assembly. The crowd is unstable and cannot last. Rallying quickly around any one capable of temporary leadership, it will disappear after the crisis as quickly as it was formed. A final characteristic of a crowd is its fickleness. Those who sang " Hosanna in the Highest " cried out a few days later " Crucify Him, Crucify Him ! "

*Characteristics of the crowd.*

By a process of education it is necessary to build up an individuality strong enough to withstand the influence of the crowd and the magic of its demagogue leader. The sensational newspaper which prints the harrowing details of crime wields a sinister power of suggestion to further crime. Social control can be developed only through the avoidance of sensationalism and through a constructive program of sane teaching,

*Importance of social control.*

intellectual self-possession, and the creation of the feeling of responsibility. An intelligent public opinion which soberly discusses questions of the day is the sole hope of a democracy. It represents the most advanced stage of the social mind, just as the mob is the lowest form of association. Social control is the collective or group mind, uninfluenced by the magic of suggestion or the blindness of imitation, intelligently cognizant of a course of action best suited to the welfare of the group. A society, free but incapable of self-control, brought about the excesses of the Reign of Terror. On the other hand, a society kept in order by the iron hand of autocracy has its Bastille or its " Mailed Fist." The aim of social progress is the development of a group capable of controlling itself in peace, liberty and intelligence. This is the problem of social control.

## QUESTIONS FOR DISCUSSION

1. Give two good results of association.
2. Contrast a static and a dynamic civilization and give examples.
3. Show some static and dynamic forces at work in our own society at the present time.
4. What are folkways?
5. How do folkways arise?
6. What come out of folkways?
7. Why is a study of a nation's folkways important?
8. Do folkways influence your own life? Explain.
9. What is social heredity?
10. Show its molding power upon the individual.
11. Show how the ideas of right and wrong vary with different groups.
12. Is the standard of morality determined by the group?
13. Give an illustration.
14. How are local customs broken and how do new ideas spread?

15. How are civilized man's customs superior to those of savages?

16. What do you mean by a "cake of custom"? By the "melting pot" of civilization?

17. Give some laws of imitation.

18. Contrast fashion and custom.

19. Show by illustration how fashion moves in cycles.

20. Show the danger of having our ideals and fashions set by a moneyed leisure class.

21. What is the social mind?

22. Show how suggestion works.

23. Under what circumstances can it be seen to best advantage?

24. Name the characteristics of the crowd.

25. How can the mob spirit be avoided?

26. What is social control?

## TOPICS FOR SPECIAL REPORT

1. Some present superstitions and their origins.

2. An interpretation of the curious customs of some primitive people (*e.g.* Eskimos or Australians).

3. The attempt of the British government to civilize and suppress certain barbaric local customs in its dependencies (*e.g.* the killing of widows in India).

4. The French Revolution and its changes in manners and customs.

5. Tarde's "Laws of Imitation."

6. Conflicting ideas of beauty and dress in various parts of the world.

7. Laws of fashion (see "Social Psychology" by Ross).

8. A personal experience illustrating the principles of mob psychology.

9. Personal experiences illustrating the power of suggestion.

## REFERENCES

SUMNER, W. G. "Folkways." Chapter I. Fundamental Notions of the Folkways. Chapter II. Characteristics of the Folkways.

Ross, E. A. "Social Psychology." Chapter II. Suggestion. Chapter III. The Crowd. Chapter IV. Mob Mind. Chapter V. Prophylactics against Mob Mind. Chapter VI. Fashion.

Chapin, F. S. "Social Evolution." Chapter VI. Social Heredity.

Ross, E. A. "Social Control."

Bagehot, W. "Physics and Politics."

Patten, S. N. "New Basis of Civilization."

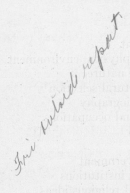

# CHAPTER V

## THE INFLUENCE OF ENVIRONMENT

I. The two factors
   1. Heredity
   2. Environment
II. Importance of physical environment
   1. Influence of nature
   2. Effect of natural selection
III. Effects of physiography
   1. Resources and occupations
   2. Accessibility
   3. Isolation
   4. Form of government
   5. Other social institutions
   6. Cultural and religious ideas
IV. Climatic influences
   1. Temperature
   2. Rainfall
   3. Weather
V. Conservation of resources
   1. Physical conservation
   2. Industrial conservation
   3. Human conservation

**The Two Factors.** — The two factors in the explanation of any social problem are heredity and environment. That

Heredity and environment.

is to say, the causes back of social phenomena are subjective, in the individual, and objective, in the environment. The prisoner behind the bars is there because of a bad heredity or an unfortunate

44

environment. Let us first more clearly define our terms.
We have spoken before of heredity, but have used the word
in two senses. In the chapter entitled " A Great Discovery " heredity was used in its commonly accepted
biological sense of physical heredity, which deals with inherent physical and mental traits. In the preceding
chapter we spoke of social heredity, which is something
entirely different, since it means the social environment of
custom and tradition inherited from the past. The word
environment is also used in two senses — physical and
social. The social environment refers to existing institutions and human surroundings. Physical environment means merely natural conditions of geography and
climate and includes, for example, a treatment of the relation between physical configuration and human civilization. It is in this sense that we use the word environment
in this chapter.

**Importance of Physical Environment**. — By the influence of physical environment we mean the effect of
nature upon man. The biologist cannot under- Influence of
stand the desert cactus or the polar bear without nature.
some knowledge of the peculiar environment of each.
Similarly, the student of society must know the tropical
African background of the American negro in order to
understand some of his present characteristics. We have
mentioned the custom among the Eskimos of killing aged
and infirm parents. This is the social effect of a physical
environment which is found in the rigorous Arctic climate
where it is difficult to procure a living.

Again, man is not exempt from the principle of natural
selection working through the environment. The Scandinavian immigrant unaccustomed to the dry sunny climate

found along the eastern coast of the United States prefers the rainy Northwest which resembles his native land. On the other hand, the negroes who migrate north-

**Effect of natural selection.** ward are not adapted to such a climate and would tend to die off in our northern states were their ranks not recruited by fresh levies from the South. Professor Boaz, after a series of experiments in which he measured the skulls of immigrants and those of their children, puts forth, perhaps without sufficient proof, the theory that the effect of the new American environment can be seen in a physical change in the shape of the head due probably to a diet of softer food. If this be true, it is very significant, for length and breadth of skull are supposed to be the most permanent of physical characteristics.

**Effects of Physiography**. — Natural resources include soil, rivers, minerals, animals and plants. The great river

**Resources and oc- cupations.** valleys of the Nile, the Euphrates and the Ganges were sufficiently fertile to support a teeming population and thus became the cradles of civilization. The possession of forest lands rich in timber for ship building, as well as proximity to the sea, made the Phœnicians great mariners. The occupations of a people are originally determined by natural environment. In one region men are fishermen, in another herdsmen, and in still another farmers. Each occupation develops its own type of culture. The story of ancient history is a record of the incursions of warlike herdsmen upon the more peaceful and more highly civilized agriculturists of the plains below. Thus, the invasion of Egypt by the Hyksos or shepherd kings lowered the civilization of that region. In ancient Greece there came into conflict the interests of the men of the shore (merchants), the men of the hills (shepherds), and the men of the plains (farmers). The location of a source of motive power is also important. The development of steam power placed the factories of England in the north where the great coal fields were located. Thus the center of population was gradually shifted from the south to the north. This principle makes us wonder what effect the development of China's resources will have upon Oriental civilization.

Rivers and bodies of water are the routes of war, of trade and of civilization. The open door into central Europe was through the river valley of the Danube and up these plains swept successive waves of invasion. Accessibility. The present race mixture in Austria and Hungary is the modern result of these invasions. Down the Rhine floated the civilization of the Christian monks. Later, this river became the trade route for the medieval commerce of the Hanseatic cities. Palestine was the highway for invading armies between Egypt and Persia. Its accessibility caused its repeated conquest by successive empires. Thus, because of fear of absorption, the people of this land have clung tenaciously to their national characteristics. Another result of accessibility may be seen in Greece. This small peninsula has the greatest seacoast of any country of similar size. Since no point is far from the sea, the people became a maritime nation. They not only had access to the earlier, oriental civilizations, such as the Egyptian, but were also able to spread their own culture throughout the Mediterranean world.

Rivers and seas, however, may also serve an opposite purpose and act as barriers to invasion. Thus England has often been saved from continental invasion because of its insularity. Witness the Spanish Armada and the

futile attempt of Napoleon to conquer England. Mountain ranges are also great barriers. The Alps have been an
Isolation. obstacle to invading armies from Hannibal to Napoleon. Note how the physical map of Europe frequently coincides with the political, and how often mountains and rivers form the boundary lines of states. The general result of geographical inaccessibility is not only to prevent the disastrous invasions of barbarian peoples, but also to hinder the peaceful spread of a higher civilization and of a foreign culture. In mountain-walled Thibet the group culture has become stagnant because of lack of intercourse with the outside world. The Scotch-Irish settlers of our early American history were among the most energetic and progressive of pioneers. How then can we explain the present backward condition of some of their descendants whom we designate as the " poor whites " of the southern mountains? The solution of the problem is found in the new environment. Shut in by the surrounding mountains, they have isolated themselves from the culture about them and the most primitive conditions prevail. Again, the climate, or rather the peculiar local environmental disease known as hookworm, has sapped their vitality and produced a peculiar type of laziness.

The people of an inaccessible land feel little need for the protection afforded by strong government. Love of liberty
Form of with perhaps a certain degree of lawlessness
government. seems to go along with a mountain environment, as illustrated by the Scotch Highlanders and Balkan patriots. Democracy is the spirit of the mountains and aristocracy that of the plains. Compare democratic Switzerland's initiative and referendum with the Junker party of agricultural East Prussia. Again, democracy

seems to be fostered by the growth of commerce. Great plains may become the seats of successive empires as in Asia, but a land broken up by seas or mountain develops the political ideal of the city-state of the Greeks and early Romans.

Other social institutions beside the state are affected by geographical environment. For example, certain environments favor pastoral life which develops a patriarchal society. Here child-bearing is the great duty and polygynous marriages flourish as shown by the story of Abraham in the Bible. In a rigorous and barren environment it is difficult to support many children, with the result that the polyandrous family flourishes. Again, let us note the history of slavery in our own country. Negro slaves were to be found in all of the thirteen original colonies. Natural conditions in the North made the institution unprofitable and legislative abolition voiced the popular feeling. In the South, however, where agriculture was the leading industry and where plantation life suited the local environment, slavery grew and flourished. A great civil war was necessary to decide whether a nation thus divided could endure.

*Other social institutions.*

The national character of a people is affected by its geographical environment. The awe-inspiring aspects of nature in India, as revealed by the enormous mountain masses of the Himalayas, the ravages of the hurricane, of the tempest and of the earthquake, as well as the fierce beasts and snakes of the jungle, inspire the inhabitants of that land with a feeling of fear and reverence rather than that of inquiry. Hence the religious spirit of that environment is strong and tradition is hard to break, as the British government has

*Cultural and religious ideas.*

*9256*

found in its dealings with the natives. Greece, on the contrary, lacks the terrifying aspects of nature, and mountains and lakes merely give variety, beauty and suggestion to the landscape. It is difficult to imagine Athenian culture growing up anywhere but in its native geographical environment. The founders of the great monotheistic religions of the world — Zoroaster, Moses, Buddha, Christ and Mohammed — belonged to the semi-tropical and desert zone. Here the thinker is impressed with the oneness of nature by the vast expanse of land, sea and sky. On the other hand, a people dwelling in a varied environment of forest, stream and hill tend toward polytheism. Trees are the homes of spirits and satyrs, while streams become peopled with nymphs and mermaids.

**Climatic Influences**. — Physical environment sets climatic limitations to human habitation. Life in the Arctics

Tempera- is hard and natural selection plays havoc among
ture.        fur hunters and gold seekers. Until recent

times the tropics have been fatal to the white man, but a scientific knowledge of the causes of disease and of methods of sanitation, as illustrated in the work of the Panama Canal Zone, is making possible a Caucasian conquest of the tropics. At the present time, however, the temperate latitudes seem most favorable to the development of an advanced civilization. The heat belt, which was the seat of many ancient cultures, has contributed little to human advancement in the last thousand years. That civilization has advanced from the south to the north, as much as from the east to the west, is seen in the successive rise of empires from ancient Egypt to modern Britain. As man has become more civilized, he becomes more accustomed to a colder and moister climate.

A moderate rainfall is just as important as a temperate climate. Too heavy a precipitation is favorable only to tropical forest and swamp. Too slight a rain- **Rainfall.** fall means aridity and the pastoral industry is the most suitable to such a region because grass is the chief kind of vegetation. That population is scanty in dry regions may be seen by a comparison of two maps, the one showing the distribution of rainfall and the other of population. Compare the population of our western states with that along either coast, or the population of Arabia with that of India. There is an interesting explanation of the historical movements of peoples into Europe. The original home of the Aryan race, having dried up because of climatic changes, was no longer capable of supporting so large a population. Hence the various waves of migration and invasion, which swept from the grass lands of western Asia into Europe.

Local and temporary climatic changes are called the weather. Clear cool weather is invigorating, while dampness and high humidity are both depressing and **The** enervating. These effects have often been re- **weather.** vealed by varying efficiency among employees and by the conduct of school children. Dry windy weather stimulates the nervous system and vitalizes human energy. This often finds expression in increased efficiency or in greater freedom of movement. The effect of the change of seasons may also be seen in the records of crime. Crime against property, like burglary, increases in winter, while crime against person, like murder, increases in spring and summer.

**Conservation of Resources.** — In view of the tremendous importance of natural resources it is evident that effective measures should be taken for their proper conservation.

Of course, so far as the life of man is concerned, the physiography of nature is practically unchangeable. But
Physical conserva- tion.
the resources of nature found in land, water and mountains are not only exhaustible, but their very utilization is the source of wealth and the mainspring of human development. If man is to progress he must utilize the soil, the minerals and the water power furnished by his natural environment. In America, the Indian failed in this utilization and the white man's justification for his conquest of America is to be found in his development of these resources. As the centuries have passed, however, our forests, our minerals and our water power sites have been ruthlessly appropriated by private individuals. It is this exploitation of natural resources that makes necessary governmental action for their conservation. Years ago European countries realized the necessity for regulation, whereby the government could control the amount of resources individually appropriated. Slowly the United States is recognizing the importance of this principle which seeks to socialize for the benefit of all the great forest lands, the wonderful mineral resources and the stupendous water power found in nature.

The principle of conservation may also be applied to industry. The aim of conservation is the elimination of
Industrial conserva- tion.
waste. Man has not only been extravagant in his utilization of natural resources, but also wasteful in industrial processes. Formerly, many products of industry were cast aside as waste, but now man realizes that such by-products, as they are called, are capable of further utilization. In fact, the great modern " trust " has often so conserved and utilized its by-products as to be able to sell its main product at a price lower than

that placed upon it by competitors. With the growth of civilization and an increasing cost of production, still greater emphasis will be placed upon the principle of conservation in industry. To be sure, this problem is economic rather than social, but it is here mentioned because of its social significance in modern civilization.

Again, the principle of conservation applies to human life. Indeed, it is in this field that conservation assumes its greatest importance. " What profiteth it a Human conman, if he gain the whole world and lose his own servation. soul? " This is equally true of national life. Without health and happiness, natural resources and industrial wealth avail little. The prime object of modern civilization should be the conservation of human life. Formerly men, women and children toiled incessantly under conditions which had little regard for their health and comfort. Sickness, accident and death followed in the path of industry without arousing the public conscience. To-day, however, everywhere we find an awakening sense of social and moral obligation in the treatment of human labor.

## QUESTIONS FOR DISCUSSION

1. Name two factors in any sociological explanation.
2. Divide the causes of some practical social problems into the hereditary and environmental.
3. In what two senses is the word " heredity " used?
4. The word " environment "?
5. Show how some plants and animals are adapted to their physical environment.
6. Show how the natural selection of a physical environment works with man and give practical illustrations.
7. Name some illustrations, other than those used in the text, of the effect of natural resources upon the occupations and life of a people.

8. What is the effect of rivers in opening up a country?

9. Give original illustrations from American history.

10. Illustrate the effect on civilization of nearness to the sea.

11. Name in order of importance several natural barriers.

12. Name a good and a bad result of natural geographical isolation.

13. Illustrate.

14. Name and illustrate the various ways that physical environment may affect the form of government.

15. The social institutions.

16. Explain the theory of the effect of natural environment upon the cultural and religious ideas of a race.

17. Can you think of any objection to this theory?

18. What are the two natural elements in climate?

19. Illustrate the effects of each.

20. How do you interpret the fact that the earliest civilizations were in warm countries and the modern great nations in temperate lands?

21. How does rainfall affect density of population?

22. What theory accounts for the migrations such as led to the overthrow of the Roman Empire?

23. Illustrate from your own experience the effect of weather influences.

## TOPICS FOR SPECIAL REPORT

1. The fertile river valleys of the Nile and Euphrates.

2. The Rhine and Danube rivers as waterways for invasions, civilization and commerce.

3. Effects of the insularity of England.

4. The Alps and the history of Italy.

5. The Allegheny Mountains as a barrier.

6. Climatic influences upon crime.

7. The conquest of the tropics by a knowledge of the causes of their peculiar diseases such as yellow fever.

8. The sanitation campaign of the U. S. Government in Cuba and Panama.

## REFERENCES

CHAPIN, F. S. "Social Evolution." Chapter V. Influences of Physical Environment.

HAYES, E. C. "Introduction to a Study of Sociology." Chapter III. Geographical Causes and their Social Effects.

SEMPLE, E. "Influences of Physical Environment" (large reference book for any selected topic).

THOMAS, W. I. "Source Book for Social Origins." Part I.

DEXTER, E. G. "Weather Influences."

HUNTINGTON, E. "Pulse of Asia."

PATTEN, S. N. "New Basis of Civilization." Chapter I.

HUNTINGTON, E. "Civilization and Climate."

PATTEN, S. N. "Development of English Thought."

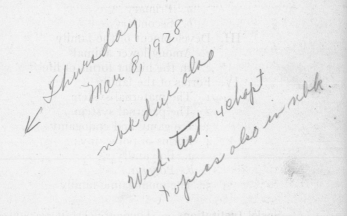

# CHAPTER VI

## HISTORY OF THE FAMILY

I. Social Institutions
  1. Their meaning
  2. Examples and origin
II. The family as an institution
  1. Its importance
  2. Its functions:
    *a*. Primary
    *b*. Secondary
III. Development of the family
  1. Among lower animals
  2. In the higher forms of life
IV. Forms of the family
  1. The maternal system
  2. The paternal system
  3. Exogamy and endogamy
  4. Forms of polygamy:
    *a*. Polyandry
    *b*. Polygyny
  5. The monogamic family

**Social Institutions**. — There are certain recognized forms of human association which have the support and approval of society. These are called social institutions.
Their meaning. There are also other forms of association not sanctioned by society, arising sporadically and lacking permanency. If the individual takes part in these non-sanctioned forms of association he incurs the displeasure of society

and often becomes a social outcast. Therefore, every normal member of society seeks activities and associations approved by the society in which he lives. After the lapse of ages these forms of association and ways of living become crystallized into social institutions. It is scarcely necessary to say that social institutions vary in different parts of the world and in different stages of human development.

Among the great social institutions of to-day are the family, the state, the church, the school and industrial society. The historical thread of each stretches far back into the dim past in a fairly continuous story. Different ages and different peoples have molded these fundamental institutions according to the particular physical environment and social heredity at hand. Thus the two great factors in social evolution — heredity and environment — lie at the roots of our social institutions. Our problem now is to trace the past development of these typical social institutions, to note the effects of physical environment and social heredity, and then to study the present organization and problems of each.

**The Family as an Institution.** — The primary and most important social institution is the family. Indeed the family, rather than the individual, may be called the unit in society, just as the cell in biology is the nucleus of all organic development. The family may be regarded as a miniature society. Since it contains both sexes, it is capable of reproducing itself and, since it includes all ages, it contains the various social relationships illustrated by the authority of the father and the obedience of the children. We may call it the primary form of association from which developed later institutions. Thus, the first industrial society was the family. In savage society the father goes upon the hunt, while the mother builds the hut and prepares the food and makes the clothing. The family of the frontiersman of our own day is practically an independent economic unit, providing for itself most of the necessary articles and utensils, as well as food and clothing. Again, religious life has centered and still should center in the family. The patriarchal father was the first high priest and the hearth-fire the seat of the earliest religious devotions. The child's earliest education is obtained at his mother's knee, and the institution of the school continues the work already begun by the family. Finally, government and the institution of the state had their roots in the institution of the family. The patriarch Abraham was a tribal chief and the Roman *pater familias*, who ruled his family, was responsible to the state for the conduct of the members of his household.

The primary function of the family is the biological one of reproduction, the perpetuation of the human species. Its functions: Primary. The industrial function of the family has, for the most part, been lost; for production, to-day, has gone from the home into the huge factory. Again, the school and the various church organizations have become modern substitutes for the educational and religious life of the family. But no social changes can undermine its primary biological function — the birth of offspring. The family is the social institution which produces new individuals for society and cares for them until maturity. Thus, the primary function of the family is to transmit physical life from generation to generation. This function is as permanent as the human race itself.

There is also a secondary function of the family, namely, to transmit social possessions from generation to genera- tion. These may be material possessions such as *Secondary* property and wealth, or the spiritual possessions *function.* of the race, such as the mother tongue or our ideals of government and religion. The transmission of these pos- sessions we call the process of socialization. This second- ary function of the family is to fit the individual for the larger life of society. It is to prepare for citizenship in the broadest sense of the word, This duty is at present in grave danger of being forgotten, unless the church and the school come to the rescue of the family. For example, the school must not only enlarge its curriculum to include work in the social sciences, but it must also introduce courses in domestic science and in vocational training in order to give that preparation for later life which was for- merly given in the home. The Sunday school has come into being to give religious training to many boys and girls who would never receive such instruction at home.

**Development of the Family**. — The lowest form of animal life, as seen in the amœba, reproduces by simple division called fission. There is no sex differentiation *Among* into male and female. Ascending the scale of *lower* life, however, sex differences become more and *animals.* more apparent. In the lower forms of life, the relation between the sexes is momentary and exists merely for the purpose of reproduction. No care is given the offspring and perpetuity of the species is obtained only by the re- production of great numbers. This stage is well illustrated by fish. Birds represent a higher stage of family de- velopment. It is necessary that they care for their eggs until they are hatched, and the pairing of male and female lasts for a season. Mammals suckle their young, who thus require increasing care, while the male secures food and protection. Hence the male and female often live together until after the birth and rearing of offspring. This we call the primitive pairing system from which developed the family. It may be regarded as a device of nature for the preservation of offspring during the period of infancy.

As we ascend the scale of life, the period of infancy becomes longer and the family more permanent. By the *In the higher forms of life.* time we reach the higher animals and those resembling man, the simple pairing system of one male and one female is very common. The gorilla and other primates live in relatively permanent family groups which are usually monogamous. Thus, the origin of the human family may be traced back to the lower animals, and monogamy began before the human stage was reached. There is a sociological theory that at one time in man's early history sex relations were so confused that primitive man had no fairly definite form of the family. As we have seen, the evidence from the higher animals contradicts this view. Again, the most primitive peoples existing to-day practice monogamy and live in relatively stable family groups. For these and other reasons, scientifically established, we are warranted in believing that primitive man had a fairly permanent and definite monogamic family which goes back to the primitive pairing system of the higher animals.

**Forms of the Family**. — From the study of societies, such as the Iroquois Indians, it has been discovered that *The maternal system.* relationship was once traced through the mother. Property and authority descended through the female line. Children took the mother's name and belonged to the mother's clan. The chief transmitted his authority not to his own son but to his eldest sister's son. This form of the family is known as the maternal or metronymic system because of the importance of the mother. It represents an earlier stage of the family through which most societies have passed. The maternal system of tracing relationship was first adopted because maternal relationship was most obvious. There was no doubt of the identity of the mother because of the physiological connection between mother and child. Hence some writers have claimed that, before the dawn of history, there existed a period of confused family relationships. As we have seen, this does not seem likely. The maternal system prevailed because the relationship of mother and child was most obvious, while the physiological importance of the father was not learned until afterward. Again, the maternal system does not mean that women were dominant politically or socially, although it is true that their position was higher in this form of the family than under the later paternal system.

The transition to a condition where descent was traced through the male line, and where the husbands and fathers were supreme, was due to a number of causes. The paternal system. War led to the custom of wife capture from other tribes. Thus we have the story of the capture of the Sabine women by the early Romans. This was succeeded by the more peaceful custom of wife purchase. Among the Zulus, where wife purchase prevails, a woman who proves childless or a poor laborer may be returned and the purchase price demanded from the girl's father. In either case of wife capture or wife purchase, the wife was regarded as the property of her husband. A third cause of the decline of the position of woman lay in the development of pastoral life. This necessitated a larger area and removed the wife far from the protecting influences of her original family. A good illustration of patriarchal society is found in examples taken from the Old Testament. Thus, the story of Jacob illustrates wife purchase by the labor of seven years for Rachel. In a patriarchal society the father is a petty tyrant wielding immense power over his family. Hence, in early Rome, the father had the power of life and death over his sons. The progress of mankind, however, has broken this authoritative form of the family and has raised the position of women and children.

Exogamy is the practice which requires a man to find his wife in some clan other than his own. Endogamy, on the contrary, is the practice of marrying within the group. For biological reasons, inbreeding is often pernicious, and perhaps natural selection favored the group practice of exogamy since it is the more common of the two customs. Again, exogamy may have arisen from the custom of wife capture from other tribes. The latter method was very common at one time and survivals of it exist in many marriage ceremonies. The bride is carried off by her intended husband, pretending to lament and struggle against her capture.

**Exogamy and endogamy.**

The institution of polygamy has given rise to three forms of the family. Polygamy really means " much married " and applies either to a plurality of wives or to a plurality of husbands or to a combination of both. Thus, among the Hawaiians, there is a curious custom known as group marriage. A small group of men, usually brothers, marry several women, usually sisters. Every woman in the group is wife to every man in the group but family ties are kept intact and regarded as

**Forms of polygamy: *Polyandry.***

sacred within this group. Polyandry, while also rare, is more common than group marriage. It is the union of several men, usually brothers, with one woman. The best illustration of this form of the family is found in the barren mountain lands of Thibet. It is a device to keep down population where the niggardliness of nature makes difficult the production of food. Another cause of polyandry lies in the social custom of female infanticide or the practice of killing infant girls. This reduces the proportion of women and leads to this unbalanced form of the family.

Polygyny is the marriage of one man to several women and represents the most usual deviation from the prevailing monogamic form of the family. This practice requires, however, a certain economic *Polygyny.* surplus. Primitive man could not have practiced it widely because his food supply was limited. Indeed, in the so-called polygynous countries of to-day, the practice of having more than one wife is confined usually to the upper and richer classes. Less than five per cent of the people of Turkey and Egypt are polygynous, although the Mohammedan religion sanctions the custom. Again, the numerical equality of the two sexes makes the spread of polygyny on a large scale impossible, unless continuous warfare decimates the male population. Wife capture and purchase favored the development of polygyny, while the desire for children, which is an important characteristic of patriarchal society, also stimulated the development of this institution.

Monogamy has been the prevailing form of marriage in all ages and in all places. Its development from the primitive pairing system is the story of the evolution of the family. Other forms of marriage, such as polygyny and polyandry, are merely local or temporary deviations from the usual form. In most civilized countries the monogamic

**The monogamic family.** family is now and has been for centuries the only sanctioned form of marriage. Aside from the moral aspects of the question, there are certain sociological reasons for its superiority. It secures the better care of children, as exemplified in a lower rate of infant mortality, and fulfills more completely the secondary function of the family, that of socialization. The monogamic family alone is capable of producing the higher affections because it fosters altruism instead of the jealousy engendered by the very nature of the polygynous family. Polygyny lowers the position of woman in every locality where it exists. It is no mere coincidence of history that the monogamic family and a higher civilization are found arising together. Each produces the other. Monogamy favors the development of altruism and coöperation which, in turn, is often the determining factor in the struggle for existence forever taking place among nations. A sound family life generally means a sound national life. The sturdy moral and military qualities of the early Romans sprang from the nucleus of a healthy family life. Luxury and vice in the later days of Rome undermined the family and thereby the nation. Thus, we can read the fall of an empire in a rising divorce rate, in a rising rate of infant mortality, and in a falling native birth rate.

## QUESTIONS FOR DISCUSSION

1. Name the social institutions.
2. What does sociology study concerning them?
3. Explain the importance of the family as the primary social institution.

4. Distinguish between the primary and secondary functions of the family.

5. Explain each.

6. Trace the development of the family up through the animal world.

7. Explain the maternal stage of the family.

8. Give the reasons for the transition to the paternal stage.

9. Give some characteristics and illustrations of patriarchal society.

10. What may cause polyandry?

11. Distinguish between polygamy and polygyny.

12. What are the causes of polygyny?

13. What are the checks to the spread of polygyny?

14. Give the social advantages of monogamy.

15. Illustrate how a healthy family and national life go together.

## TOPICS FOR SPECIAL REPORT

1. Evidences of family life among birds.

2. The matriarchate of the Iroquois Indians.

3. The patriarchal family of the Old Testament.

4. The powers of the Roman father.

5. The effect of polygyny upon the civilization of Mohammedan countries.

6. Polyandry in Thibet.

7. Marriage customs of the Greeks and Romans.

## REFERENCES

ELLWOOD, C. A. "Sociology and Modern Social Problems." Chapters IV to VII inclusive.

HAYES, E. C. "Introduction to a Study of Sociology." Chapter XXIX.

BLACKMAR, F. W., and GILLIN. "Outlines of Sociology." Chapter V. Organization and Life of the Family.

PARSONS, E. C. "The Family." (Illustrative material.)

WESTERMARCK, E. "History of Human Family." (Reference.)

F

HOWARD, GEO. E. "History of Matrimonial Institutions." (Reference.)

FAIRBANKS, A. "An Introduction to Sociology." Chapter IX. Family as a Social Unit.

DEALEY, J. Q. "The Family in its Sociological Aspects."

# CHAPTER VII

## THE DEVELOPMENT OF THE STATE

**Nature and Origin of the State.** — Like the family, the state is another important institution of society. It is a society organized politically for the purpose of preserving the group and of protecting the in- Definition. dividuals composing it. We may define the state as a community of people inhabiting a definite area, fairly well

67

unified under some sort of government and ruled by officials under a body of written law or in accordance with unwritten custom. Its purpose is social control for the common good through coöperation.

The origin of the state is difficult to trace because of its divergent roots and because of the numerous fanciful

Origin:
*Fanciful theories.*

theories that obscure its early history. Almost every people has its tradition of an ancient lawgiver, like the Greek Draco or the Roman Numa. These wise men, if they ever really existed, did not give to the people by divine inspiration a new and brilliant code of laws, but merely collected and put into written form the customs and traditions of many generations. Each nation looks back to some mythical hero, claiming him as its founder. Thus Rome had its Romulus and England its Arthur. Later in history appeared the " Divine Right " theory of the state, by which kingship was viewed not as a political development, but as a divinely ordained institution. Under this view the church and the state could not be easily separated. The English Stuarts claimed their power from God, and in France so absolute was this type of government that Louis XIV could say, " I am the state." This view of the state was followed by the " Social Contract " theory of such philosophers as Hobbes, Locke and Rousseau. It was claimed by these writers that mankind originally lived in a state of nature, characterized by war, confusion and individual liberty. In order to secure protection, the people voluntarily surrendered this natural liberty to some chief whom they selected to rule over them in order that they might have peace and civil liberty.

The foregoing theories were the products of tradition, or of a speculative philosophy, or of the desire to justify despotic rule. The true origin of the institution of the state is not to be found in such simple explanations. Its basis lies in man's social instinct, that is in his *The socio-* inherent desire for the companionship of group *logical view.* life. Another factor is coöperation, which developed group solidarity in the conflict with other peoples. Slowly there developed from rude and simple beginnings the modern state. It was a gradual development of political control made necessary by the attempts of men to live together harmoniously within a given area. As the patriarchal family expanded, there was no conscious effort to build up a state. Custom developed into law and the patriarch into king. War, since it required organization for successful prosecution, furthered the evolution of the state. The temporary leader in battle tended to become the permanent chief. Again, in times of peace, the enforcement of group folkways and customs made authority necessary. This authority was rather religious than political, but in primitive society there was little differentiation between church and state.

**Functions of the State.** — The primary function of the state is to protect its members in the enjoyment of their rights of life and property. As we have seen, **Primary** this was one reason for its origin. When the **functions.** state can no longer afford protection from foreign attack, it ceases to exist and confusion reigns. The fall of the Roman Empire was succeeded by feudalism and the individual looked to his nearest and most powerful lord for protection. Internally, the function of the state is to preserve the social order, that is, to protect each member of society in the enjoyment of his rights. It must hold in check the unsocial individual who would infringe upon the privileges of others. Thus, the state is the guardian of property and regulates its transfer and inheritance. It seeks to define crime and also to punish it by the administration of justice in its courts.

With the decline of the functions of the early family, the power and activity of the state have increased. The Secondary functions. modern ruler, taking the place of the patriarchal father, governs a great community stretching over an enormous area. The function of protection expands into diverse forms of which our early ancestors had no conception. Thus, the state now regulates trade and industry, coins money, establishes standards of measure and formulates tariffs. The regulation of transportation, of the public health and of sanitation has come within its jurisdiction, as well as the control of education which formerly rested with the church or the school. Lastly has come the care of defectives and dependents for whom little systematic provision was formerly made. With the growth of industry and the increase of population, the modern state has become almost paternalistic. Thus the functions and powers of the state have increased with the growing culture of society. The ideal of citizenship is becoming that of social service.

**Stages of Development.** — The two roots of the state lie in kinship or blood-relationship and in the institution of The patriarchal family. private property. The state grew up with the development of the idea of private property for the protection of which government came into existence. Kinship is the other basis of the state, for the patriarchal family expanded into the *gens*, the *phratry*, the tribe and finally the nation. The primitive social group or " horde," as it is sometimes called, was composed of several family groups, the patriarchal family being much larger than the modern one. The family in the modern sense of the word includes merely the parents and offspring; for to-day when each son marries, he is regarded as forming another family. In former days, however, he did not escape his original family jurisdiction, but merely brought his wife into his father's household. The patriarchal father ruled over all his sons, their wives and their sons' families. The oldest surviving male was head of this large patriarchal family. He was judge, high priest and ruler, often possessing power of life and death over his little community. He was the custodian of the folkways, or unwritten law, and the administrator of justice and of religious sacrifices. After death, he was deified by the ceremony of ancestor worship.

The family expanded in numbers not only by natural increase but also by adoption or fictitious kinship. A stranger might be brought into the group and, The gens after going through a ceremony of initiation, or clan. was regarded as a true member of the family into which he had been adopted. Thus the patriarchal family expanded into a larger group called the *gens* or clan. This was a union of several families who possessed similar religious ceremonies and beliefs. The binding social tie expanded from kinship into common religion. The heads of the *gentes* or clans became officers of some importance. By further expansion, a union of several *gentes* or clans was called *curia* by the Romans or *phratry* by the Greeks. The purpose now became more political than religious. Covering a greater area, the new group contained the germs of local government. The first Roman assembly sat according to *curiæ* which have been likened to the wards of a modern city. We can observe this process among the Iroquois Indians who formed a federation of six tribes. Each tribe was divided into two *phratries*, each of which was subdivided into several clans named after various animals. There were, for example, the clans of the wolf, the bear and the turtle.

More important than either the clan or the *phratry* is the larger unit called the tribe which often represents the

**The tribe.** group as a whole. Among many peoples the development of the state never gets beyond the tribal stage. The Iroquois Indians, by a federation of tribes, were beginning to develop a nation when the white man appeared. The chief purpose of tribal organization is to secure coöperation in war. A capable chief or war leader is generally chosen from the heads of the clans. In many cases the *phratry* does not seem to be so important, although the custom varies with different peoples. The chief leads all the clans in war and in times of peace acts as presiding officer or judge. As the group organization perfects itself, the chief becomes king. His office tends to become hereditary and his power despotic as long as war continues.

The most ancient type of the nation is that which we call the city-state, so well illustrated by early Rome and by

**The city-state.** the small independent communities of ancient Greece. These were often based upon tribal units. Early Rome, for example, was made up of three tribes, each consisting of ten *curiæ*. The early city-states were very small, consisting merely of a single walled town and the surrounding territory. Each was an independent self-governing community, making war, negotiating peace, and demanding allegiance from its citizens.

The early city-state expanded into the nation either by the process of war or by the struggle of one city-state against another and the incorporation of the **The nation.** conquered by the conquerors. An economic factor in the conquest lay in the desire for booty or the more modern desire for commercial expansion. The successful nation became constantly larger by devouring its rivals. The field of history is strewn with the wrecks of conquered civilizations, like those of Troy, Etruria and Carthage. While the process of external expansion is going on, there is taking place internally the differentiation of political organs and functions such as is found in the modern state. Church and state tend to separate, while the government divides itself into the executive, the legislative and the judicial. Separate institutions like senate, assemblies and courts appear. The trend of development is not always toward a greater degree of democracy, because men are often willing to live under a despotism which protects their lives and their property. As Aristotle has pointed out, a frequent cycle of political change is from monarchy to aristocracy and from aristocracy to tyranny. When the rule of the tyrant becomes unbearable, the tyranny is succeeded by a democracy which, upon becoming corrupt or inefficient, gives place once more to monarchy.

**Institutions Related to the State.** — The process of war brought about the amalgamation of the state. In the patriarchal days each family avenged a wrong **Nature of** done to one of its members. In a later stage of **war: *Causes*.** political development, the warfare was carried on between tribes. In modern times war is waged between nations or between groups of nations. With the growth of the political unit, the area affected has become constantly larger. War may be regarded as the group phase of the struggle for existence. As population increases and presses upon food supply, the group tends to expand territorially. This necessity for expansion brings the group into conflict with its neighbors and war results. Besides this economic factor, racial antagonism and the clash of cultures or religions are potent causes of war. Man's primitive instincts are easily aroused, and the havoc of conflict is too apparent to need mention. Many regard war to-day as an anachronism, a relic of the primitive days of barbarism. The economic stakes for which it is waged fade frequently into insignificance when compared with the loss of property involved. The appalling loss of life is sometimes in vain, for unfortunately right is not always victorious.

Nevertheless, so long as man's primitive instincts remain, war seems to be a necessary part of the struggle for existence. *Results.* War, too, often stimulates the hardy virtues of a decaying people. It develops patriotism and serves the purpose of moral regeneration. Another good result of war has been the development of a higher degree of social organization, for conflict made group solidarity necessary. Government often arose around some competent leader who led his people to victory or safety. Thus the law-giver Moses led the children of Israel out of Egypt, guided them during their period of war and migration, and around him crystallized the slowly forming nation. The dangers of war tend to make the ruler's power more autocratic, and kingship developed in Judea after the long wars with neighboring peoples. Another result of past wars was the breaking of the " cake of custom " by a cross-fertilization of cultures. Captive Greece conquered, by her civilization, the victorious Romans. War resulted also in the formation of social classes, for the conquerors often held the conquered as slaves or as a subject class, like the Helots of the Spartans. So, in England, there existed for a century a great gulf between the upper class Norman nobles and the lower class conquered Saxons.

Thus the institution of slavery developed with war. The lives of the conquered were spared in order that they might relieve the conquerors of the burden of monot- **Rise of** onous labor. Because of the creation of a slave **slavery.** population, industry ceased to be the lot of women as was the custom during the savage or hunting stage. Slavery disciplined many subject peoples to habits of steady work and enabled the conquerors to live a. life of leisure. The cultures of Greece and Rome were products of slave civilizations. Slavery has been common in the past and has been justified by the folkways and moral standards of the group practicing it. Gradually, the lot of the slave improved, until the final disappearance of this institution from civilized society.

Laws, as we have seen, originated in folkways and unwritten customs which were later codified into legal systems by able statesmen. They reflect group stand- **Develop-** ards of conduct. The rise of the state and **ment of law** the progress of law are parallel developments. **and property.** One reason for the existence of law is the protection of the individual in his rights of property. Among primitive peoples the only recognized private property is a personal possession, such as a weapon or a bodily ornament. The belongings of another are respected merely out of regard for the owner or fear of him. The institution of private property gradually develops as the group mind or public opinion considers property rights as distinct from the individual himself. The enforcing of justice upon the thief is no longer an individual matter of the aggrieved party, but becomes a group function for which the state comes into existence. Primitive people are generally more or less communistic. Hunting grounds belong to the group and not to the individual. The Australian hunter, for example, regards the game he kills as belonging to others besides himself, and explicit rules for its disposition are found in the folkways. Individual rights are difficult for most savages to understand. The growth of civilization has been marked by the development of the idea of individual property rights as distinct from primitive savage communism.

## QUESTIONS FOR DISCUSSION

1. Give a brief definition of the state as an institution of society.
2. What are the four elements necessary?
3. Name three theories of the state.
4. Explain each.
5. What is the basis of the state in human instinct?
6. Show the rôle of coöperation.
7. Explain the idea of evolution as applied to the development of the state.
8. What made authority necessary in times of war?
9. In peace?
10. What is the primary function of the state?
11. When does feudalism arise?
12. Can you give any illustrations other than medieval Europe?
13. Name some other functions of the state.
14. Show how its sphere of activity has grown.
15. Give a description of the patriarchal family as a unit of government.
16. Explain the clan and the *phratry*.
17. What were the differences between them?

18. Give the organization of the Iroquois Indians.

19. Discuss the tribal stage of political development.

20. Define and illustrate the city-state.

21. Show the process by which nations developed from small city-states.

22. Illustrate the growth of political institutions and the development of separate organs of government.

23. How does this illustrate the evolutionary principle of development from the simple to the complex?

24. Give Aristotle's cycle of government.

25. Give some good results of war.

26. What is your opinion about its abolition in the near future?

27. Give two good results of slavery in the past.

28. Do you think our Southern slaveholders believed the institution to be just?

29. What are the two roots of the state?

30. Trace the development of the idea of private property.

## TOPICS FOR SPECIAL REPORT

1. The city-state of the Greeks.
2. The clans of ancient Rome.
3. Aristotle's defense of slavery as typical of the ancient Greeks.
4. The social contact theory.
5. The theory of the divine right of kings.
6. Communism.
7. Conditions necessary for the abolition of war.
8. Some famous lawgivers of antiquity.

## REFERENCES

HAYES, E. C. "Introduction to a Study of Sociology." Property, pp. 519–520; State, pp. 538–541; Slavery, pp. 536–538.

BLACKMAR, F. W., and GILLIN. "Outlines of Sociology." Chapter VII. Origin and Development of the State. Chapter VIII. Theory and Functions of the State.

ELLWOOD, C. A. "Sociology and Modern Social Problems." War, pp. 47–51.

DEALEY, J. Q. "Sociology." Chapter VI. Development of the State.

FAIRBANKS, A. "Introduction to Sociology." Chapter X. The State as an Organ of Social Activity.

FOWLER, W. W. "The City State of the Greeks and Romans."

WILSON, W. "The State." Chapters I and II.

# CHAPTER VIII

## The Problem of Population

**Growth of Population**. — The problem of population is a national aspect of family life. We have seen that reproduction or the creation of new members of society is the primary function of the family, and that an increase of

Its importance. population is essential to the development of the state or national life. Other things being equal, the relative importance of a group tends to rise or fall with an increase or decrease in its numbers. Mass is a considerable factor in survival, a principle of highest significance in times of fierce warfare.

While no reliable statistics are available, it is generally believed that the population of Europe during the Middle

Its modern increase:

*Early conditions.*

Ages was stationary. Conditions prevented any considerable growth of numbers for, while feudal warfare devastated the crops, famine and pestilence swept the land. The few walled towns and cities of that time were filthy, unsanitary and congested centers, through which the Black Plague could make terrible headway. In spite of the enormous death rate, a correspondingly high birth rate kept medieval population up to the limit fixed by the productivity of the land. This was not great, however, for the area under cultivation was small and the methods of farming crude. When the Council of Clermont preached the First Crusade in 1095, one argument advanced in its favor was that it offered a means of escape from over population in France. Throughout the Middle Ages and during modern times, until the opening of the nineteenth century, population increased slowly.

During the last century, however, a remarkable increase took place in the population of the civilized world. From

*Causes of increase.*

1800 to 1900 European Russia increased in population from forty to one hundred six millions, Germany from twenty-seven to fifty-six, France from twenty-five to thirty-nine and Great Britain from twenty-five to forty-one millions. Increase of population means a surplus of births over deaths, and this surplus during the nineteenth century was due to a fall in the death rate rather than to a rise in the birth rate. The advance of medical science and of public hygiene has prolonged human life by cutting down the death rate. Again, during the last century, the existence of a larger population was made possible by improved economic conditions due to various inventions and discoveries. No longer did a third of the land lie fallow as in the Middle Ages, but rotation of crops was practiced. Increased knowledge of agriculture and new inventions, such as the machine plow and the combined harvester and reaper, multiplied many times the food supply. The rise of the factory system and the development of steam transportation have made luxuries commonplace and famines exceptional. The civilized world had passed from an economy of pain to an economy of pleasure, as Professor Patten so aptly phrased it. Finally, the geographical area for production has been widened. The great plains of the Mississippi, of South America, of South Africa and of Australia have been developed. These vast regions, originally possessed by a very sparse native population, are now producing foodstuffs for the European population.

From what has been said it will be seen that there is a close connection between growth of population and increase of food supply. Because of this relationship, writers have been tempted to lay down laws of population. Thus in 1798 an English economist named Thomas Malthus published " An Essay on Population." He originally contended that while food supply increased only in an arithmetical progression, popu-

*Laws of population: Theory of Malthus.*

G

lation tended to increase in a geometrical ratio. This theory was later modified to the mere assertion that population tended to increase faster than the food supply. Positive checks upon population are those factors which increase the death rate. Good examples of these are war, pestilence and famine. Negative or preventive checks are those which decrease the birth rate, such as the higher age of marriage and the development of a feeling of responsibility. Such in brief was the theory of Thomas Malthus who believed the source of most human misery lay in the tendency of population to outstrip the means of subsistence. His writings were so widely read that there soon grew up around him a pessimistic school of philosophers. Little hope was held for the future of society, and war, famine and pestilence were regarded as necessary evils to keep down surplus population. The very century in which Malthus died disproved his melancholy theory, mentioned here merely because of its historical importance. As we have seen, not only were new areas of production opened, but also upon old lands intensive farming was practiced. A progressive society, characterized by invention and coöperation, can set no arbitrary limit to its productivity. Again, the same century produced a falling birth rate which, as a negative check, makes unnecessary the operation of such positive checks as war and famine in the process of adjusting population to food supply.

It may be stated that, while the growth of population is limited by food supply and general economic conditions,
*Modern opinion.* it is impossible to lay down any exact laws upon the subject. Savages in the hunting and fishing stage do not develop a dense population. The American Indians were probably not more numerous in the days of

Columbus than at present, but had apparently reached their maximum growth of population. A whole continent can support only a sparse population so long as it is used as a hunting ground. When the pastoral stage is reached, a given area will support more people, but a wandering life necessitates large areas inadequately developed. A fairly dense population develops only when the agricultural stage is reached. The fourth stage, that of commerce and manufacturing, has produced a congestion in cities and a density of population unparalleled in history.

The 1920 census found over 117,000,000 people living under the American flag, 105,000,000 of whom resided in continental United States. In point of numbers China with its four hundred millions comes first. Should this nation take hold of western civilization as did Japan, it is destined to become a mighty factor in the world of to-morrow. We have compared the populations of the nations of western Europe in 1800 with the figures for 1900 and have seen the remarkable increase during the past century. Let us compare the latter figures with those for 1910 and see what the future may promise.

European Russia jumped from one hundred six to one hundred thirty-four millions, Germany from fifty-six to sixty-five, France from thirty-nine to thirty-nine In foreign and one-half millions, Great Britain and Ireland countries. from forty-two to forty-five, Austria from forty-five to forty-nine, Italy from thirty-two to thirty-five, Spain from eighteen and one-half to nineteen and one-half millions and the United States from seventy-six to ninety-two millions. Looking over the figures for Europe we notice first of all that, generally speaking, there was no diminution in the rapid rate of increase which marked the last century.

Of course this does not take into account the effect of the World War upon present population. In the second place, the rate of increase varies greatly in the different countries and, if continued, this difference will greatly affect their future relative importance. In spite of a high death rate, Russia leads the list because of an enormous birth rate. Thus that nation may become a still greater factor in future European politics, although a high birth rate and a high death rate indicate a relatively low plane of civilization. France and Germany afford an interesting comparison. While Germany comes second in rate of increase, France is last in the list, for her population is little more than stationary. If the ratios for the first ten years are typical of the century, the relative importance of these nations will be greatly affected. A century from now, a country of forty million people will be of little more importance than Holland or Belgium is at present.

Immigration has been largely responsible for the enormous increase in the population of the United States. At the time

In the
United
States.

when our independence was achieved there were about three million people inhabiting the thirteen original states. Since then, in every generation of thirty years, our population has doubled itself. Naturally, the increase has been greatest in the newer states of the West. The following table shows the result of each census:

| | | | |
|---|---|---|---|
| 1790 — | 3,929,214 | 1850 — | 23,191,876 |
| 1800 — | 5,308,483 | 1860 — | 31,443,321 |
| 1810 — | 7,239,881 | 1870 — | 38,558,371 |
| 1820 — | 9,638,453 | 1880 — | 50,155,783 |
| 1830 — | 12,866,020 | 1890 — | 62,947,714 |
| 1840 — | 17,069,453 | 1900 — | 75,994,575 |

1910 — 91,972,266
1920 — 105,708,771

**Distribution of Population**. — About <u>one-half</u> of the <u>world's population lives in Asia</u> and one-quarter in Europe. The remaining dry land of the globe including Geographical Africa, Australia, North and South America distribution. contains little over a quarter of the world's total population. In Europe the industrial nations of <u>Belgium</u> and <u>England</u> are the most densely populated. Before the World War the population of Belgium averaged six hundred thirty-six per square mile. <u>Italy and Germany</u> came next with a respective density of one hundred six and one hundred four people per square kilometer. The least densely populated of all Europe are Russia and Scandinavia. As compared with western Europe, the United States is sparsely peopled. Germany, for example, is ten times as densely populated as our own country. The average density for the United States as a whole is thirty-one per square mile, varying from five hundred eight in Rhode Island to less than one in Nevada. The center of population, however, has been moving steadily westward from the older states along the Atlantic seaboard. When the first census was taken in 1790 this center was located near Baltimore, but it has moved steadily westward through Maryland, Virginia, West Virginia, Ohio and Indiana. The 1920 census located it in Owen county in southwestern Indiana. The dry climate and high altitude of our mountain states of the West make a dense population improbable in that region. The density of population in the eastern states is much greater than in the western, for the East is the commercial and industrial section where numerous large cities flourish. Indeed, at present, over half our entire population lives in cities of twenty-five hundred or more inhabitants. During the last ten years our urban population has increased three times as fast as the rural. About five per cent of our entire population is within the limits of greater New York City.

About nine-tenths of our population is white, while the remaining one-tenth is negro, most of whom are located south of the Mason and Dixon line. There are about one-fourth of a million Indians, and about one hundred fifty thousand Mongolians, chiefly located in California. This number of Mongolians may be divided fairly equally between the Chinese and the Japanese.

*Other methods: Race.*

About eighty-five per cent of our present population is native born, the remaining fifteen per cent being foreign. The number of those of foreign parentage is quite high and reaches a maximum in the New England and Middle Atlantic States of over twenty-five per cent. As we shall see later, there is a great tendency of our foreign-born population to become congested in the cities.

*Nativity.*

How nature provides for the approximate numerical equality of the sexes is a problem of biology, but that such is the case may be seen by examining large numbers of birth records. As men are more likely to migrate than women, new countries like our own, affected by immigration, will show a slight excess of males over females. Older countries, affected by emigration, show a slight excess of females. War tends to reduce the proportion of males. In the United States there is an excess of two and one-half million males over the number of females. In Europe, before the World War, there was a slight excess of women.

*Sex.*

The average age in the United States as found by the census of 1920 was approximately twenty-six years. The

suffrage laws vary in the different states, but the proportion of those over the legal age of twenty-one is slightly over one-half.    The proportion of males of military age from eighteen to forty-five years is about  *Age.*
one-fifth the population or approximately twenty millions. About the same proportion makes up the school population of the country.

**Vital Statistics**. — Under vital statistics are included the records of births and deaths in a nation.    These are reckoned according to every thousand of the
population.    Thus, a death rate of nineteen and  **Meaning.**
seven-tenths would therefore mean that in a given year, in a given community, an average of slightly over nineteen people died out of every thousand of the population. Death records are fairly accurate, but in spite of legal requirements the registration of births in our country is far from complete.

We have seen that the population of Europe, before the World War, was increasing.    This was true in spite of a falling birth rate, for the death rate had also fallen so that there still was a considerable excess of births over deaths. Let us examine the birth rates of three typical nations:

BIRTH RATE

| | 1871–1880 | 1881–1890 | 1891–1900 | 1900–1909 |
|---|---|---|---|---|
| Germany . . . . . . . | 39.1 | 36.8 | 36.1 | 34.0 |
| England and Wales  . . . | 35.5 | 23.5 | 30.0 | 27.6 |
| France  . . . . . . . | 25.4 | 23.9 | 22.1 | 20.8 |

The above table is evidence of a declining birth rate in three leading countries of Europe.    This fact is extremely significant, for it seems to indicate that a high civilization is characterized by a low birth rate. Again, the difference

A falling
birth rate:
*In Europe.*

in the birth rates of Germany and France is most striking. There are many reasons for this difference, but perhaps the most important is the economic. Germany in the last generation made great industrial progress and became capable of supporting a large population, while in France economic and social conditions were not so favorable to the growth of large families. For example, French law requires an equal division of the father's property among the children. This plan has encouraged small families among the peasants so that the holdings of each son may not be too small. This low birth rate has been a problem to French statesmen and a scheme of taxation has even been proposed to meet the situation. According to this plan, the highest tax would fall upon bachelors, whereas a father of three children might be entirely exempt from taxation.

In America, a similar but not so pressing a problem exists, for we are facing a decrease in the birth rate of our

*In America.*

native white stock. The average size of the American family has decreased from five and six-tenths in 1850 to four and five-tenths in 1910. Thus in the last half century it has decreased by more than one person. The falling birth rate is most noticeable in New England, so that the very phenomenon occurring in France is equally visible in Vermont and New Hampshire. This decrease is most apparent when we compare our native birth rate with the birth rate of our immigrants. In 1910, in Massachusetts, the native birth rate was fourteen and eight-tenths, while the birth rate of the foreign born was forty-nine and five-tenths. The death rates of native born and foreign born were sixteen and three-tenths and fifteen and five-tenths respectively. Hence the native stock in Massachusetts is decreasing, since the birth rate is actually lower than the death rate. Among the foreign immigrants, however, the surplus of births over deaths is enormous. What will be the future of Puritan New England if this situation continues and who will inherit the land of the Pilgrim fathers? In the South, however, the situation is not so serious, for there the native white stock is holding its own.

The most important cause of the declining birth rate among our native white stock is found in the economic situation. American standards of living have been constantly rising, while wages have not *The causes.* risen proportionately. This relatively lower increase in wages has been attributed to the lower standards of immigrant laborers who, in their competition with native laborers, force down wages. As a consequence, the American seems to be delaying the age of marriage, and the result is the small family. If he wishes to give to his children desired advantages, a moderate income will not permit him to rear a large family. The increase in the cost of living has exceeded the increase in wages and far outstripped the salary of the so-called middle classes. As a result, the birth rate falls rather than the standard of living. Curiously enough the size of the family seems to vary inversely with the extremes of income. What has been said above applies mainly to the great middle class. Comparing the so-called upper and lower classes of American society, based of course upon income, we find that the birth rate of the " laboring class " is much higher than that of the " social set." In this latter case a desire for luxurious ease and comfort often militates against large families. In addition to selfishness, there are many other causes, beside the economic, which help to explain the declining birth rate of native white Americans.

From the following table we may observe a falling death rate in three leading European countries:

|  | 1875–1899 | 1900 | 1900–1909 |
|---|---|---|---|
| Germany . . . . . . . | 24.4 | 22.1 | 19.5 |
| England and Wales . . . | 19.3 | 18.2 | 15.8 |
| France . . . . . . . . | 22.0 | 21.9 | 19.8 |

This fact of a falling death rate is also true of our own country. Thus the death rate in Massachusetts was nineteen and three-tenths in 1890 and seventeen and seven-tenths in 1900. In the same decade, the death rate in the state of New York fell from nineteen and six-tenths to seventeen and nine-tenths. The stage of civilization attained by a people may be read in the death rate of a nation, for enlightened countries attempt to prolong human life and to lessen preventable diseases. Modern medical science has done much in this direction. In the last century the death rate of cities has been cut in half by a knowledge of public hygiene and sanitation. One by one the causes and carriers of disease are being discovered and conquered. The elimination of typhoid by a more careful disposal of sewage, of yellow fever by the extermination of the mosquito, and of small-pox by compulsory vaccination are the triumphs of medical science. The crusade against tuberculosis is still being waged. However, infant mortality, although decreasing,

*A falling death rate: The reasons.*

is still high. Baby-saving campaigns have resulted in popular education upon this subject. Clean milk and fly-less homes will accomplish marvels. At the present time, however, one-half of all infants born die before the age of five years. In 1900, in the registered area of the United States, sixteen and two-tenths per cent of all children born died within the first year.

War is an obviously important factor affecting the death rate. Economic depression raises the price of food and with it the death rate. Industrial accidents *Other* kill thousands annually in the United States *influences.* alone, and occupational diseases take a terrible toll. Climate and season are two other important factors influencing the death rate. In cold climates winter is often fatal, while in warm lands summer brings the dreaded fever. It would seem that sex and conjugal condition are also factors in longevity, for apparently males are shorter lived than females and bachelors do not live as long as married men.

## QUESTIONS FOR DISCUSSION

1. Why do you think the population of Europe during the Middle Ages was stationary?
2. Show the great increase during the nineteenth century.
3. Give reasons for it.
4. State the theory of Malthus.
5. Criticize it and show the falsity of his fears.
6. What is the "law of diminishing returns"?
7. What relation does it bear to Malthus' theory?
8. Show the relation between occupation and density of population.
9. Compare the countries of Europe in respect to their present rates of increase.

10. Show the enormous rate of increase in the population of United States.

11. To what is it due?

12. What continents are most densely populated?

13. What countries of Europe are the most and what the least densely populated?

14. What is the average density of population in the United States?

15. How does it vary from East to West?

16. How does it compare with Europe?

17. Show how the center of population has moved westward.

18. Show how our population is distributed by race; by nativity.

19. Distribute population according to sex; according to age.

20. What are vital statistics?

21. Compare the birth rates in France and Germany.

22. Compare the birth rates in America of the native and the foreign born.

23. What will be the result if this difference continues?

24. Give reasons for our falling native birth rate.

25. Where is it most, and where least, apparent?

26. Show the falling death rate in Europe; in America.

27. How has the advance of medical science prolonged human life and cut down the death rate?

28. Discuss infant mortality.

29. Describe some factors that influence the death rate.

## TOPICS FOR SPECIAL REPORT

1. The opening of new areas for the production of food.

2. The possibilities of scientific farming.

3. The pressure of the population of China upon its resources; of India.

4. The effects of the theory of Malthus upon later writers.

5. An explanation of the alleged static population of France.

6. The rapid increase of population in Germany.

7. The possibility of further lowering the death rate in civilized countries.

8. The falling of the birth rate of the native white Americans.

## REFERENCES

ELLWOOD, C. A. "Sociology and Modern Social Problems." Chapter IX. Growth of Population.

WRIGHT, C. D. "Practical Sociology." Chapter II. Population of U. S. Chapter III. Status of the Population of U. S. Chapter IV. Native and Foreign Born.

BAILEY. "Modern Social Conditions."

United States Census Reports.

*Contrast settlers at different times & different sections*

# CHAPTER IX

## THE AMERICAN PEOPLE

**Method of Growth.** — Increase of population may take place by either of two methods. There may be a growth of the native population due to a natural surplus of births over deaths. This was the theme of the preceding chapter. A second method of increase which we are now to investigate is by immigration from foreign **The two ways.** lands. Both these methods have played an important part in the great numerical expansion of the American people. There is, moreover, a very interesting relation between the native birth rate and the rate of foreign immigration, as will be seen by a study of the following table:

| Year | Per Cent of Total Increase | Per Cent by Immigration | Per Cent by Birth |
|------|---------------------------|------------------------|-------------------|
| 1840 . . . . . | 32.67 | 4.66 | 28.01 |
| 1850 . . . . . | 35.87 | 10.04 | 25.83 |
| 1860 . . . . . | 35.58 | 11.12 | 24.46 |
| 1870 . . . . . | 22.63 | 7.25 | 15.38 |
| 1880 . . . . . | 30.08 | 7.29 | 22.79 |
| 1890 . . . . . | 25.50 | 10.46 | 15.04 |
| 1900 . . . . . | 20.73 | 5.86 | 14.87 |
| 1910 . . . . . | 21.02 | 11.57 | 9.45 |
| 1920 . . . . . | 15.00 | 4.50 | 10.50 |

This table shows that, generally speaking, as the rate of foreign immigration has increased the native birth rate has fallen. Hence Professor Walker argues that **An odd theory.** it is doubtful whether foreign immigration has actually increased the sum total of our population which was increasing as rapidly before the enormous wave of immigration as afterwards. Again, although the South has received little immigration since the Civil War, her population has increased proportionately just as rapidly as the population of the North has been recruited by foreign immigration.

However this may be, the volume of foreign immigration has been sufficiently great to play an important part in our national life. We shall discuss in this chapter the past story of immigration and in the following the present problem confronting us.

**The Original Groups.** — In 1607, at Jamestown, was founded the first permanent English colony in America. The South: From the earliest times to the present, the New *Early* World has been regarded as a land of boundless *settlement.* possibilities. The first English colonists in Virginia expected to find gold and precious stones and to return to the mother land with the wealth of the New World. Instead, death and starvation faced them, while the life of the new colony hung by a thread. The cultivation of tobacco, however, gave the South a permanent industrial basis. The nationality of the immigrants was almost purely English, but of the most varied character and social condition. After the execution of Charles I and the establishment of the Commonwealth, a number of royalist families fled to Virginia rather than submit to political conditions at home. The exodus of the cavaliers to the New World is responsible for such names as Washington, Marshall, Monroe and Madison in American history. Many of the first families of the South had their roots in the aristocracy of Old England. Many also were sprung from the country gentry and from the middle class who came to America to escape political vexation or to recruit a failing fortune. The lower classes also sent their quota. Indentured servants came over at the rate of a thousand a year. Kidnappers smuggled over victims snatched from the streets of London, while prisoners were often given the choice between the gallows and the New World. Dr. Johnson considered Americans " a race of convicts " who " ought to be content with anything we allow them short of hanging." This comment of an old English pedant should be remembered by the descendants of these same Americans, not because of its inaccuracy, but rather to prevent ourselves from falling into a similar error with regard to our own present-day immigrants.

The founding of Georgia by Oglethorpe, as an asylum for debtors languishing in English prisons, should be interesting to the student of social problems. The cultivation of indigo in the Carolinas played *Social life.* the same rôle as the cultivation of tobacco in Virginia. Cotton did not become king in the South until after the invention of the cotton gin. Slavery was introduced and, as in Spanish America, it was especially suited to plantation life. A broad and fertile land made agriculture the natural industry, while large estates developed a landed aristocracy. The home of the planter was magnificently located upon a hill overlooking a river, up which came the yearly ship from England to discharge its cargo of luxuries and to receive its crop of tobacco. Living at a distance from each other, travelers were royally entertained and Southern hospitality became justly famous. The county system of local government, instead of the township, was the natural political development of a widely scattered population engaged in agriculture. The established church was the Anglican.

Plymouth Rock is still the shrine of tourists, for here in 1620 landed the Pilgrim fathers. For the sake of conscience, they sailed the stormy Atlantic and endured the bleak shores of New England. In their old home, state and church were united and the Anglican form of worship was obligatory. After a

New England: *How founded.*

H

brief stay in Holland, the Pilgrims were granted the right to settle in America where they could worship God as they pleased. The restoration in 1660, like the persecutions of Archbishop Laud, drove to the New World thousands more of dissenting Puritans. In this great exodus several regicides took refuge. Virginia had been the Mecca for royalists for whom, a short time before, the parliamentary Commonwealth had become unsafe. New England, after the restoration of the Stuart king, became the haven for the adherents of the " Roundhead " party.

Like Virginia the early settlers of New England were purely of English stock, but of very different character. *Compared with the South.* We have spoken already of the political and religious differences between them. The cavalier type in the South was merry and pleasure loving, while the New England Puritan was grave and stern. Roisterers, gossips and Sabbath breakers were punished. In America, to-day, the Puritan traditions of the Sabbath still linger in spite of the broadening spirit of the twentieth century. The climate, the hilly nature of the land and the fear of the Indians prevented agriculture from developing into the plantation system. For the same reasons, the township system of local government developed with its school and meetinghouse. Self-government became a passion with the Puritan, who fought for freedom from the days of the Boston tea-party to the time of the abolition movement against slavery. Puritan blood has sometimes been responsible for narrowness and bigotry in our national character, but it has always been willing to fight for a cause that it believed to be just.

The Middle Colonies had a rather checkered career and their origin, unlike that of the other two sections, was not

INTERIOR OF A NEW ENGLAND PIONEER'S HOME.

purely English.   Let us trace their racial heredity.   The
Dutch were the first to settle New Amsterdam as a trading post with the Indians for furs.   Their line **Middle**
stretched from Fort Nassau (now Gloucester, **Colonies:**
N.J.) to Fort Orange (now Albany, N.Y.).   *Their origin.*
Long after the English occupied their territory,   Dutch
names like Schuyler, Astor and Van Rensselaer continued
to appear in American life.   The customs and characteristics of the Knickerbockers have colored New York.   The
Swedes settled at the mouth of the Delaware and named
Christiana Creek after their queen.   They were absorbed
in turn, however, by the Dutch and English.   Pennsylvania and Maryland are two famous examples of colonies
founded as asylums from religious persecutions, by William
Penn for the Quakers, and by Lord Baltimore for the Roman
Catholics.   Religious liberty characterized the Middle
Colonies.   This toleration affords a good illustration of
the liberalizing effects of a cross fertilization of cultures.

The Swedes and the Dutch lost their colonies to the
English, who continued to migrate to America in large
numbers.   A new element, however, was found *Another*
in a large wave of German immigration which *element.*
began to pour into Pennsylvania about this time.   William
Penn had advertised his colony in a pamphlet directed to
the oppressed of all nations.   This was circulated widely
through the Palatinate region of Germany.   There the
peasants had suffered greatly from the horrors of the
Thirty Years' War and in the wars with Louis XIV of
France.   Many dissenting Protestant sects, like the Dun-
kards and the Mennonites, sought liberty in the New World.
So vast was this alien tide that it was feared the English
would be outnumbered by the German population which

settled the rich agricultural valleys of Pennsylvania. Among the great men of this group we may mention Pastorius, the German Quaker, who settled Germantown, Rittenhouse, the mathematician, and the patriot Muhlenburg.

Louis XIV of France revoked the Edict of Nantes which had granted toleration to the Protestant Huguenots. Under *Later addi-* pain of conformity or persecution this enterpris-
*tions:* ing and industrial class of French citizens fled to
*Huguenots.* Holland, England and America. New Rochelle, named after the old Huguenot stronghold in France, was founded near New York. South Carolina also had a sprinkling of this immigration which furnished such names in American history as Paul Revere and John Jay.

Among the most aggressive of our early settlers were the Scotch-Irish. They were the Protestant Scotch, *The Scotch-* mostly Presbyterians, who had settled northern
*Irish.* Ireland in the days of James I. Through them Ulster became a great industrial center, but the growing linen industry was deliberately killed by an act of the English parliament. Again, conformity to the established Anglican church was necessary to the enjoyment of many rights of citizenship. Therefore, at the beginning of the eighteenth century, a great wave of Scotch-Irish migration to America took place. As the seacoast was already occupied, they settled along the frontier marked by the Allegheny Mountains. Their line stretched from New Hampshire and Vermont, through central Pennsylvania west of the German settlement, and down through the Shenandoah Valley into Virginia and the Carolinas. The Scotch-Irish were of that pioneer type who cleared the forests and fought back the Indians. They won the West

for a later generation and have kept alive ideals of democracy. To this group belong many illustrious statesmen and generals, like Patrick Henry, Andrew Jackson and General Grant.

**National Expansion**. — Such were the people who settled the thirteen original states and such was the racial heredity of the young nation. At the time when independ- Territorial ence was achieved only the seacoast back to the growth. mountains was occupied. The movement of population across the Appalachians was just beginning. In Jefferson's administration was acquired the great Louisiana Purchase which moved our western limits from the Mississippi River to the Rocky Mountains. Land could be had for the settling and a long train of prairie schooners swept westward. The later discovery of gold in our new possession of California was an additional attraction. Canals, public roads and steam transportation opened up this vast region. The divergent elements in our colonial stock first began to amalgamate in this western melting pot of races.

The development of the American people illustrates two results of migration as a factor in social evolution. First of all, immigration acts as a selective pro- Social cess because it picks out of a foreign population results. the stronger, the more restless and the more energetic elements. They are the pioneers who brave the dangers of travel across the sea and the unknown fate of a strange land. Another result of immigration is the intermingling of peoples. The crossing of nationalities in America has been well-nigh universal, so that pure strains of racial blood are comparatively rare. Cultures have mingled as well as blood. The " cake of custom " having been broken, the new land became heir to the culture of numerous civilizations out of which America is now molding its own.

At the same time that our national domain was expanding westward, waves of migration were coming to America from Europe. As water seeks its level, so population moves from dense to sparsely settled regions. The countries principally contributing to our early immigration were Great Britain and Ireland, Germany and Scandinavia. Between 1820, the first year for which we have statistics, and the present time, over thirty million immigrants have come to America. Half of this number has arrived since 1890, which date marks the beginning of immigration on a large scale. The sources of immigration have steadily shifted from northern Europe to the Mediterranean lands. For this reason we speak of the early, and of the later, immigration of the nineteenth century.

*Waves of immigration: Number.*

In 1820 the number of immigrants was eight thousand. This group increased slowly, not passing the one hundred thousand mark until the forties were reached. Two significant dates are 1846 and 1848. The former marked the failure of the potato crop in Ireland, while the latter ushered in the political revolutions of Central Europe. Both events sent large numbers of immigrants to America, but the increase of numbers was checked by the outbreak of the Civil War. In the seventies the numbers rose again, growing still larger in the eighties. The proportion declined, however, during the nineties. With the opening of the twentieth century and up until the outbreak of the World War, immigration to the United States assumed enormous proportions, passing the mark of one million annually. It is interesting to note how the

*Causes.*

fluctuations in immigration have corresponded to economic conditions in the United States. The curve of migration corresponds almost exactly with the rise and fall of national prosperity in this country.

**The Early Immigration of the Nineteenth Century.** — Because our institutions are modeled largely upon those of Great Britain, American history has its beginnings in England. Her contribution to The Irish. the early colonists was numerically the greatest, — English, Scotch and Welsh immigration to this country continuing long after the war for independence. Ireland, however, has occupied a unique position in American history. From 1820 to 1850 the Irish made up two-fifths, and, during the fifties, one-third, of our total immigration. The population of the island was reduced one-half by famine and emigration. There are probably now more Irish in America than in Ireland itself, and the people have decidedly colored our national character. At first the Irish immigrant was received into the " pick and shovel caste," but he has risen rapidly from the ranks of unskilled labor to positions of honor and trust in the community. Many Americans prominent in public life are of Irish descent, for they have shown rare capacity in executive positions. Many, however, have not advanced because the Irish-American, as compared with the German-American, seems to fall into extremes of conduct.

The German-American element in our population is of equal importance. Over five millions of Germans have come to this country during the last century. The At first, as we have seen, this migration was due Germans. to religious oppression, but later it was the result of political oppression. As compared with the Irish, this group of immigrants was steady, thrifty and provident. Because of different language and customs, the German element in this country has been more difficult to assimilate than the Irish. Germans tend to settle in communities like those in Pennsylvania, Missouri, Illinois and Wisconsin. They have become skilled artisans, small tradesmen and have also attached themselves to the soil. The Irish have been fond of competitive sports and athletic games, but the German-American has found interest in gymnastic societies, festivals and choruses requiring coöperation rather than competition. The Irish policeman and the German band are typical of opposing racial characteristics.

At the present time there are probably over a million people in the United States who were born in Norway,

The Scandinavians. Sweden or Denmark. Norway has given to us a greater percentage of her people than any other country except Ireland. The home of the Scandinavian immigrant has been the Northwest, including the states of Minnesota, Wisconsin, Illinois, North and South Dakota and Iowa. The Irish immigrants were almost entirely Catholic, but the Scandinavians were Protestant. This group has recruited the rural farming population of our country and has also played an important part in the lumbering and transportation industries. In point of literacy this group leads. Like the German and the Irish migration, the Scandinavian immigration to this country has about ceased.

## QUESTIONS FOR DISCUSSION

1. In what two ways may population increase?
2. What is the relation between them?
3. Explain Professor Walker's theory.

4. Describe the character of the Virginia settlers.

5. Compare the New Englanders with them.

6. Compare the different institutions of the two regions.

7. What alien peoples settled in the Middle Colonies?

8. Give some of their characteristics.

9. What was the effect of this mixture of races and creeds?

10. Give the motive and character of the Huguenot settlers.

11. Of the Scotch-Irish.

12. Where did these people settle?

13. State the ancestry of some famous Americans.

14. What was the effect upon immigration of the territorial expansion of our young nation?

15. Give two effects of migration upon social evolution.

16. Trace the rise and fall of immigration and show its relation to conditions in Europe and in the United States.

17. From what countries did the early immigration of the nineteenth century come?

18. Make a list of the various causes.

19. Give the number and characteristics of the Irish immigration.

20. Of the German immigration.

21. Of the Scandinavian immigration.

## TOPICS FOR SPECIAL REPORT

1. The historical background in England for the settlement of Virginia and of New England.

2. Geographical environment as an explanation for differences in the institutions of New England and the Southern colonies.

3. The contributions of non-English nationalities to the life and customs of the Middle Colonies.

4. The rôle of religious persecution in the settlement of America.

5. The Scotch-Irish pioneer in American history.

6. German immigration to this country.

7. The effects of the potato famine in Ireland.

8. The revolutions of 1848 in continental Europe as affecting emigration.

## REFERENCES

THWAITES, R. G.  " The Colonies."

ROSS, E. A.  "Old World in the New."  Chapters I to IV.

WARNE, F. J.  "Immigrant Invasion."  Chapter IV.

COMMONS, J. R.  "Races and Immigrants in America."  Chapter II.

ELLWOOD, C. A.  "Sociology and Modern Social Problems."  Chapter X.  Immigration Problems.

*Contrast early*
*immigrants & later*
*source*
*type*
*cause*
*effect*

# CHAPTER X

## THE PROBLEM OF IMMIGRATION

I. Present sources
  1. The change
  2. The Italians
  3. The Slavs
  4. The Russian Jews
  5. Other groups
II. Distribution of immigration
  1. Geographical
  2. Industrial
III. Effects of immigration
  1. Economic effect
  2. Social effect
  3. Political effect
  4. Illiteracy
  5. Poverty and crime
  6. Other social effects
IV. Asiatic immigration
  1. Its history
  2. Its problems
V. Restrictions upon immigration
  1. The usual restrictions
  2. The proposed remedy

**Present Sources.** — In the last two decades of the nineteenth century a remarkable change began to take place in the character of American immigration. Previously the supply had been drawn from **The change.** northern Europe in the Teutonic and Celtic countries

107

of Scandinavia, Germany, Great Britain and Ireland. Now the source of supply began to shift to the southeast, including the countries of Italy, Austria, Hungary and Russia. This change is easily perceived by a study of the following table, which gives the percentage of immigration for six groups:

|  | 1882 | 1907 |
|---|---|---|
| Great Britain and Ireland . . . | 22.8% | 8.8% |
| Germany . . . . . . . . . | 31.7% | 2.9% |
| Scandinavia . . . . . . . | 13.3% | 3.9% |
| Total . . . . . . . . | 67.8% | 15.6% |
| Italy . . . . . . . . . . | 4.1% | 22.2% |
| Austro-Hungary . . . . . . | 3.7% | 26.3% |
| Russia . . . . . . . . . | 2.7% | 20.1% |
| Total . . . . . . . . | 10.5% | 68.6% |

This table shows that, during recent times, the percentages of immigration from the countries of northern and southern Europe have been practically reversed. The change in the character of the immigration is likewise significant. A line drawn diagonally across Europe from northeast to southwest separates two distinct civilizations. The northern area (except France, from which we receive few immigrants, and Ireland) is Protestant and, generally speaking, has been accustomed to some degree of political freedom. The southern area is Catholic in religion and, as yet, not altogether accustomed to free institutions. Such a geographical line would also separate literacy from illiteracy, and the intelligent artisan and farmer from a backward peasantry scarcely removed from serfdom. Finally, it would separate the Teutonic races from the Latin and the Slav. The European type north of this imaginary line is similar to our colonial stock and is capable of adjusting itself to American institutions. The races to the southeast, however, present a more difficult problem of amalgamation. Whereas in earlier times the immigrants to America often sought a refuge from religious and political persecution, the cause of the more recent immigration is largely economic.

Before the World War, Italy was sending to our shores between one-quarter and one-half million immigrants annually. The reason for this Italian immigration is entirely economic, for in the native land **The Italians.** living has become precarious. The rich resources of America call the Italian from his impoverished and overpopulated land. The Italian immigration has settled largely in the North Atlantic states, showing a great tendency to congest in cities. Often an entire village has been transplanted to one street in the ghetto of a great city. Only one-fifth of the immigrants are women, and the absence of family ties encourages a migratory life. Hence many shift from place to place, borne along with the tide of a fluctuating labor market. After acquiring a little of the new world's wealth, they often seek to return to their native Italian village. A distinction, however, should be made between the North and the South Italian stocks which are fundamentally different. The racial distinction may be read in physical characteristics, while traits of character are also divergent. The better class of north Italian stock often seeks Argentina and other South American lands, where it becomes an important factor in industrial enterprises. The occupations of the Italian in America include construction work, trading and farming, as well as many forms of unskilled labor.

At the present time there are nearly two million Slavs in the United States, half of whom are Poles.  So great

**The Slavs.** is the number of the various Slavic groups that their European habitat is a Babel of tongues and a mass of confusion.  In numerical proportion we find, after the Poles, the following groups, — Bohemians, Moravians, Slovaks from the Carpathian Mountains, Slovenes from the head of the Adriatic, Croatians, Dalmations, Russians (exclusive of the Hebrews), Bulgarians, Servians, Montenegrins, Slavonians, Ruthenians, Lithuanians and Letts.  Three-fourths of these immigrants are males and their illiteracy is extremely high.  The Slavs belong almost entirely to the class of unskilled labor which finds occupation in the mines and in the great manufacturing industries where brawn, not brain, is essential.  They have settled mainly in the mining and industrial region which has its central point in western Pennsylvania.  An exception is found in the case of Poles and Bohemians who settle upon farms.  The Slavs are remarkable for their fecundity.  Large families and a high birth rate are the rule.  They are slow in assimilation and many of their different groups seek to found in the new world a nationalism impossible of attainment in the old.  The future of Slav immigration is of vital importance, for immigration has scarcely touched the millions of Slavs in Russia.  So far most of this immigration has been largely Hebrew in character.

At the present time there are over two million Hebrew immigrants in America, so that one-fifth of all the Jews

**Russian Jews.** in the world reside in the United States.  America is, indeed, the " Promised Land."  As compared with other groups, the Hebrew seeks to bring

Courtesy of the Charles Beseler Company.

MODERN "PILGRIMS" COMING TO AMERICA.

over his entire family and to make America his permanent
home. The Jews have settled almost entirely in the
cities, preferring commerce and trading to manual labor.
Garment and cigar making are more attractive to them
than ordinary unskilled labor. The sweat shop industries
are good examples of the exploitation of the Jewish immigrant. There are comparatively few Jews in prison or in
the almshouses. Intellectually, they rank higher than
other immigrants, as may be readily seen by the records
of school children in foreign districts. Out of the six
million Jews in the Russian pale, nearly two million have
been forced to America by the fire of persecution. A
background of centuries of race prejudice has so cemented
this group that religious and other traditions prevent
their quick absorption into American civilization. However, they do assume outward American characteristics
and the rise of the Hebrew in wealth and social position
is marvelous.

The attempted Russification of Finland has driven thousands of these people to America. Like the Swedes, the
Finns have become farmers in our great North- Other
west. The Magyars or Hungarians are partly groups.
Mongul in blood and descended from the Asiatic invaders
who settled in the plains of the Danube River. There
are a quarter of a million of these Hungarians in our land
and, like the Slavs, they may be found in the mining and
industrial regions of America. Many return to Europe
with their American earnings, leaving behind, not infrequently, an undesirable record. During the last fifteen
years, about one hundred and fifty thousand Greeks have
come to us from the land of Homer. Among this people,
as well as the Italians, the padrone system of labor flourishes.

Many boys live under a master, by whom and for whose benefit their labor is exploited. From Asiatic Turkey come not only the Turks, but also the Armenians and Syrians, who peddle anything from olive oil to costly rugs. These people are subject to rigid immigration inspection, for the disease of trachoma or granulated eyelid is common among them.

**Distribution of Immigration.** — We have seen the tendency of immigrants to congest into groups and have Geographical. noted the favored spot of each national group. The figures for 1907 showed that sixty-five per cent of those who came that year settled in the North Atlantic states, twenty-three per cent in the North Central states, but only four and one-half per cent in the South, and six per cent in the West. From the following table, compiled from the census of 1910, we may observe the percentage of foreign population in certain typical states:

| STATE | PERCENTAGE OF FOREIGN BORN | STATE | PERCENTAGE OF FOREIGN PARENTAGE |
|---|---|---|---|
| Rhode Island | 32.8 | Minnesota . . | 71.5 |
| Massachusetts | 31.2 | North Dakota | 70.6 |
| New York . | 29.9 | Rhode Island | 68.7 |
| Connecticut . | 29.5 | Wisconsin . . | 66.8 |
| North Dakota | 27.1 | Massachusetts | 66.0 |
| Minnesota . | 26.2 | Connecticut . | 63.1 |
| New Jersey . | 25.9 | New York . | 63.0 |

The seven states on the left show that over a quarter of their population has been born in foreign lands. In addition to this fact, the seven states on the right show that two-thirds of their population are of foreign parentage.

This table indicates not only the size of the foreign element in our population, but also the fact that it is largely located in our North Atlantic and Middle states in the East, and in the North Central states of the West.

The congestion of foreign immigration in urban centers may be shown by a similar table (also taken from the 1910 census) for five leading American cities:

| CITY | PERCENTAGE OF FOREIGN BORN | PERCENTAGE OF FOREIGN PARENTAGE |
|---|---|---|
| New York . . . . . . . . | 40.4 | 78.6 |
| Chicago . . . . . . . . . | 35.7 | 77.5 |
| Philadelphia . . . . . . . | 24.7 | 56.8 |
| St. Louis . . . . . . . . | 18.3 | 54.2 |
| Boston . . . . . . . . . | 35.9 | 74.2 |

We have already seen the characteristic industries of the different nationalities of our immigrant population. As a general conclusion, it is safe to say that Industrial. four-fifths of our recent immigrants belong to the group known as unskilled labor. The important industries in which they are engaged are mining, construction work, transportation and domestic service. Agriculture does not play an important part in the life of the immigrant.

**Effects of Immigration.** — The economic effect of immigration is well illustrated by the attitude of organized labor upon the question of unrestricted immigra- Economic tion. Organized labor asserts, with much truth, effect. that immigrant labor has lowered wages by its willingness to submit to a lower standard of living than that accepted by the American workman. Therefore, just as the Amer-

I

ican manufacturer is protected, so should American labor be safe-guarded, in order that the higher standards of living of American workmen may not be lowered by the low wage of immigrant labor. On the other hand, there may be an economic need for unskilled immigrant labor to perform the work spurned by American labor. Hence there seems to be a real place for immigrant labor in the United States. For example, great construction enterprises are carried on by gangs of immigrants, who toil in our mines and foundries to make America an industrial leader. Instead of going upon the farm, colonies of foreigners settle around great industrial centers. As a result, the exploitation of the immigrant has been great. He is thrown into the maelstrom of industry, with its long hours of work, dangerous trades and unhealthy working conditions. This problem we shall meet again, but it is most acute among the ignorant immigrant classes. If the American worker has been displaced by his lower waged rival, he has more often been lifted into the higher plane of skilled industries. He has left, rather than been forced out of, the ranks of unskilled labor.

The recent immigrants from southern Europe are racially different from native Americans and from the earlier Social representatives of northern Europe, who were effect. close to us in blood and civilization. Consequently, they are more difficult to assimilate. Of course, America is the " melting pot " of nations, where there is brewing a national character whose exact nature is difficult to foretell. Whether the new mixture will be sociologically inferior or superior to the old, it is impossible to predict. Only its future development in the new environment can answer that question. The public schools are doing the wonderful work of Americanizing the children of the immigrants, and the rapidity of the process among the second generation is remarkable. Community centers and night schools are solving the more difficult problem among the older immigrants, who seek to learn at least the rudiments of our language. The homes in the congested immigrant section are frequently unhealthy and the position of woman is often unfortunate. More than anything else do we fear the lowering of American ideals and standards of living.

The political effect of immigration may be seen especially in the conduct of municipal government in the United States. Massing in large groups in our **Political** great industrial centers, immigrants have come **effect.** to wield political power. Often the " declaration of intention " to become citizens of the United States has been sufficient qualification for voting in municipal elections. Consequently, the political " boss " has rallied around him the foreign vote of our large cities in exchange for favors and rewards of various kinds and descriptions. If America is to have clean and efficient municipal government, our cities must be purged of this form of political bribery. Recently, it was feared that the foreign vote and influence might play an insidious part in national politics and in international policies. However, this fear of the so-called " hyphenated " American seems to be groundless.

A large amount of the illiteracy in the United States is due, partly to the negro in the South, and partly to the immigrant in the North. In 1920 there were over **Illiteracy.** 7,000,000 adult illiterates in the United States. The number of illiterates among the foreign born was about equal to that among the native born, in spite of the fact that the foreign born comprised only a minority of our total population. In Massachusetts, the percentage of illiteracy for the native population was five-tenths per cent, and for the foreign born twelve and seven-tenths per cent.

A special prison census taken some years ago showed that twenty-three and seven-tenths per cent of the male **Poverty** white prisoners in the United States were foreign **and crime.** born, while for the same year twenty-three per cent of the total male white population over the age of fifteen years were foreign born. Hence, our immigrants do not seem to show an undue proportion of crime. The South Italian group, however, has an unenviable police record and shows a high proportion of serious crime. The children of immigrants also show a remarkable tendency toward crime. This is due more to the bad social environment of the city slums in which they are reared than to a criminal tendency in their racial heredity. In the matter of poverty and dependency, the immigrants also have an undesirable record. The number of foreign born in our almshouses is greater than the number of native-born whites, although this group constitutes less than one-fifth of the total white population. More stringent laws regarding immigration will undoubtedly cut down this excessive proportion of dependency among the foreign born.

Among the recent immigrants, there are about three times as many men as women. This has affected the **Other social** proportion of sexes in the United States and has **effects.** produced a slight excess of males in our total population. A numerical disproportion of the sexes is undesirable. Again, the social evil of vice and immorality has been accentuated by immigration. Inspectors must keep a vigilant watch to prevent the importation and exploitation of women for immoral purposes. Another social effect of immigration is the tendency to keep down the native birth rate. In America, the birth rate of the foreign immigrant is much higher than that of the native white stock.

**Asiatic Immigration**. — European immigration has come to this country by way of the Atlantic and at first settled largely in our eastern section. A smaller Asiatic immigration has crossed the Pacific and settled *Its history.* along our western coast, principally in the state of California. The immigration of the Chinese began with the discovery of gold in 1849. They later crossed in such large numbers that Congress in 1882 passed a Chinese Exclusion Act. This deliberately and completely forbade the entrance of Chinese of the laboring class into this country. The proportion of Chinese has therefore declined until, at present, there are only about seventy-two thousand in the United States. They are found as small tradesmen, in domestic service and in the fruit and truck industries of California. Our colonial possessions in the Pacific Ocean also have a large proportion of Mongolians. These islands have been stepping stones to America, although numerous stories are current as to how the Chinese have smuggled themselves across the northern border from the Dominion of Canada. British Columbia has a similar problem in the immigration of cheap Hindu laborers known as coolies. As yet, the number of these people in our own land is insignificant. The Japanese on our Pacific coast, however, have been a problem of

more or less importance. Although these Asiatics did
not begin to cross over to America until after the Chinese,
they numbered 91,000 in 1920. They have also settled in
the cities and agricultural valleys of the Pacific slope, a
considerable proportion of the fruit industry of California
being in their hands. As their numbers increased, the
industrial competition and race friction grew more acute,
and, to-day, a slight race problem exists in California.
The legislation of the state discriminates against the
Japanese in matters of land holding and public school
education. This situation has caused the national government some uneasiness and has often strained the friendly
relations between the two great nations. There is no
Japanese exclusion act, but a " gentlemen's agreement "
between the two governments prevents Japan from issuing
passports to Japanese laborers who would seek to immi-
grate to America.

The problems arising from Asiatic immigration are
more intense than those resulting from the European
immigrant. Illiteracy is high among Asiatics,
Its problems.  as is also the disproportion between the sexes,
for Oriental immigration is almost entirely male. Many
also have not sought to make America their permanent
home, but to return to Asia with the wealth secured in
the new land. The industrial problem of low wages and
low standards of living is intensified with Asiatic immigration, while the political objection to such immigration
also holds. More important than either, however, is the
social effect of Asiatic immigration, for the Mongolian
presents an almost impossible problem of assimilation.
The Asiatics are so homogeneous that race difference
presents in their case a barrier regarded by many as in-

superable. If this Oriental immigration were not excluded, America would be confronted with a Mongolian race problem in the West similar to the Negro problem in the South. We have seen that, other things being equal, immigration tends to move from a dense area of population to a rich and sparsely settled region. Hence, the pressure of the millions of over-populated Asia upon the thinly settled lands of the new world. To overcome this undesirable mixture of such totally alien groups, a policy of exclusion seems to offer the only effective remedy.

**Restrictions upon Immigration**. — Except for the exclusion of Asiatics, little restriction has been placed by our national government upon foreign immigra- The usual
tion. Because our territory seemed boundless restrictions.
and our resources limitless, we welcomed European settlers to help us lay the foundations of our future greatness. But now our national boundaries seem fixed, and free land in the United States is nearly exhausted. Again, the character of our immigration has changed and the South European stocks bring us a different racial heredity. The older immigrants delight to call themselves Americans and would exclude as " undesirable " the newer arrivals. In this, there is an element of truth. Many European nations have often used the United States as a " dumping ground " for criminals, paupers and defectives. Agitation for restriction upon immigration goes as far back as the " Native American " and " Know Nothing " parties of the *ante bellum* days. In 1875, a law was passed excluding criminals and immoral women from our shores. In 1888, the labor unions succeeded in having Congress pass a law prohibiting the importation of foreign contract labor. Numerous immigration laws have been passed in

recent years, and inspection offices have been created to keep out the following classes of undesirables: (1) contract labor; (2) anarchists; (3) those immigrating for immoral purposes; (4) criminals (except for political offenses not recognized by the United States); (5) paupers and those likely to become public charges because of lack of visible means of support; (6) mental defectives such as the insane and feeble-minded, and (7) those having infectious diseases such as tuberculosis or trachoma. Steamship companies, which formerly made large dividends from their steerage cargo, are now required to transport back to their native land all immigrants who fail to pass our inspection laws. If this were done in European ports, the futile journey across the sea would be avoided. At present, Ellis Island near New York is the great inspection point and clearing house for arriving immigrants.

These restrictions do not seem stringent enough for the leaders of organized labor, who oppose the competition of **The proposed remedy.** the low-waged immigrant. Many advocate a greater head tax or possession by the immigrant upon his entry into America of a considerable sum of money. The most popular scheme is the literacy test, which requires the applicant for admission to our shores to be able to read or write in some language, not necessarily English. Such a bill passed Congress at different sessions, but was vetoed successively by Presidents Cleveland, Taft and Wilson. However, this bill has now finally been enacted into law over President Wilson's veto. Such a test cuts down the amount of immigration, if this is the only end desired. It is easy of application and may be applied at foreign ports, thus saving the passage to America of many otherwise disappointed immigrants. Many, however, do not desire this restriction of immigration because they feel America needs a supply of unskilled labor. Again, others feel that the infusion of new blood, as well as the various cultures of Europe, will make the future America richer and better after the difficult process of adjustment and assimilation is passed. Granting, for the sake of argument, that it is necessary to restrict the amount of immigration, will the literacy test be most productive of good results? The easiest way is not always the best. Ability to read and write does not necessarily mean good citizenship. A literacy test may not be the best means of selection, because it is neither an accurate valuation of the biological worth of a national stock, nor a measure of individual character and native ability.

## QUESTIONS FOR DISCUSSION

1. What European countries formerly sent us the greatest number of immigrants?

2. What nations now lead in the number sent us?

3. Show this change from statistics.

4. When did it begin to take place?

5. Compare the civilizations of Northern and Southern Europe with respect to the type of immigrant each sends us.

6. Compare the causes of the earlier and later immigration.

7. Give the causes of the Italian immigration.

8. Compare the North Italian with the South Italian type.

9. Give the characteristics of the Slav group and compare it with the Italian.

10. Give the characteristics of the Hebrew immigrants from South Russia.

11. Name and describe the other lesser groups.

12. Show the geographical and industrial distribution of our immigrants as a whole. Give statistics.

13. Where geographically, and in what particular industries, does each immigrant group tend to settle?

14. Name some states which lead in the number of foreign born, giving statistics to illustrate the point.

15. Indicate the states having the highest percentage of those born of foreign parentage.

16. Give some figures to show the percentage of foreign born and the percentage of foreign parentage in our leading cities.

17. Explain the economic problem resulting from immigration.

18. Try to trace back your own descent.

19. Explain the social problem resulting from immigration.

20. Explain the political problem.

21. State the effect of immigration upon crime.

22. State the effect of immigration upon pauperism.

23. Give the history of Asiatic immigration to America.

24. Where, and in what industries, have the Orientals settled?

25. Why was the Chinese Exclusion Act necessary?

26. What is the situation with Japan in this respect?

27. What is the economic basis of the so-called "Yellow Peril"?

28. What groups of immigrants are now excluded?

29. Make out a case for and against the literacy test.

30. What is your own opinion with respect to restrictions upon immigration?

## TOPICS FOR SPECIAL REPORT

1. Ellis Island.
2. The various nationalities in Austria-Hungary.
3. Russia's past treatment of the Jews.
4. The effect of the present war upon immigration.
5. Our recent law for the restriction of immigration.
6. The Americanization of the immigrant.
7. The unskilled immigrant and organized labor.
8. The steerage passage to America.
9. The foreign quarter in your own locality.

## REFERENCES

Ross, E. A. "The Old World in the New." Chapters V to XII.

Commons, J. R. "Races and Immigrants in America." Chapter IV.

Steiner, E. A. "On the Trail of the Immigrant."

Warne, F. J. "The Immigrant Invasion."

Brandenburg, B. "Imported Americans."

Steiner, E. A. "From Alien to Citizen."

Antin, Mary. "The Promised Land."

Riis, J. A. "Making of an American."

Zangwill, I. "The Melting Pot."

Fairchild, H. P. "Immigration."

Hourwich, I. A. "Immigration and Labor."

Coolidge, M. R. "Chinese Immigration."

Kawakami, K. K. "Asia at the Door."

Steiner, E. A. "The Immigrant Tide."

# CHAPTER XI

## The American Race Problem

I. Background of the Negro
   1. Origin of race
   2. The African environment
   3. Slave trade
   4. Slave life
   5. Negro characteristics
II. Number of Negroes
   1. The increase
   2. The distribution
III. Problems of the Negro
   1. Reconstruction
   2. The political problem
   3. The social problem
   4. Crime and pauperism
   5. Industrial problems
   6. Education and leadership
   7. The solution
IV. The Indian
   1. Early treatment
   2. Present condition

In addition to the foreign immigrant, the Negro is another extraneous element in our population. He possesses a still different racial heredity and presents a difficult problem of readjustment to a new physical and social environment.

**Background of the Negro**. — The biological evolution of mankind was probably from some one, rather than from several, of the more primitive species. From this common stock race differentiation probably took place. Whether the earliest man was white, black or of a Origin of still different type cannot be positively asserted. race. Primitive man migrated in several directions from his original home in some central portion of the eastern hemisphere. The natural selection of different geographical environments seems to have slowly developed the different branches of the human race. An imaginary line drawn from England to Java is rich in fossil remains of primitive man. Such a line also separates the Mongolian to the northeast in Asia from the Negro to the southwest in Africa. The Caucasian race lies midway between the two regions and its different branches occupy the various geographical environments along this line. Hence, some writers believe that here may be found the origin of the human species. One branch migrated to the northeast into Asia, another to the southwest into Africa, while still others, remaining in their original home, became the progenitors of the Caucasian race. The dark skin and other physical characteristics of the present negro had a survival value in the tropics of Africa. In the Asiatic environment there was a different set of survival values and natural selection worked here to produce the Mongolian race. Long before the dawn of history, the natural selection of different environments thus slowly developed a differentiation into races of the primitive human stock.

The tropical environment of the negro helps to explain his racial heredity, which in turn enables us to understand many of his present physical and mental traits. The nature and permanency of his physical characteristics are obvious. The mental traits, however, are less apparent but equally important. The natural selection of a tropical environment, operating for thousands of years, has

The African environment. produced in the negro qualities which cannot be overcome by a few centuries of civilization. A few examples will illustrate this point. Severe physical exertion is fatal in the tropics, so that the very energetic are usually eliminated. Again, nature furnishes a bountiful supply of food and natural selection places no premium upon industry and foresight, as it does in colder climates of the North. Since the death rate is high, the birth rate must be correspondingly high in the group that survives. Thus, certain writers seek to explain the instability and the rapid rate of increase of the negro as part of his racial heredity, which developed during thousands of years in the African tropics.

The Spanish planters in the West Indies developed negro slavery before a Dutch trading ship discharged its human cargo at Virginia in 1619. Many Englishmen of

The slave trade. Elizabethan days sought to monopolize this carrying trade. The gallant sea rovers who sailed the Spanish Main were merchantmen or pirates, slavers or men of war, as the occasion demanded. Hawkins made a fortune out of the slave trade and proclaimed this fact upon his family coat of arms. That enormous numbers of negroes were carried to America is attested by the large percentage of negro blood in the mixed races of Latin America. Many of the leading families in the present republics of South America and the West Indies have a strain of colored blood coursing through their veins. The population of Haiti consists largely of the descendants of slaves. In colonial days, there was a famous triangular voyage in which certain mariners from the North sold slaves to their southern cousins. The slaves were brought from Africa to the Spanish and English plantations, where molasses was taken on board for New England. Here it was made into rum with which to buy more slaves in Africa. This was not difficult, for this institution flourished in that country where frequent tribal wars furnished a ready supply of slave labor. In some parts of Africa it was difficult to get three men to go on a journey together, for fear that two might conspire to sell the other into slavery. Later, the Portuguese and Arabs monopolized the business of procuring slaves for sale on the coast. The passage to America was known as the middle voyage, and the negroes were crowded between the decks, which were so low that in many cases it was impossible to sit upright. So close together were they packed that the group must turn over in mass at a given signal. The mortality was enormous because the sick, the crazed and the blinded were often thrown overboard. Slavers calculated upon delivering but a part of their human cargo. This traffic was a dark blot upon American history, made darker by the fact that later the Mayflower was desecrated by use for such purpose. The National government forbade the importation of slaves after 1808, while the Congress of Vienna, held in 1815 at the close of the Napoleonic wars, legislated against the traffic in human lives.

There are two sides to the story of slavery. In America, the negro became Christianized and learned of a higher civilization. In some states, however, it was **Slave life.** illegal to teach slaves to read and write. Conditions of life under slavery were not always so bad as they have been depicted. The material comforts of the American slave compared favorably with the life of European peasants of the same day. In most cases they were well housed, well fed and well cared for, because the self-interest of even the cruel planter dictated such a course as profitable to himself. Slave trading was most pernicious, however, because it broke up the family. At auction sales, mother and children, husband and wife, were often separated. Most of the slaves accepted their fate stoically, for their moral ideals were low and their conceptions of family life undeveloped. Again, slavery was not calculated to develop in the negro a regard for the property rights of others. It was difficult for the slave to understand the institution of property when his own most sacred possession — life itself — was taken from him. As the master planned the present and future of the slave, it was unlikely also that slavery would develop individual initiative and self-control. Slavery thus hindered the development of independent manhood and, merely from the economic standpoint, its evils far outweighed its advantages.

We have seen the effects of a tropical environment upon the racial heredity of the negro. Some of these slavery **Negro characteristics.** accentuated as, for example, irresponsibility and an undeveloped moral sense. Under these circumstances may we expect the family ideals of the negro to compare favorably with our own? Is it natural, too, that slaves suddenly freed from compulsion should readily acquire habits of steady industry? The inefficiency of negro labor is due partly to his improvident recklessness, and partly to his newly acquired freedom. Prohibition has established itself in the South to make negro labor more efficient and to diminish crime. The negro's ignorance and superstition are proverbial, while his uncleanliness exacts a terrible toll. He is deeply religious, but relics of African folkways are to be found in his fabric of Christianity. His imagination and childish love of story telling often lead to an almost unconscious exaggeration and untruthfulness. The negro represents a nature people, unmoral rather than immoral. Not only is he affectionate, but he is singularly free from vindictiveness. The Civil War showed frequent evidences of the loyalty of the negro to the household of his master who was fighting to perpetuate the institution of slavery. He is not only cheerful and happy, but his folk songs constitute a real contribution to American music.

**Number of Negroes**. — The census of 1910 showed nine million eight hundred and twenty-seven thousand negroes in the United States. The 1920 census showed The more than ten millions in this country. Although increase. their number has doubled since the Civil War, the percentage of negroes in our total population has gradually diminished from about fifteen per cent at that time to about ten and one-half per cent at present. Although their birth rate is high, their death rate is correspondingly high. This is particularly true in the cities, where the negro death rate is often half as high again as the death rate of the whites. That the negro is not adapted to the environment of the northern states is shown by the fact that his race would die in the North were it not recruited by fresh migrations from the South. There are two conclusions concerning the negro's rate of increase. In the first place his numbers are not proportionately increasing as rapidly as is the white race. On the other hand, the negro is absolutely increasing in number, and there is no indication that the race will die out or become numerically insignificant like the Indian. The future of America still holds the solution of the negro race problem.

K

Since the home of the negro is in the South, the race question has often been called the Southerner's problem.

The distribution. Nearly nine-tenths of all our negroes live south of the Mason and Dixon Line. The " Black Belt " is a broad agricultural plain extending from Virginia to Texas. Here live eight-tenths of all the negroes whose rate of increase in this section is very high. The census of 1910 shows the following percentages of negroes in our southern states:

| | | | |
|---|---|---|---|
| Mississippi | 56.2% | Florida | 41.0% |
| South Carolina | 55.2% | Virginia | 32.6% |
| Georgia | 45.1% | North Carolina | 31.6% |
| Louisiana | 43.1% | Arkansas | 28.1% |
| Alabama | 42.5% | Tennessee | 21.7% |
| | Texas | 17.7% | |

This table shows that, in the two states of Mississippi and South Carolina, there are actually more negroes than whites. Before 1861 the negroes lived almost entirely upon the plantations and picked the cotton crop. Since then many have gone to the northern states, but we have seen how natural selection has operated there to keep down their numbers. There has also been a considerable movement into the cities. A similar sad fate has awaited them here, for the negro does not seem adapted to city life. In spite of this fact, in certain cities like Jacksonville, Charleston and Savannah, about one-half of the population is composed of colored people.

**Problems of the Negro.**—Slavery, threatening the existence of the Union, gave rise to the great conflict which re-

Reconstruction. sulted in its abolition. The Emancipation Proclamation issued by President Lincoln was a war measure, the legality of which was later established by constitutional action. The Civil War thus resulted in the passage of the thirteenth, fourteenth and fifteenth amendments. The first abolished slavery, the second granted the negro citizenship and the third enfranchised him. A Freedmen's Bureau, created to protect the black man in the enjoyment of his new rights, began the work of education. Suddenly, and with no preparation, between four and five million slaves became American citizens. The later enfranchisement, without training or preparation, led to sad results. The " carpet bagger " directed the ignorant colored vote for his own benefit and an era of negro domination followed the war. Colored legislators sat in the proud halls of southern capitals, while illiterate ex-slaves wasted the public funds in a wave of corrupt and foolish extravagance. Federal troops organized military districts and made more fearful the dark days of the Reconstruction period. Under President Hayes the troops were withdrawn, and the South recovered but did not forget the era of negro rule. As the whites obtained gradual control, the negro was driven from politics.

The new constitutions of many southern states, adopted since the war, provide for the practical disfranchisement of the negro. Mississippi led this movement **The political** in 1890 when the new constitution provided **problem.** that every voter should be able to read or to interpret a clause of the constitution. The negro has found this task difficult before a Southern election board. Other states have added a " Grandfather's Clause " which exempts from the literacy test the descendants of those who voted prior to 1860. Although legally the negro is kept from voting, not because of race, but by reason of illiteracy, yet the spirit of these laws is undoubtedly contrary to the fifteenth amendment. By the political problem of the negro, we mean therefore that arising from the franchise and from the principle of equality before the law. " No taxation without representation " might be the cry of the negro as well as that of any other disfranchised group.   In the South, the negro has little share in making the laws and but slight participation in their administration.   The negro has been guilty of hideous crimes, but has sometimes been convicted without due process of law and without sufficient proof of guilt.   This method of punishment occasionally results in scenes of mob violence and anarchy, such as were witnessed in Atlanta in 1906.   Mob spirit, both dangerous and contagious, presents a serious problem in social control.   It feeds upon ignorance and prejudice. Enfranchisement, however, might increase rather than diminish race friction.   Lynchings also occur in the border states of the North where the negro possesses the right to vote.   A greater social control and a more intelligent citizenship are necessary to prevent such disorders.   Another effect of negro suffrage is to increase political corruption, for the negro is ignorant and illiterate.   In northern cities, the negro vote is as easily controlled as the immigrant's.

American civilization has made a great gulf between the two races in all lines of social life and activity.   According **The social** to modern standards, one drop of colored blood **problem.** makes a man a negro doomed to suffer social ostracism.   The laws of many states forbid the intermarriage of negroes and whites.   This is regarded by intelligent men of both races as a wise prohibition.   A crossing between the negro and the white may not be biologically disastrous, and the physical qualities of the offspring may not necessarily be lowered; but the social consequences of such a union are disastrous, for the offspring is always relegated to the negro group. Careful students estimate that between one-third and one-half of our negro population shows an infusion of white blood. This mixed group is composed of extremes. Since the mulatto is often the product of conditions of vice, it is not surprising that he frequently lives up to the traditions of his origin. Born and surrounded by a bad social environment, his tendency toward crime is natural. The ambitious and forward mulatto is often regarded with suspicion by both races, to neither of which is he able to adjust himself. On the other hand, this mixed group has produced many of the great leaders of the colored race.

The amount of crime among the negroes is far in excess of that warranted by their proportion to the total population. This tendency seems to be increasing rather than decreasing. It is greater in the border states of the North than in the South, where tradition has fixed Crime and the negro's place in society. The maximum of pauperism. crime among negroes is reached in the city, where the congested negro quarter furnishes the cause of numerous disturbances for the local police authorities. Furious religious revivals and festivals are regarded as dangerous to these temperamental people. Strong drink may make the docile and good-natured negro quarrelsome and criminal. A serious crime committed by a colored man may throw a whole district into a fever of excitement, whereas the same deed committed by a white man attracts little attention. Vice as well as crime exists among the negroes. The proportion of illegitimate births among the colored population is much greater than that among the whites. Indeed, in some quarters, a permanent family life hardly exists. Negro pauperism is also high for, unfortunately, the negro group contributes an undue proportion of its members to the almshouses and to the various charitable institutions of our great cities. Students have estimated that from a half to three-fourths of the negroes live below the poverty line.

The industrial problem of the negro is often regarded as fundamental in the matter of race adjustment. Its es-
**Industrial problems.** sence is the making of the negro an efficient and dependable factor in economic production. Economic independence will help the race to solve the problems of crime and pauperism. The negro must learn habits of steady work, the lessons of thrift and industry, and accustom himself to a system of labor by free contract. Much has been accomplished since the break-up of the old system, when the freed slave was turned loose upon a new and strange economic environment without either land or capital. However, much remains to be accomplished, for the industrial progress of the negro has been slow in comparison with that of many immigrant groups. The typical negro is a farmer and may be found in the cotton fields of the " Black Belt." Only in rare cases does he own the land, for a survival of the plantation system flourishes in the large estates of the white landlords. These are broken up into small tracts worked by the negroes. Since most of the negroes are poor, the landlord supplies not only the tract of land with its little cabin, but also the few tools and other instruments of production. There is often a plantation supply store at which the negro has a charge account for the food and other supplies which he purchases. After the cotton crop is picked, it is sent to the neighboring gin

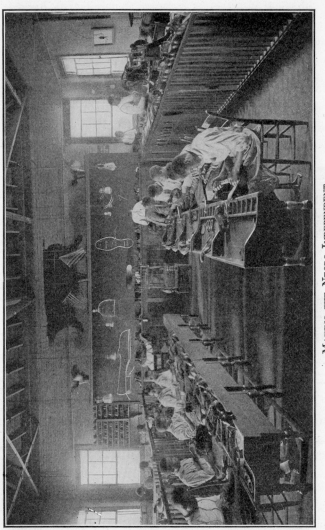

MAKING THE NEGRO INDEPENDENT.

and a settlement made. When the rent, the account at the plantation store and other charges are deducted, the balance is turned over to the dusky farmer. This is small enough, for prices are high and the interest upon credit purchases is heavy. A contract has been signed which holds the negro to his job and fugitives are severely treated by the law. In some places a system closely resembling peonage has been uncovered. The planter, however, often finds it difficult to secure negroes for steady work.

The great cry of the developing South is for labor and more labor. Hence some of our immigration, like the Italian, is going south and competing with the negro upon the farm and cotton field. In spite of race friction, the Southerner seems to prefer the labor of the negro around whom his native traditions cluster. The negro is better off, working steadily upon the farm, than floating haphazardly in the current of unskilled labor. A migratory negro of the ignorant laboring class often gets into trouble and is regarded suspiciously in the South. Negro ownership of land is as desirable in the South as native peasant ownership in Ireland, where the agrarian problem is somewhat similar. Slowly, progress is being made and many negroes own considerable property. The per capita wealth of our colored population has increased, but among the masses poverty is still the rule.

Industrial education is the crying need of the negro, if he is to be trained to habits of steady industry and to rise above the group of unskilled labor. Great Education trade schools, like Tuskegee and Hampton, and have done much to create intelligent workers leadership. and good citizens. Booker T. Washington, the late principal of Tuskegee, who emphasized this side of negro education, was regarded as the great leader of his race. A different view is held by Dr. Wm. E. B. DuBois, who pleads for the higher and more cultural education of the negro. Undoubtedly, this kind of education is necessary to provide colored teachers for the negro race. The negro must help solve his own problems and this is impossible without intelligent native leadership. From the negro universities of Atlanta, Fisk and Howard have come scores of intelligent colored men and women equipped to serve as professional teachers in the colored schools of the South. In the distribution of public and private funds between the colored and the white schools, the basis of determination should be one of need and necessity. That this work merits hearty financial support is beyond question. It has borne fruit in many directions, for both men of letters and race leaders may be cited among the negroes. Paul Laurence Dunbar is a poet of note, while one of the pictures of Mr. H. O. Tanner hangs in the galleries of the Luxembourg.

The present negro problem is the natural outgrowth of early economic and social conditions. Let us remember, **The solution.** that the negro is here not at his own request, but as a result of the action of our ancestors. " But what shall we do with the negro? " is the oft-repeated question. Liberia was founded as a colony in Africa for the freed slaves of America. The experiment, however, cannot be called successful and the precedent is not likely to be followed. The transportation of ten millions of negroes, even if desired, is impracticable. In his present stage of economic development, it is difficult to see how the negro could properly support himself. He might even lapse into a state of barbarism. Some sensational writers fear the assimilation of the freed negroes with our own Caucasian stock. This is alike undesirable and improbable, for such infusion cannot take place without the consent of both parties. There is no one patented solution for any social or economic problem, nor may future conditions be prophesied. The present policy seems to be that of a separate, but friendly, coexistence of the two races. An intelligent leadership and sound industrial education will develop the negro into a useful and law-abiding citizen. When he becomes an efficient producer, his own poverty and crime will diminish. Then the South will be more likely to grant him genuine political rights. In the meantime, an intelligent understanding of the negro problem will tend to remove many of the difficulties involved in its solution.

**The Indian.** — In addition to the Negro and the Mongolian, America has the Indian. His problem is interesting only historically. In comparison with the number of negroes in this country, the present quarter of a million Indians is insignificant. Like the Negro, however, the Indian has been the victim of conditions over which he had no control. The European settlers drove him from his hunting grounds and appropriated for themselves his original home. In the wars of conquest many regarded the dead Indian as the only good Indian. To be sure, William Penn and Roger Williams stand out as pleasing contrasts to this opinion. Before the advancing Caucasian tide, the Indian, like the buffalo, has disappeared below the horizon. There are probably as many Indians to-day as when Columbus discovered America. The Indian population has decreased relatively because his birth rate is much lower than that of the whites. Contact with European civilization seemed fatal to these nature people.  They learned its vices rather than its virtues. Alcohol, it is said, has killed more Indians than the white man's bullet.  An indoor life, with its resulting tuberculosis, seems also singularly fatal to the Indian.

The United States Government has set aside reservations for the Red Man and appropriates funds for supplies **Present** and maintenance.  While this may be a just **condition.** policy, the lack of necessity on the part of the Indian for self-support is bound to encourage laziness and undermine independent manhood.  Again, our dealings in the past with these people have not always been free from corruption and injustice.  It is hoped that a better day is dawning.  Government schools, like Carlisle, seek to teach the Indian habits of industry and to give him vocational training.  As a result, many Indians have adopted our civilization and are being assimilated into the American population.

## QUESTIONS FOR DISCUSSION

1. Discuss the origin of race and show the working of natural selection in race development.

2. Show the effect of the tropical environment of Africa upon the racial heredity of the negro.

3. Sketch the history of the slave trade.

4. Give the good and the bad effects of slavery.

5. Give some characteristics of the negro.

6. Explain some of these in terms of his physical and social environment.

7. How does the rate of increase of the negro compare with that of the whites?  What of the future?

8. Where is the negro not increasing in numbers?

9. Give figures to show that the negro is the race problem of the South.

10. What states have a greater colored population than white?

11. Where and what is the "Black Belt"?
12. Sketch the political status of the negro.
13. How is the fifteenth amendment circumvented?
14. What is your opinion as to the political equality of the negro?
15. Is the negro protected in his rights of citizenship?
16. What is the extent of infusion of white blood in the negro?
17. Discuss the unfortunate social consequences.
18. Show that the mulatto group is made up of two extremes. Why?
19. Discuss crime and pauperism among the negroes.
20. What is the extent of poverty in this group?
21. What is the essence of the negro industrial problem?
22. Discuss the system under which the "Black Belt" is farmed.
23. Compare the two types of negro education.
24. Name some leaders of the race.
25. What is your idea regarding the outlook of the negro problem?
26. How has the Indian been treated by the European settlers? by our national government?
27. How has contact with civilization affected the Indians?
28. Is the Indian dying out?

## TOPICS FOR SPECIAL REPORT

1. The various negro races of Africa.
2. Legislation against the slave trade.
3. Conditions of the negro under slavery.
4. The family life of the negro.
5. The life and work of Booker T. Washington.
6. Tuskegee Institute.
7. Institutions for the higher education of the negro.
8. The negro and city life.
9. Industrial efficiency and negro labor.
10. The "Black Belt."
11. The Freedmen's Bureau and Reconstruction days.
12. The negro and the franchise.

## REFERENCES

MERRIAM, G. S. "The Negro and the Nation."

MILLER, KELLY. "Race Adjustment."

DuBois, W. E. B. "Souls of Black Folk."

WASHINGTON, B. T. "Negro Problem."

WASHINGTON, B. T. "Story of the Negro."

WASHINGTON, B. T. "Up from Slavery."

WASHINGTON, B. T. "Working with the Hands."

WASHINGTON, B. T. "Future of the American Negro."

STONE, A. H. "Studies in the American Race Problem."

BAKER, R. S. "Following the Color Line."

HOFFMAN. "Race Traits."

MURPHY, E. G. "Bases of Ascendency."

TILLINGHAST, J. A. "Negro in Africa and America."

SMITH, W. B. "The Color Line."

McKENZIE, F. A. "The Indian."

"Negro Education" Bulletin, 1916, nos. 38 and 39, Bureau of Education, Department of the Interior.

# CHAPTER XII

## THE PROBLEM OF THE CITY

CLOSELY connected with the problem of immigration is that of city life. In fact, cities have always been powerful magnets attracting not only the foreign population, but also the discontented ambitious element in rural life. It is desirable, therefore, to trace the development of the city from early times to its present imposing position in modern society.

**The City in the Past.** — Ancient history tells us of some famous cities. The proud city of Nineveh was the metropolis of the Assyrian Empire, and Babylon, along whose walls several chariots might run abreast, is said to have had a million inhabitants. Although Athens has determined the content of culture for hundreds of years, its size was insignificant when measured by modern standards. The City of the Acropolis in the flower of its growth had perhaps a hundred thousand inhabitants; while Rome, when destroyed by Nero, probably contained a half million people. The Romans, however, were fond of urban life and their civilization was characterized by many famous towns. These declined during the Middle Ages when population, then largely rural, lived upon the feudal manors of that day. The development of commerce revived some of the old cities and stimulated the growth of others. As the towns grew from manorial villages, many purchased or forcibly secured their independence from the lord to whom allegiance had been due. The Renaissance was born in the city-states of northern Italy, and the Reformation was fostered in the free cities of Germany. The cities of Europe continued to grow slowly in size, but even the great capitals of that day were insignificant when compared with their present counterparts. As late as 1815 the Congress of Vienna sat within the walled town which had not yet expanded from its shell. The rapid growth of cities has taken place only within the last hundred years, in the period following the Industrial Revolution. Four-fifths of London's growth took place during the last century, and a like expansion is equally true of Paris and of Petrograd. The recent development of Tokio shows that Oriental cities, affected by Western civilization, may experience a similar mushroom growth.

*Its history.*

The medieval town was characterized by narrow, crooked and unpaved streets. Garbage and refuse were thrown from the window often to the discomfort of pass- *Early* ing pedestrians. Street cleaning was unknown *conditions.* because rain occasionally accomplished the desired result. The houses were gabled with projecting upper stories which, to-day, still give the picturesque effect of early times. Signs, placed before the various shops, pictured the wares whose names few could read. At night apprentices fastened huge shutters to the front of the shop and the doors were bolted. Along the dark narrow streets roisterers were frequently attacked by footpads, and to keep the peace a night watch, with arms and lantern, was employed. In later times, the night watch sang the hours and with it, perchance, a bit of scriptural advice. Chains were fastened across the streets and the town gate was kept shut until sunrise. The romance of time has given color and picturesqueness to the scene, but the towns and cities of the past were unpleasant and evil places as compared with those of modern times. With no knowledge of sanitation or public hygiene, the death rate was enormous. Numbers were recruited by fugitive serfs and by those drawn thither by the comparative peace and the possibility of commercial gain. Plagues, like the Black Death, and great fires, like that of London, brought fearful destruction to life and property.

**Urban Conditions in the United States**. — The United States Census Bureau classifies communities with a population of 2500 or more as urban. There are *Growth of* three such groups: (1) those having a popu- *American* lation from 2500 to 25,000, constituting a small *cities.* city; (2) those from 25,000 to 100,000, classified as medium-

sized cities; and (3) those over 100,000, or large cities.
In 1800 there were only five cities in the United States
with a population of over 10,000 ; while the census for
1910 showed over six hundred cities of such size or over.
Indeed, they made up thirty-seven per cent of our population. According to the 1920 census the figures relating
to the population show that our urban population is 51.9
per cent of the total population. In the decade between
the census of 1900 and that of 1910, our urban population
increased eleven millions while the rural advanced only
six millions. If, under rural population we exclude all
towns and limit ourselves strictly to the dwellers in the
country, we find that urban population in the United States
increased six times as rapidly as the purely rural population. Our urban population is concentrated largely in
the northeastern section of the country. The states of
Massachusetts, New York, Pennsylvania, Ohio and Illinois contain half of our country's total urban population.
The combined New England and Middle Atlantic States
contain almost one-half of the total urban population. If
we include the North Central States the proportion is
two-thirds. The census for 1910 showed the following
percentages of urban population for these states:

| | | | |
|---|---|---|---|
| Rhode Island | 96.7% | Pennsylvania | 60.4% |
| Massachusetts | 92.8% | New Hampshire | 59.2% |
| Connecticut | 89.7% | Ohio | 55.9% |
| New York | 78.8% | Washington | 53.0% |
| New Jersey | 75.2% | Maine | 51.4% |
| California | 61.8% | Maryland | 50.8% |
| Illinois | 61.7% | Colorado | 50.4% |

The above states thus contained an urban population
of one-half or over. It is interesting to notice how this

distribution corresponds to the proportion of immigrants and of those of foreign parentage. Note, also, that these states, with few exceptions, constitute our great commercial and industrial centers. The southern and western sections of our country are not only more thinly populated, but their proportion of city dwellers is also much lower, because of the different nature of the occupations of the people in those regions. A comparison with European conditions will also be interesting. Although European countries are more densely populated, the proportion of city dwellers is not so high as in some of our industrial states. The urban population of England and Wales is seventy-eight per cent, Germany fifty-seven per cent and France forty-one per cent; while Russia has a proportion of city dwellers as low as thirteen per cent. It is evident, therefore, that there has been an unprecedented growth of cities since the Industrial Revolution of the eighteenth century. In America, this growth has been especially rapid.

The Industrial Revolution, introducing the factory system and modern industrialism, has been the prime cause of the development of cities. Cities have grown up around manufacturing centers, for superior *The causes.* transportation facilities make an urban location of industry advantageous. Hither are brought raw materials, which are converted into finished products and shipped to far distant places. Again, the city furnishes an excellent labor market. Since trade and commerce are as important as manufacturing, the city is generally located upon some point favorable for commerce and often arose where a natural break in transportation occurred. The famous cities of northern Italy, like Venice and Genoa, occupied

L

a central position in the commerce of medieval Europe. Across the Mediterranean, their ships sailed to and from the Orient. From them the goods were sent by the rivers of Germany and France to points in northern and western Europe. When the commercial world shifted its center from the Mediterranean to the Atlantic, these ports lost their strategic position and suffered decline. In Europe and America, we find cities located upon navigable waters, New York upon a bay, Chicago upon a lake and San Francisco upon the coast. A city, located upon a modern commercial route, may be the outlet for the products of the local environment as well as the distributing point for incoming goods. Thus, Chicago taps the cattle and grain industry of the West and New Orleans exports much of the cotton of the South. New York, the largest city in America, is as cosmopolitan in its commerce as in its population.

The superior advantages of the city constitute another attractive force. Higher wages and more varied opportunities lure many ambitious country lads to the city where they seek fame and fortune. The use of machinery in agriculture has also decreased the proportion of men needed on the farm. The combined harvester and reaper can do the work of many men, and other agricultural inventions have temporarily displaced scores of farm hands. The period of adjustment, which the introduction of machinery necessitated, came later in farming than in manufacturing; hence the exodus from farm to city. The city also offers superior educational advantages. Again, its varied life contains more opportunities for comfort and amusement; for, until recently, modern pleasures and conveniences, such as are found in city homes, did not exist upon the farm.

So rapid has been the development of cities in America that the consequences have often been unfortunate. No one would have dreamed that the site of Fort City Dearborn would become in fifty years the great planning. city of Chicago. Because of the rapidity of urban growth no provision was made for the future development of the city. Crooked streets naturally grew up along early roads, like the cow paths of Boston. Hideous slums have arisen to house the poorer groups who have crowded into them. Incidentally, however, it might be wise to realize that such conditions existed also in the great cities of antiquity, where overcrowding and its attendant evils were great. In the development of many American cities, no system has characterized municipal building operations, and much confusion exists which might otherwise have been avoided. Frequently, river fronts have been monopolized by manufacturing plants and shipping concerns have thought only of their own interests. Unfortunately, individual gain has come before civic beauty and welfare. Grotesque contrasts in buildings offend the eye. Europe saw the danger before America, and Continental cities resolved to protect the health and comfort of the city dweller. Half a century ago Paris, in spite of the enormous expense involved in the demolition of valuable property, remodeled itself by a magnificent system of boulevards.

Washington is one of the few American cities that was designed in advance and properly planned for future growth. Hence it has saved the expense which Paris incurred. Many American cities, like Philadelphia, are facing a great public expenditure, which could have been avoided by a carefully designed plan for future development. German cities are also beautiful and well planned.

Vienna is one of the most magnificent cities in the world, while the glory of Budapest is unsurpassed. The water fronts of many European cities are a source of beauty, as well as a highway for commerce and industry. Splendid stone bridges, monuments, parks and drives are to be found. The location of industry is prescribed by the municipality and a large portion of the water front preserved for the people. In some German cities a zone system has been established, whereby one section is reserved for factories, another for business houses, and still another for residences.

A comprehensive planning of transportation lines and of city streets is highly advantageous to urban development. Many American cities have followed the checkerboard plan of William Penn, who is said to have taken his idea from ancient Babylon. This scheme is simple and systematic, but it often causes congestion on the few streets that lead into the central business section. The best plan, perhaps, is to map out the city in the form of a wheel. Its central throbbing section would correspond to the hub and the main streets to the spokes, while the cross streets would be a series of rings. The construction of buildings should then be planned in accordance with principles of architectural beauty and symmetry. Municipal buildings might well be grouped in the civic center where the wide avenues and broad boulevards converge. Ample provisions should be made for squares, parks and public places, which serve not only as sources of communal pleasure, but also as essential factors in public health. Suburbs for the working man at low rentals are more needed in the modern city than villas for the richer group. Such a scheme in connection with a system of cheap and rapid transportation will materially help to solve the problem of mass conges-

"How the Other Half Lives."

tion. This has been tried in certain cities of England where a special commutation rate to workers has enabled them to live in the outskirts of the city. This plan seeks to prevent, rather than to cure, the problem of congestion.

The growth of cities has been attended by a development of the so-called " slum " districts. In them the housing conditions are such as to arouse alarm for the physical and moral condition of their inhabitants. The basis of this problem, like many others, is economic; for, as the city increases in population, real estate rises in value. The result of this tendency is a greater density of population in a given area. While the city has grown outward in many districts, it has likewise grown upward in others. Of this the modern " skyscraper " is witness. What has happened in the business section has also taken place in the congested living quarters of a great metropolis. Thus the tenement house has sprung into existence. This is a large building, or series of buildings, several stories high and capable of accommodating a large number of families. The law in New York defines a tenement house as the residence of three or more families, each independent of the other and each providing its own cooking facilities. In fact, the number of cooking stoves is often used to determine the number of families. Congestion may also result from the occupancy of old shacks in alleys unfit for human habitation.

The tenement house has arisen in many of the formerly fashionable quarters of the city now converted into business sections. As the former inhabitants have moved out, the poorer groups, often foreign immigrants, have occupied their homes. These old houses, many of which are fairly large, are used to accommodate a number of families. The

problem of housing is aggravated by the existence of the
lodger. We have seen that, with the foreign immigrants,
the number of men predominates. Many of these laborers
may room together or become lodgers with one family.
Desire for gain is strong among this group and that, as
well as poverty, has led to very low standards of living.
Housing commissions and various charity organizations
have discovered some alarming facts. Two or more families
often occupy the same room, and many beds are never
free from human burdens.

Congestion and housing conditions affect not only
physical health but moral character. In the first place
*The results.*  congestion results in the spreading of contagious
diseases, while lack of air and sunshine permits
the spread of tuberculosis. " Bandbox " houses of one
room upon another, situated to the rear of high buildings,
possess no adequate facilities for light or ventilation.
Another common evil is the lack of water and of a proper
system of drainage. Many families use but one hydrant
and the amount of washing enjoyed bears a direct relation
to the adequacy and nearness of the water supply. Drainage facilities are so inadequate that refuse water is often
emptied into a back yard, which also serves as a dumping
ground for garbage, ashes and rubbish. Toilet facilities
are extremely inadequate. Flies become efficient carriers
of disease, while bacteria flourish in the dark, damp and
unclean environment. Infant mortality runs high in congested quarters, where hot summers and cold winters reap
a rich harvest of human life. The moral dangers of congestion, although perhaps less apparent, are none the less
real. In one small room, individuals of all ages and both
sexes congregate. Under these conditions it is impossible

to develop proper ideals of morality and family life — the very foundations of human society. Such conditions breed the criminal, the immoral and the degenerate element in American society.

What remedies may be suggested for these housing conditions so fatal to the life and character of modern peoples? Since congestion is the root of the *The* evil, the problem must be approached from this *remedies.* standpoint. Either congestion itself must be removed or its evils mitigated. The former method has been sought by the advocates of comprehensive city-planning. According to this plan, the great congested quarters of the city would be denuded of their surplus population by their removal to suburban districts to which adequate means of transportation would be established. The success of this plan depends upon its cheapness. Unless rentals are reasonable and transportation rates low, the plan cannot succeed. Again, paternal schemes have been tried, such as that of the Krupps at Essen in Germany, and the experiment of the Pullman Company near Chicago. Philanthropists, like Ruskin and Peabody, have also attempted to improve the housing conditions of the laboring class. Perhaps the most practical plan is that of strict government regulation and municipal inspection of housing conditions in the more densely populated sections of the city. Regulations must be enacted and rigidly enforced to guard the health, comfort and safety of those living in congested quarters. A campaign of education will accomplish much in developing in the community a realization of " how the other half lives "; while a sound solution of the problem of immigration will materially lessen the evil of congestion.

The growth of the modern city bears a vital relation to the problem of public health. We have already seen the effect of bad housing conditions, with all their attendant evils, upon the health of the congested sections of a great city. But in addition to proper housing conditions, many other factors enter into the health and safety of urban populations. Of first importance is the water supply. This should be plentiful and free from contamination. Because of the lack of proper waterworks and an adequate filtration system, many cities have suffered from a poor and contaminated water supply. Again, it is imperative for the maintenance of public health that the city should be supplied with an adequate system of underdrainage and an effective sewage disposal plant. The proper disposal and collection of garbage, together with the elimination of unclean rubbish, is a most important factor in the maintenance of public health. A pure milk supply is only second in importance to a clean water supply. Because of carelessness and ignorance in the preparation of the milk diet, thousands of babies are sacrificed annually in every great city. Pure food regulations and cold storage restrictions are also made necessary by the conditions of urban life. Protection, too, should be afforded against the spread of contagious disease. Houses must be fumigated to kill the germs of tuberculosis, scarlet fever, diphtheria and smallpox. The health department of a great city holds as many lives in its care as are intrusted to the police and fire departments. Many hospitals maintain free clinics and dispensaries, some of which include a special social service department. To-day, in our great cities, the public schools employ nurses and physicians to examine the eyes and to care for the teeth of thousands

*Public health.*

The Ghetto of New York City.

*Courtesy of the New York Child Welfare Committee.*

of children. Likewise, the playground movement has begun and recreation centers are located in many school yards. Public baths are a source of both pleasure and bodily cleanliness, while the parks of the city afford relief to the thousands who never ask themselves where they will spend the summer.

The city is the great laboratory for the study of society. Here are intensified the great social problems of race, immigration, crime and poverty. It is not that the city is inherently more wicked than the country, but the fact of great numbers accentuates the problem. We have seen that the problems of immigration and of city life are inseparable. It is also in the city that the negro problem shows some of its worst evils. The crowding together of whites and blacks often results in considerable race friction and disorder among the ignorant classes of each race. Poverty and pauperism are more common in the city than in the country, for many unfortunates drift in from the surrounding rural districts. Urban charitable institutions support during the winter the migratory group which leaves with the advent of spring. Many cases of permanent relief formerly lived in the country and came to the city with no definite means of support. It has been estimated that a third of the population of many big cities live below the poverty line, and in some of them as high as ten per cent have required the assistance of charity. The city's record of crime is unenviable and is often twice as large as that of the country. Vice seems associated with city life; but illiteracy is not so great among the native born in the city as in the country.

But what of the future? The " city beautiful " is the

ideal of those who would remodel city life upon more artistic lines by inaugurating an era of city-planning for future development. A second ideal centers in public health. The examination of men for military service in the great World War will disclose valuable statistics concerning the health of city dwellers. There is no doubt, however, that the urban death rate is shrinking. The city, which was formerly regarded as extremely unhealthy, is becoming more sanitary with the advance of scientific knowledge. Preventable disease, however, can be still further cut down by greater civic coöperation. A third ideal is that of reform in housing conditions, and committees of citizens have determined that the slum must go. The political ideal seeks a municipal government which is both efficient and democratic. Some American cities have already adopted a commission form of government to insure better civic housekeeping. Let us hope that the future will not bear out the words of Ambassador Bryce, the great student of American institutions, that municipal government has been the great failure of American democracy.

*The future.*

**Contrast between City and Country.** — The more rapid increase of urban population as compared with rural has already been indicated. The appeal of the city to the country boy was ever present, and, in the past, rural districts were frequently drained of the ambitious element qualified for future leadership. Country schools were often few and poor, while the school term was shortened to meet the demands of farm life. Higher education could only be obtained in the city. Work on the farm was hard and the hours of labor long. Indeed, the farmer and his family have probably been exploited as

*The past.*

much as any other element in American society. He has patiently suffered a working day from sunrise to sunset, while his wife has not only performed the chores of farm life but also reared large families. The farmer, himself, has endured longer hours of work than those permitted by many trade unions. In the past, his daughters and sons have sought an escape in city life from the hard rigor of the farm.

In recent years, however, a change has gradually taken place. A decreasing proportion of food producers and an increasing proportion of food consumers has elevated the importance and economic position of the farmer. Higher prices and better living conditions combine to make his life more enjoyable. No longer is he necessarily confined and bound by tradition. The creation of a federal department of agriculture has been beneficial in the dissemination of better methods of farming. Expert advice upon seeds and soils can be had for the asking. Education has advanced with material prosperity and the modern farmer is beginning to see the value of sending his boys to school. The country high school has appeared upon the landscape. The rural free delivery of mail, the newspaper and the telephone help the farmer to keep abreast of the times. The mail order offices of the big department stores send their catalogues to his door, while the interurban electric trolley takes him quickly to town. Finally, the advent of the automobile has produced better roads and promoted sociability. Thus the former isolation of country life is fast disappearing.

The new era.

## QUESTIONS FOR DISCUSSION

1. Name and describe some famous cities of antiquity.

2. What stimulated the growth of towns in the Middle Ages?

3. Describe their appearance and sanitary conditions.

4. What modern industrial changes caused an unprecedented growth of cities? Illustrate from European cities.

5. Compare urban and rural development in America.

6. What is the distribution of urban population in the United States?

7. What are the causes of the growth of cities in recent years?

8. Give the result of such a rapid growth of cities.

9. Outline the advantages of a comprehensive system of city planning.

10. How would it help solve the problems of congestion?

11. Describe some conditions of bad housing with which you are familiar.

12. Give the effects of such conditions upon public health and morality.

13. Give some remedial suggestions.

14. What do you think of municipal tenements and corporation villages?

15. What should housing legislation prohibit and what should be demanded?

16. Show the relation between public utilities and city health.

17. Show some definite ways in which pure food laws protect the public health.

18. Describe the activities of a bureau of public health.

19. Why is a social service department a valuable addition to a hospital staff?

20. What social ills are intensified in a city?

21. How do city and country compare in poverty and crime?

22. What should be the ideals of the future city?

23. Describe the change which has taken place in rural life.

## TOPICS FOR SPECIAL REPORT

1. The government of European cities as compared with that of the average American city.
2. The water fronts of French and German cities.
3. The possibilities of city-planning in America.
4. The water supply of your city.
5. The tenement problem of a large city.
6. Housing conditions in some slum district near you.

## REFERENCES

WILCOX, D. F. "The American City."
ROBINSON, C. M. "Modern Civic Art."
ROWE, L. S. "Problems of City Government."
ALLEN, WM. H. "Efficient Democracy."
SMITH, S. G. "Social Pathology."
WEBER. "Growth of Cities."
BAILEY, L. H. "The Country Life Movement in the United States."
GODFREY, H. "The Health of the City."

# CHAPTER XIII

## THE RISE OF INDUSTRY

**I.** The institution of industrial society
   1. Definition and origin
   2. Stages of development
   3. Characteristics of industry
**II.** Before the age of machinery
   1. The manorial system
   2. The gilds
   3. Later changes
**III.** The industrial revolution
   1. The invention of machinery
   2. The factory system
   3. Social effects on England
   4. Parliamentary legislation

**The Institution of Industrial Society.** — The origin and development of the family and of the state have already **Definition** been traced. Another important institution is **and origin.** that of industrial society, which may be defined as a society organized for economic production. Primitive society was simple and unorganized. Social evolution has developed complex organizations within the group and has separated or differentiated various specialized institutions. Herbert Spencer compared this process of differentiation to organic evolution in the field of biology. Lower organisms have little differentiation of structure, but in higher forms specialized organs are to be found. Nervous, reproductive, digestive and circulatory systems begin to appear. Primitive society had few distinct social institutions. These were developed in the slow process of social evolution by a growth of organization and coöperation. Thus, the state became an institution distinct from the family, just as industrial society became independently organized. All social institutions, however, are closely related to, and easily affected by, each other. Just as we have seen the beginnings of the family in the animal world, so we have examples of industrial societies among the lower animals. Note, for example, the organization and coöperation of beavers in building a dam, or of bees in making honey. However, it is instinct, not intellect, that characterizes most of the industrial activities of lower animals.

Social evolution divides the development of industrial society into the following stages: (1) hunting and fishing; (2) pastoral; (3) agricultural, and (4) industrial. Stages of development. There is no clear-cut line of demarcation between these economic stages. Like other periods of history, one fades gradually into the other. Often we may see both existing side by side. Again, some groups advance more rapidly than others and arrive earlier at an advanced stage. With the passing from the hunting and fishing period to the pastoral, and then to the agricultural stage, there are developed the early handicrafts like weaving and pottery making. When the fourth economic stage is reached, society has usually attained a high degree of civilization.

The development of industrial society is marked by certain definite characteristics. In the first place, social organization and coöperation may be read in a greater division of labor. This is absent among primitive groups where each family is a complete economic unit.    In more advanced societies there is a specialization of effort; one

Character-
istics of
industry.

man farms, another makes shoes, and still another exchanges the goods produced in the community.    In addition to the growth of social organization, there goes on a process of invention and discovery within the group, whereby man has been enabled to utilize more fully his economic environment.    Discoveries and inventions, such as the rotation of crops, the expansive power of steam and the modern mechanical inventions, have multiplied enormously the productivity of nature.    This has been called man's conquest of nature and is part of the process of the evolution of industrial society.    The twin forces of invention and social organization have created a social surplus, that is, a surplus of goods above what is needed for present consumption. Each new invention or change in organization means a problem of social adjustment and the transition period may be one of hardship.    Another characteristic of industry may be found in the formation of social classes, whose existence is due to the development of industrial society, as well as to the growth of the state, the effect of war and numerous other forces.    The earliest division of labor and of social classes was based on sex.    In savage societies the women worked while the men hunted.    Later, society was divided into a slave and a leisure class.    We have seen how the conquering group exploited the labor of the conquered by the institution of slavery.    Upon it developed many ancient cultures and civilizations.    Modern industrial society involves social distinctions based upon labor and capital.    These groups, however, should not be antagonistic, but complementary and interdependent.

**Before the Age of Machinery**. — During the Middle Ages, when agriculture was the prevailing occupation, population was widely scattered throughout the country districts of Europe. The institution of feudalism, determining the economic as well as the military organization of society, made the manor the unit of agricultural production. The serfs, who tilled the soil, lived in small villages close to the protecting walls of the neighboring castle or manor house. Their wretched huts, with thatched roof and crude interior, often sheltered both man and beast. On all sides lay the lord's estate composed of woodland for hunting, meadow land for grazing and the lands for actual farming. Some of these farm lands the lord kept for himself, but the remainder was divided into strips for the serfs, who worked not only their own lands but also their lord's. The serf also paid the lord a rent in the form of a share of the produce derived from the land which he tilled for his own support. Not only were methods of agriculture crude, but one-third of the land lay fallow every year. The manor, shut off from the outside world and supported by its own activities, had little intercourse with the rest of Christendom.

*The manorial system.*

The medieval towns were the birthplaces of commerce and manufacturing, which were carried on by an organization of trade and craft gilds. A trade gild included the merchants of that particular town and a craft gild the makers of a special commodity. Not only was a fraternal spirit maintained in each group, but a practical monopoly was secured by the members, who excluded outsiders from participation in the production of that particular commodity and also placed restrictions upon their own activities. The quantity and quality of

*The gilds.*

M

the goods produced were carefully regulated. Medieval production was, of course, carried on by hand and under the careful eye of the master. A boy worked as an apprentice while he learned a trade. After the period of apprenticeship had expired, he became a journeyman and could then work for wages. Upon the accumulation of a little capital, he might set up a shop for himself and become a master workman. Medieval trade and commerce was carried on at certain markets and by great annual fairs.

The Crusades, stimulating commerce, helped to break down feudalism; while the Black Death hastened the gradual decay of serfdom. When the manorial *Later changes.* system began to decline, a class of farm laborers appeared to take the place of the medieval serf. With the decline of gilds, great trading companies came into existence, like the London and East India Companies, which planned to carry on commerce with the new lands that had been discovered. The craft gilds were replaced by the domestic system of manufacturing, whereby artisans could now set up hand machinery in their own homes and there carry on production free from the protection of the gild. The necessity for some sort of protection in industry, together with the decline of feudalism, led finally to the development of strong national governments.

**The Industrial Revolution**. — The textile industries were the first to be revolutionized by the use of machinery. *The invention of machinery.* Under the domestic system, weaving was done upon the hand loom by the father of the house, assisted perhaps by a journeyman, while the women did the spinning on the primitive spinning wheel. But, during the second half of the eighteenth century, a great series of mechanical inventions took place which completely altered these simple processes. Hargreaves and Arkwright invented a " spinning jenny " which could spin several threads at once out of the raw material, while a power loom superseded the slower method of weaving by hand. Another Englishman, named Watt, gave to the world the steam engine. Eli Whitney's cotton gin increased the supply of raw cotton for the manufacture of cloth. These were the first of a series of great mechanical inventions which have continued down to our own day. The movement began in England in the manufacture of textiles, but has spread to other lands and other industries. The locomotive and the steamboat have revolutionized means of transportation as much as the earlier inventions revolutionized methods of manufacturing. The last century has been called the age of steam and machinery.

The new machinery was responsible for the change to the factory system of manufacturing. The cumbersome mechanical inventions were too large and costly **The factory** for the cottage weavers and spinners to set up in **system.** their homes. Large factories were therefore built to house the new machinery, and production went from the home into large specialized industrial plants. Since this method required great sums of money, a new capitalistic class, who owned the instruments of production, sprang into existence. The laborers, who had formerly owned their own tools, now became a group of machine operators who no longer worked for themselves. Population shifted to the regions where coal and iron were to be found and great industrial towns grew up. Many of the estates, which had formerly been regarded as common pasture land, were inclosed for the benefit of the local landlord, who raised sheep in order to procure a supply of raw wool for the manufacture of cloth. This change worked hardship to the rural laborers, many of whom came to the towns to seek employment in the factories. Again, the new machinery drove many of the hand weavers out of employment. In alleys and cellars some kept up a futile competition for a lower wage, while others retaliated by burning and destroying the new machinery. A period of adjustment was necessary before labor could adapt itself to the new industrial environment. During this period of transition there was considerable disorder and distress. In the long run, however, machinery, like any other improvement, was of great benefit to society. It not only multiplied the output, but made possible the lowering of prices to such a level that the new goods could come within the reach of all. The factory system, however, divided society into the opposing camps of labor and capital, whose apparently conflicting interests have created many modern social problems.

The Industrial Revolution was largely responsible for England's proud position of industrial and commercial **Social effects on England.** leadership, which continued undisputed until the economic expansion of Germany and America. Looking overseas at the great colonial empire, Englishmen might well be proud of their country's achievement; but, glancing inwardly at industrial conditions, the picture was not inspiring. In fact, the social effects on England of the great industrial revolution were alarming. The early factories were unhealthy and the housing conditions equally bad. Hours of labor were so long that a working day of twelve, thirteen and fourteen hours was not unusual. Great evils of child labor and of women in industry sprang into existence. Children were sent into the factories by their parents at the age of eight and indeed younger. Pauper children from the poorhouses were bound over to the manufacturers into a virtual slavery. They were given food of the coarsest description which they often ate while working. The children were abused and driven to their work which lasted twelve hours a day. Accidents were frequent, disease common, and the excessive toil often put an early end to their unhappy lot. In the mines equally bad conditions were found by an investigating committee. Women and men worked side by side, almost naked, in the damp unwholesome shafts of the mine. A part of the work of the smaller women and children consisted in dragging carts of coal through underground passages frequently three feet or less in height. Little girls carried a half hundredweight of coal up steep ladders to the surface. A mere recital of this testimony before Parliament made unnecessary any discussion of the desirability of reform in mining conditions.

But in spite of the real dangers of the new industrial conditions, England was rather loath to pass social legislation for their betterment. The *laissez faire* theory of government was popular. It held that government regulation of industrial conditions would interfere with the natural operation of economic laws. This attitude was consistent with the national policy of free trade and the repeal of the corn laws. Greedy manufacturers prophesied disaster, if they should be deprived of their supply of female labor. But the fear of physical degeneracy of the workers at length made government action imperative. A famous factory law was passed the year following the Great Reform Bill of 1832. No children under nine years of age were to be employed, and those from nine to thirteen were to work only eight

Parliamentary legislation.

hours a day. Young persons from thirteen to eighteen could not work over twelve hours, and none of these at night. A corps of inspectors was created and factory regulation became a reality. A subsequent act of 1847 limited the work of women to ten hours a day. Since it was unprofitable to work the factories by men alone, without the aid of women and children, a ten-hour day gradually became the common standard for all. In 1842 a law had been passed regulating labor in mines. It prohibited all underground work by females and by boys under thirteen. In recent years the British Parliament has passed other factory laws, and the new era of government regulation has been strikingly characterized by an increasing amount of social legislation.

## QUESTIONS FOR DISCUSSION

1. Define industrial society.
2. Describe its evolution.
3. What are the four stages of development?
4. Compare society to an organism — showing the process of evolution taking place in each.
5. How was industrial society brought about?
6. State the advantages of an industrial society over an agricultural community.
7. Why does an industrial society combine at the same time so many benefits and evils?
8. Enumerate both benefits and evils.
9. Give the characteristics of the development of industrial society.
10. Describe the organization of a feudal manor.
11. What two kinds of gilds were there?
12. Describe the regulations and advantages of the gilds.
13. What factors influenced commerce during the Middle Ages?
14. What was the original meaning of the word "manufacture"?

15. What economic changes took place at the close of the Middle Ages and at the beginning of the modern era?

16. Name some of the great mechanical inventions that introduced the Industrial Revolution.

17. Explain the effects of the factory system.

18. What social evils resulted in England?

19. Sketch the history of parliamentary legislation and give the important bills.

## TOPICS FOR SPECIAL REPORT

1. Woman's share in primitive industry.
2. The gild system of production.
3. The domestic system of manufacturing.
4. The advent of machinery and steam power.
5. The effect of the Industrial Revolution upon the skilled artisan.
6. Child labor in England before 1832.
7. The important factory laws of England (*e.g.* that of 1833).
8. Contemporary social legislation in England.

## REFERENCES

Munro, D. C.  "A History of the Middle Ages."

Cheyney, E. P.  "Industrial and Social History of England." Chapters II–IX (inclusive).

Seager, H. R.  "Principles of Economics."  Chapters I and XXX.

Ashley, W. J.  "English Economic History."  (Reference.)

Cunningham.  "Growth of English Commerce and Industry." (Reference.)

Spencer, H.  "Principles of Sociology."  (Reference.)

Toynbee.  "Industrial Revolution."

# CHAPTER XIV

## Social Effects of Industry

I. Child labor in the United States
   1. History and extent
   2. Causes and remedies
   3. The effects
   4. Recent legislation
II. Women in industry
   1. Similarity to child labor
   2. The sweat shop
   3. Low wages
   4. New occupations
III. Occupations of risk
   1. Dangerous trades
   2. Industrial accidents:
      *a.* Extent and character
      *b.* Railroad accidents
      *c.* Other accidents
   3. Proposed remedies:
      *a.* Social insurance
      *b.* Compulsory state insurance

THE effects of the Industrial Revolution manifested themselves in America in a manner similar to that which characterized the growth of industry in England. But the United States, unlike England, was a young agricultural country when the factory system first wrought its havoc in the Old World. In recent years, however, the growth of manufacturing in America has been rapid and has been accompanied by a number of industrial problems which have had marked social significance. Among the most important of these are the problems of child labor, of women in industry and of dangerous trades and occupations.

**Child Labor in the United States.** — The early effects of the factory system in America somewhat resembled the conditions already described in England. Al- History though the opening of our mines was not at- and extent. tended by such horrors as prevailed in the Old World, the early situation in the textile mills was reprehensible. In New England, where manufacturing began, children under sixteen often worked twelve, thirteen and fourteen hours a day. The first important legislation upon child labor in this country was passed by Massachusetts in 1836. More stringent laws were subsequently enacted and other states followed her example. But America labors under a peculiar disadvantage in securing such legislation. Many social questions, which in Europe are matters of national legislation, in our own country fall within the sphere of state action. Hence, great variations occur in the realm of laws dealing with accidents, child labor, women in industry and like problems. The action of the federal government in such matters can be obtained only by a constitutional amendment, or by a liberal interpretation of its control over interstate commerce. At present, therefore, the child labor situation varies with the different laws of the several states. New England, which in this regard formerly held an unenviable reputation, has now by appropriate legislation materially improved the child labor situation. With the growth of an industrial South, this evil has appeared in the southern cotton mills to an alarming extent. Much of the cotton is also picked by child labor. In several southern states the National Child Labor Committee estimated that half of the children between ten and thirteen years of age in that section could be classified as wage earners. A large proportion of child labor is used in agriculture, but this is not considered so harmful in its physical effects as life in the mill. Many children in country regions leave school, temporarily or permanently, for the occupation of fruit and berry picking. Many are also at work, legally or illegally, in the great canneries of the South and Middle States.

The introduction of machinery and the minute sub-division of labor, accompanying the factory system, lessen Causes and the need for the skilled artisan. Little strength remedies. and intelligence are required to feed and attend many machines in the modern factory. Hence the labor of children will often suffice in modern industrial life. As compared with that of men, such labor is cheap and plentiful, and it is therefore necessary to enact special legislation in order to protect such workers, who often fall a prey to the thoughtless or selfish employer. An indifferent public is a second factor in the child labor problem. Cheap goods will sell in spite of the fact that this cheapness is often secured at the price of the child's health and welfare. The Consumers' League has done much in a campaign of popular education to inform the public concerning the social cost of such production. It has an honor list of industrial firms, whose working conditions are good, and whose patronage is worthy of public approval. The Christmas slogan of " Shop early " has accomplished much good for the young men and women employed in department stores. A third factor in the problem is the child himself. Poverty is one cause of child

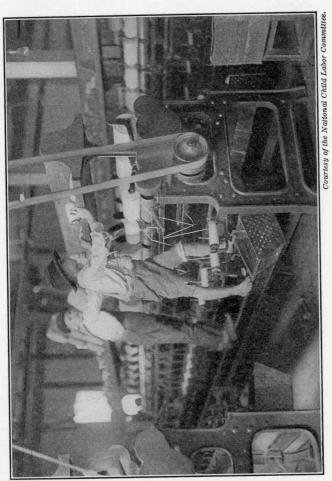

The Dangers of Child Labor.

labor, because the child's small wages are often needed to supplement the family income. Again, the child himself may be glad to leave school because it does not appeal to him. It is often far removed from practical life and the discipline is irksome. Later, this short-sighted policy will be apparent, when the child who has remained in school forges ahead of those who have left before completing the course. It is perfectly true, however, that the modern school should provide a curriculum sufficiently diversified to appeal to the needs of all classes of children.

The effects of child labor are injurious to the child, to society and to industry. Even under the most favorable working conditions, such labor is highly in- **The effects.** jurious from the physical point of view. Childhood is the period of physical growth requiring an abundance of fresh air, freedom and activity. It is also the period of mental growth and development. The monotony of repeated operations of the same character is a poor substitute for self-expression and intellectual training. Again, in the factory, the moral atmosphere of the child's surroundings is frequently bad and he comes into contact with many existing evils before the age of innocent childhood has passed. In the second place, child labor has injurious effects upon society. It tends to break up family life by taking the child out of his normal place in the home. The young wage earner very quickly tends to become independent of parental authority. His opportunity to rise is limited, and he becomes accustomed to low wages and standards. It is also well to remember that these child laborers will become the fathers and mothers of the next generation and that they are not receiving proper training for their future in society. Finally, a word should be said of the effect of this problem upon industry. Child labor in the long run is not always the cheapest labor. It lowers the efficiency of the worker for, generally speaking, every dollar earned before the age of fourteen is taken from later earning capacity. Moreover, the labor of children is wasteful. They are unreliable and their carelessness is a frequent cause of accidents.

Most of our recent child labor laws have been passed since 1895. A National Child Labor Committee, organized Recent in 1904, has urged reform in many states and legislation. suggested model laws for enactment. Since each state enacts its own laws, the employers affected by the proposed legislation threaten to remove their plants to other states. New York and Illinois have excellent child labor laws, and the Pennsylvania legislature in 1915 passed a law decidedly improving the child labor situation in that state. A happy augury for the future is found in the recent creation of a Federal Child Labor Bureau, although a law prohibiting child labor in interstate industries has been declared unconstitutional. A model child labor law must not only be clear and distinct in language, but must also provide an effective machinery for the enforcement of its provisions. A salaried corps of inspectors should be created with power to prosecute violations of the law. While many employers seek to coöperate in enforcing the law, others have been guilty of evasion.

It is generally agreed that a model child labor law should cover certain well-defined points. The maximum working day should be one of eight hours instead of ten, as found in some states. Night work should also be prohibited and a closing hour fixed. The minimum age at which the child is permitted to work should be fourteen. Some states still have a limit of twelve years of age, and certain southern states make an exception even to this age in the case of the children of pauper parents. Children between the ages of fourteen and sixteen should have duly signed working papers. The state laws on child labor should be correlated with those upon compulsory education. No children should be permitted to enter what are called the " dangerous trades " and these should be specified in the law.

**Women in Industry.** — Women as well as children became workers under the new factory system. The economic causes of both problems are much the same **Similarity to** and their effects quite similar. For physical **child labor.** reasons, the efficiency of woman is sometimes not so high as that of man; while her health and vitality are often seriously impaired through the strain of industry. Again, the entrance of woman into industry is marked by low wages and inferior standards of living. From the standpoint of society the effect upon family life may be equally bad, especially in the case of mothers forced to leave small children. The secondary function of the family is that of socialization, or the preparation of children for the life of society. This cannot be accomplished in a disrupted family life. However, woman cannot be denied her right to independence and self-support; for this movement is but a part of the larger field of equality into which she has entered. Nevertheless, it is necessary to protect her in the exercise of this new freedom. Therefore laws have been passed to regulate the industries into which she may enter, so that her surroundings may be healthful and sanitary. There exists as great a discrepancy in the various laws of the different states upon these matters as upon child labor.

The number of women employed is very high in the manufacturing states of our North Atlantic section and also in parts of the South. At the present time there is a total of nearly eight million women engaged in various industries in the United States. This means that about one female in every five is gainfully employed. Not only has the total number of women in industry increased but also the proportion to the total population has advanced.

Because many of those concerned are women, a word may be said here about the sweat shop system. This is **The sweat** found principally in large, congested cities, and **shop.** especially in the clothing industry located in these centers. The cloth, after being cut for garments in the principal establishments, is distributed to various small shops and private houses in the neighborhood. Here men, women and children make the finished garment. Employment is irregular and wages are determined by the " sweater " who takes advantage of the immigrant, the aged, the children, the inexperienced and those in dire need. Hours of labor are long in the busy season, and the surroundings, where the work is done, are often detrimental to the health of the worker. Factory laws are vain against these abuses because the sweat shop may be located in the home of the individual.

In most occupations the wages of women are much lower than those of men. Therefore, many women have raised **Low wages.** the cry of " equal pay for equal work." However, while most women have only themselves to support or simply the family income to supplement, men usually bear the burden of the entire family support. Again, competition with women has resulted in a lowering of the wages of men. To supplement the income, other

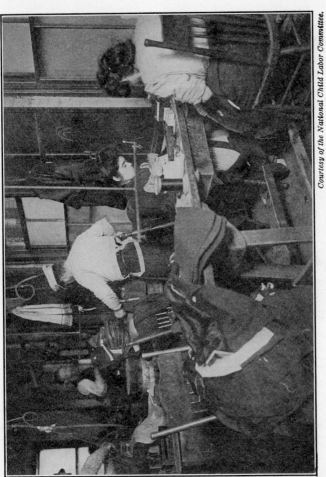

*Courtesy of the National Child Labor Committee.*

A TYPICAL SWEAT-SHOP.

members of the family have sought gainful occupations. Hence, many argue that this whole movement is that of a circle with nothing gained in the end. They therefore look with disfavor upon the entrance of women into business and industrial life. Certain special investigations have shown that, in some industries, the wages of women are criminally low. The wage allowed precludes any possibility of maintaining a decent standard of living for those women who must support themselves. The result is bad housing, insufficient food and clothing, and little, if any, means of recreation. To escape this, many women, it is claimed, have been tempted to lives of immorality. Hence, several states have passed minimum wage laws which fix the lowest wage that may be paid women workers in certain employments. Massachusetts led this movement in 1912. It would seem that the state can only protect women from exploitation by refusing to permit them to work for a wage insufficient to maintain a decent standard of living.

The occupations of women may be grouped under the following heads: (1) domestic service; (2) agriculture; (3) industry; (4) commerce and business; (5) professional life. Domestic service em- New occupations. ploys a large number of women, but has been exempted from many laws dealing with women in industry. Although American women have not engaged in agriculture to any great extent, European immigrants sometimes pick fruit and berries. In the South a large part of the cotton crop is picked by colored women. The great change, however, has come in the last three groups of occupations. We have seen the entrance of women into industry and have noted its causes and effects. Of more recent years, women have invaded commerce, business and the professions.

Formerly the only profession open to women was that of teaching. The great universities, however, have now begun to open wide their doors to women who desire to study law or medicine or the new profession of social service. Formerly, women were rarely seen in the mercantile pursuits, but now they are repeatedly taking the places of men as clerks, stenographers and saleswomen. Since the age of marriage has advanced, women have assumed such positions in order to provide for themselves a means of support. Many women desire the economic independence secured through a professional or business career. In most cases, however, women are simply " loaned " to industry and eventually find their rightful place in the home.

**Occupations of Risk**. — In the path of the Industrial Revolution there followed certain occupations of risk that Dangerous have left a deep impression upon society. The trades. name " dangerous trades " is applied to them because the very nature of the occupation is dangerous to the health and safety of the worker. These may conveniently be considered from the point of view of the chief sources of danger inherent in such trades. One source of danger lies in the poisonous character of the materials used in certain branches of industry. The effect of such work upon the individual is frequently seen in the disease known as lead poisoning, which often occurs in the manufacture of white lead. This substance enters the system through the skin or by way of the alimentary canal, when the worker is not careful to wash his hands before eating. Paralysis, insanity and finally death may result. Several European countries have greatly reduced the mortality in this trade by forbidding such practices as dry rubbing, and by insisting upon the necessity of certain precautionary measures. Workers with phosphorus frequently contract a characteristic disease, singularly fatal, known as phosphorus jaw. This is one of the few dangerous trades against which our government has legislated.

A second source of danger lies in those industries which expose the lungs to an excessive amount of dust. Nature has furnished protection for occasional exposure to a normal amount of dust, but continual exposure to this irritant is extremely dangerous. The lungs become spotted with foreign particles which make fearful ravages upon the delicate membrane. Tuberculosis and other diseases of the lungs and bronchial tubes affect the respiratory organs. This dust danger is well illustrated in coal mining. By screening the coal wet, the amount of coal dust in the air may be reduced. A similar pernicious effect often results from the dust generated by stone cutting and by metal grinding, and from the lint in textile mills. Suction tubes and blowers should be used to draw off this vitiated air from the atmosphere. Certain gases and fumes may also be both dangerous and poisonous. In such cases, the work should be done in a helmet or under a hood with a forced draft. In many of the chemical trades the work is of a dangerous character.

A third source of danger lies in sudden changes of temperature and air pressure. When steel workers, or those employed near hot furnaces, feel the outside contact of the cold blast of winter, they become an easy prey to pneumonia. Underground workers in mines, tunnels and subways often develop peculiar diseases due to changes of air pressure. Although higher wages are sometimes paid to workers in certain trades, because of their acknowledged dangerous

N

character, society must still further protect them from the unusual strains of industry. The law must prescribe precautionary measures and insist upon their enforcement. Shorter hours and frequent periods of rest are absolutely essential to the health and safety of such workers.

The industrial accident, impairing if not altogether destroying the efficiency of the worker, is another product of the factory system. Although this problem is economic in character, it must here be mentioned because of its great social significance. The report of the first Coöperative Safety Congress showed that, on the average, one worker was killed in every sixteen minutes and one injured in every sixteen seconds. This is the price in human life that America has paid for speed. The responsibility for this condition rests upon both the employer and the worker. The worker is sometimes careless, indifferent or ignorant; while the employer is often negligent in supplying safety devices and in rigidly enforcing the law. Of recent years a campaign of popular education has been inaugurated with the slogan "Safety First." A national organization for the safety of the worker uses the "white cross" to stand for prevention, in the same way that the "red cross" stands for first aid to the injured. Industrial accidents may be commonly classified according to occupation, as railroad, mining, factory and building accidents.

*Industrial accidents: Extent and character.*

The Interstate Commerce Commission carefully compiles the statistics relating to railroad accidents. It would seem that in an average year one employee is killed for every four hundred employed by the railroad. This of course does not include thousands of passengers who have been killed or injured in the wrecks.

*Railroad accidents.*

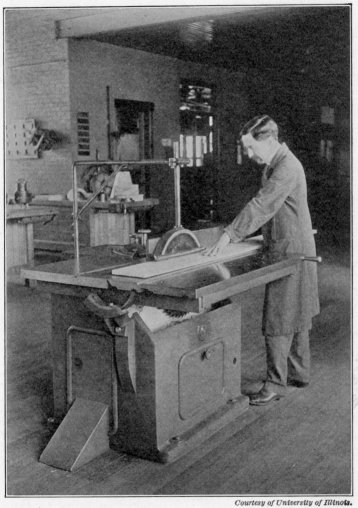

CIRCULAR SAW GUARDED TO PREVENT ACCIDENT.

A comparison with certain European countries, like England and Germany, shows that there is no justification for such an appalling loss of life. Remedial measures should apply to company and workman alike. The corporation should not only install the latest and most approved signal devices, but should also use steel coaches wherever possible. Unfortunately, the financial condition of some railroads has prevented an expenditure of funds for such purposes. A federal law requiring automatic couplers has reduced markedly the number of casualties among trainmen. The employee, however, cannot be relieved of his individual responsibility. He must be constantly on the alert for his own safety and for that of others. From the railroad point of view it is an absolute waste to employ ignorant, careless or unsteady workmen. On the other hand, hours of work should not be so continuous as to produce fatigue and lowered efficiency.

Statistics regarding mining accidents are compiled by state inspectors and are neither so complete nor so accurate as those regarding railroads. Of mining accidents, those in coal mines are the most numerous. *Other accidents.* In the coal-producing countries of Europe the output has increased greatly, but the number of deaths per thousand has decreased. This is due to legislation concerning the operation of mines and to the establishment of testing stations for the study of problems relating to safety in mines. Much has been accomplished by government regulations concerning the use of safety lamps, explosives and the proper support of small passageways. In regard to manufacturing, we find the same incompleteness of statistics, because of the system of state inspection of factories. The chief source of danger here lies in the use of unguarded machinery. Safety appliances are often discarded in the "speeding up" process. Inefficient labor and long-continued work upon the same monotonous operation frequently result in careless accidents. The effects of industrial accidents and dangerous trades are more than an impairment of individual efficiency or a sacrifice of life and limb. They also represent an enormous loss of productive power. Again, the burden of such injuries falls not only upon the worker himself, but also upon his family and the community. Loss of the services of the breadwinner may make the family destitute of proper support and thus dependent upon society.

In view of these marked effects of dangerous trades and industrial accidents upon society, it is important that the **Proposed remedies:** individual affected be provided with legal machinery whereby he may be reimbursed for injuries suffered at the hands of his fellow men. *Social insurance.* That is, society must offer some means of protection to the workman or to his family for social injuries. The first step toward social insurance is found in the Employer's Liability Act, under which the injured workman may bring suit against the employer to recover damages for injury suffered. However, because of the doctrine of contributory negligence, it was often impossible for the workman to receive any recompense for his injury, if it could be proved that such injury was partly caused by his own carelessness or by that of his fellow workers. It, therefore, marked a great step in advance for the workman when society evolved the idea of a Workman's Compensation Act, whereby the expense of lawsuits is generally eliminated. According to this act, the workman, for his injury, receives automatically a percentage of his wages or a certain sum in proportion to the injury sustained. Even though the fault may be largely that of the workman, the employer must bear the brunt of the financial burden, and in this way accept financially the risk which the laborer assumes physically. Hence the employer is more apt to consider the safety of his employees. In 1897, to supersede the older Employer's Liability Act, England passed a Workman's Compensation Act. In the United States, this legislation is largely a matter of state action and several commonwealths, including Pennsylvania, have enacted such laws.

A final step in the process of social insurance is that of compulsory state insurance. Germany early adopted this plan. In 1884 a law was enacted requiring em- *Compulsory* ployees to become members of mutual accident *state* insurance companies supervised by the govern- *insurance.* ment. Germany also has compulsory insurance against illness, to which fund both employees and employers contribute. A third form of state insurance is represented by old age pensions. To this fund not only the employer and employee contribute, but the state also bears a portion of the burden of every annuity. These plans have usually been regarded as paternalistic by liberal democratic countries and, for this reason, have not yet been generally adopted. However, with the increase of governmental activity along the lines of social welfare, it is more than likely that the near future will witness even the most democratic countries taking such action.

## QUESTIONS FOR DISCUSSION

1. Sketch the history of child labor in the United States.

2. What states and industries are conspicuous in this regard?

3. Why is it more difficult in the United States than in England to legislate against this evil?

4. Give some causes of child labor and suggest remedies.

5. State fully the effects of child labor.

6. What points should a model child labor bill cover?

7. What organization has done much to lessen child labor? How?

8. Compare the child labor problem with that of women in industry.

9. Discuss the evils of the sweat shop.

10. Show the relation of women in industry to men's wages.

11. What are some results of an inadequate wage for women?

12. How and why have some states tried to regulate this problem?

13. Give five classes of women's occupations.

14. Show how woman's sphere of activity has increased.

15. What do you think will be some results of it?

16. Classify some dangerous trades and tell what the source of danger is in each.

17. Can you name any others beside those in the text?

18. Give an estimate of the annual number of industrial accidents.

19. Who are to blame and why?

20. What occupations lead in this respect and how may conditions in each be improved?

21. What are the social effects of industrial accidents?

22. Compare American and European conditions with regard to industrial accidents.

23. Find out what you can about the "Safety First" movement.

24. What is the meaning of social insurance?

25. Compare the Employer's Liability Act with the Workman's Compensation Act.

26. Show what Germany has done in the field of compulsory state insurance.

## TOPICS FOR SPECIAL REPORT

1. The child labor laws of your own state.
2. The work of the "Consumers' League."
3. Minimum wage laws.
4. Working conditions in our mines.
5. Working conditions in some factory or department store near you.
6. The railroads and industrial accidents.
7. Government regulation of dangerous trades in the United States and other countries.
8. Contemporary social legislation in the United States.

## REFERENCES

ADAMS and SUMNER. "Labor Problems." Chapter II.
Report of the National Child Labor Committee.
SPARGO, JOHN. "Bitter Cry of the Children."
CLOPPER, E. N. "Child Labor in the City Streets."
KELLEY, F. "Some Ethical Gains through Legislation." Chapters I, II, III.
Reports of Consumers' Leagues.
MANGOLD, G. B. "Child Labor Problems." Book 3, Chapters I–V.
ABBOTT, EDITH. "Women in Industry."
BURCH, H. R., and NEARING, S. "Elements of Economics." Chapters XII, XIII.
SEAGER, H. R. "Social Insurance."
OLIVER, T. "Dangerous Trades."
OLIVER, T. "Diseases of Occupation."
VAN VORST. "The Woman Who Toils."
SEAGER, H. R. "Principles of Economics."

# CHAPTER XV

## The Problem of Adjustment

**Nature of Adjustment.** — In the preceding chapters we have seen numerous examples of maladjustment, that is, of the failure of society to adjust itself properly to great changes in the social environment. In a country like China, where the force of tradition is potent,

*Maladjustments.*

184

these maladjustments are explicable. It is not difficult to understand why, in spite of rich natural resources, the specter of poverty stalks the land and the death rate rises to enormous proportions. The ways of the fathers interfere with the utilization of the environment. In the United States, however, there is little justification for maladjustment. America is a new country, full of modern ideas and untrammeled by tradition. It is rather startling therefore to find, in a land of popular education and democratic ideals, a society that fails to change the environment of law and custom in order to meet the new conditions brought about by the Industrial Revolution.

That revolution, culminating in the factory system and in large scale production, transformed our economic life and made social adjustment necessary. In the present age, therefore, a number of unsettled **Need of adjustment.** problems of an economic and social character have survived the transformation of our industrial environment. Housing and health conditions do not conform to scientific knowledge and present ideals. In a land of riches, poverty still exists and women and children labor for long hours in unhealthy factories. Men still work unrestricted in the dangerous trades, while every year human lives are sacrificed in industrial accidents. Friction between labor and capital results in strikes and lockouts and from such industrial conflicts society suffers. In view of all these circumstances, the need of adjustment is evident.

Adjustment is the removal by society of apparent obstacles in the path of progress. These obstacles come down to us from the past in the form of customs, laws, **Meaning of adjustment.** fixed ideas and methods of living. They have been suited to an older environment — either physical or social — but are out of harmony with present conditions. Society must, therefore, change this social heredity so that to-day the life of man may reach its full fruition. For example, the traditions of hard continuous toil, of low wages, of bad housing conditions and of unhealthy working surroundings have come down to us from an age when such ideas were an outgrowth of meager physical resources and of lack of scientific knowledge. But to-day, in normal times, an eight-hour day, high wages and good working conditions are easily attainable. Society, therefore, must change from the old to the new régime. This process of change is called adjustment.

All life is a process of adjustment. We find it at work in the physical world, in organic life and in society. In the Principles of physical world the process is unconscious. But, adjustment. when society seeks to change environing social conditions in order to meet the needs of man's present life, it proceeds on two principles. First, it acts on the theory that man himself is capable of improvement and for the most part unfettered by laws of physical and mental inheritance. While, of course, the existence of certain inherited physical and mental handicaps is recognized, society, in working out the process of adjustment, proceeds on the principle that the vast majority of mankind is inherently capable of progress. In other words, man's future is not regarded as already determined by his biological past. The son of a pauper may have in him the germs of greatness as much as the child of the millionaire. In the second place, the process of adjustment is accomplished through the principle of coöperation. Society, working together, must accomplish the changes in the social environment necessary to man's freedom and development.

Compared to the organized force of society, individual effort is powerless. Never will great changes be wrought in the social order, until the doctrine of unshackled individualism is recognized as belonging to the past age that gave it birth.

Although much remains to be accomplished, society has already made many adjustments. Serfdom and slavery have been abolished, while the death knell **Results ac-** of autocracy has been sounded. No longer do **complished.** men toil so incessantly as when conditions of life were precarious. Professor Patten in his " New Basis of Civilization " discusses the social and economic gains of the last century. Production has so increased that many goods, formerly regarded as luxuries, are now consumed by all. Inventions have not only lightened the burden of labor, but have also resulted in more leisure time for the worker. The wealth of our natural resources is so abundant that exploitation is no longer necessary. Higher ideals prevail and public opinion will no longer tolerate what was once regarded as necessary and normal. For this reason, society is more seriously than ever considering the problem of adjustment.

The process of adjustment must be continuous with every change in the social and economic environment. For example, if society has created an enor- **The social** mous amount of surplus wealth, it will inevi- **surplus.** tably follow that certain adjustments will have to be made by society for the disposition of that wealth. For many years past, in the United States, an enormous amount of surplus wealth has been created. It exists in the form of railroads and canals, as well as in " trust " products and land values. This wealth has been called the social surplus because it is regarded, not so much as the result of individual, as of social action. In other words, the social surplus is primarily the result of coöperation, and its increase is characteristic of an advancing civilization. Primitive man lived from hand to mouth without the accumulation of any surplus. In the little that he consumed, however, he was rather communistic, because the land and game were shared by all. But modern men produce collectively great quantities of goods which are subject to individual appropriation and consumption. In the production of these goods, thousands of men have united. Without this coöperation, they could not have been produced. Hence, the term social surplus has been applied to them. In the process of modern manufacturing, for example, the final product is possible only by means of the principle of division of labor and by the complete coöperation of all the labor involved. The creation of this social surplus by our modern industrial system has led to a new problem of adjustment.

**Methods of Adjustment.** — How has society attempted to meet the new problem of adjustment made necessary by the creation of a social surplus? That is to say, through what channels may this socially created wealth be returned to the worker and the community? With the hope of solving this problem, certain groups in society have advocated special methods of adjustment. It is our purpose here to present the main outlines of these plans, rather than to pass judgment upon their respective merits.

One method of adjustment that society has generally accepted and usually advocated is that of organization. Of course, capital and labor are equally essential to production. With the advent of the Industrial Revolution, society, aside from the landowner, became divided into two great classes — those of capital and labor. In the nineteenth century, the capitalistic class became highly organized. It owned the tools of produc- *Through organization:* tion, offered the worker employment, and paid *How capital* him wages. It was therefore in the form of wages *organized.* that labor received its share of wealth. The determination of these wages rested largely with the employer. For, as the capitalistic class became thoroughly organized, it could fix wages at the level desired. It must be remembered that, when capital became organized in the form of the great "trusts" of the latter part of the nineteenth century, these combinations attempted to crush competition and to wield great monopoly power. This exercise of monopoly power brought with it certain advantages. For example, capital, so organized, could control the product from raw material to finished article, reduce the cost of production, utilize by-products and, through specialization in industry, secure the highest possible efficiency. From a social point of view, these gains to industry might result in tremendous advantages to the community.

But how did this power, wielded by organizations of capital, actually manifest itself? As far back as the beginning of the nineteenth century, its effect on labor *How labor* was apparent and, toward the close of the same *organized.* century, its effect upon society was equally apparent. Instead of the advantages of organized capital redounding to the benefit of labor and the community, they were largely appropriated by the capitalists themselves. Low wages, long hours of work and unsanitary working conditions forced labor to form equally powerful organizations; and, later, high prices and inferior products forced the community to take similar measures for its protection. In other words, the advantage of decreased cost of production, instead of going to labor in the form of higher wages or to the community in the form of lower prices, went to the capitalistic class in the form of higher prices and larger profits. Labor organizations were first looked upon as conspiracies and their leaders severely punished. To-day, however, they have secured a firm place in the social and economic system. The American Federation of Labor is one of the most influential organizations in this country, wielding enormous power in behalf of its members. Labor relies upon this organization to secure a larger share of the social surplus. This it accomplishes by securing higher wages, shorter hours and better working conditions. It employs the weapons of the strike, the lockout and the boycott. Of course, the exercise of this power is often dangerous to the community, as well as to the worker and employer. The great anthracite coal strike in Pennsylvania was sufficient evidence of this danger, while the bold threat of the Railroad Brotherhoods (1916) shows the tremendous power now exercised by such organizations as well as their possible danger. The Industrial Workers of the World is a later organization of labor that shows to what extremes labor will go to gain a larger share of the social surplus. It openly advocates violence and destruction of property. Such illegal and anarchistic methods deserve society's severest condemnation.

We have also seen that the community has suffered from the organization of capital in the form of the *How society* trust and other great industrial combinations. *organized.* The decreased cost of production, brought about by large scale production, should, however, appear in lower prices and better goods for the community. Society thus demands its share of the social surplus. When, therefore, it was found in the latter years of the nineteenth century that prices were rising out of all proportion to cost of production, and that the consumer was becoming a victim of organized capital's monopoly power, society began to take measures for its own protection. In 1887 the Interstate Commerce Commission had been established and in 1890 the Sherman Anti-Trust Law was passed. The former applied primarily to railroads and the latter to trusts. These acts have later been strengthened by a number of amendments and new enactments for the protection of the public. In this manner, society is seeking an adjustment to the new economic conditions. The public, through lower prices and better goods, seeks to break the undue monopoly power exercised by organized capital. With the abnormal conditions brought about by war, society sees still further the necessity for self-protection.

Another method of appropriating the social surplus is through taxation. In this country, during the last century, the system of taxation employed caused the burden to fall largely upon the poor and the great middle class. Nine-tenths of our revenue was formerly derived from customs duties and excise taxes. Duties, of course, are laid upon imported articles, while excises are internal taxes. The former fall upon a multitude of goods, including wool, sugar and other articles in daily use; while the latter are laid chiefly upon tobacco and other luxuries. All of these taxes are indirect, that is, the burden of paying them may be shifted from the producer to the consumer. In this

*Through changes in taxation: Usual forms.*

manner, the support of the government fell largely upon the poorer classes in society because the goods taxed were so largely consumed by them. From a social point of view, this system of taxation had the effect of discriminating in favor of the wealthier classes in society.

Consequently, with the growth of the idea of social welfare, society began to work out changes in the method of *Newer forms* taxation. Here was an enormous social surplus *of taxation.* — wealth socially created — that was largely escaping taxation and remaining in the hands of private individuals. How was this surplus to be returned to the society that created it? In other words, what change in environing conditions, in laws and traditions, was society obliged to accomplish in order to bring about necessary readjustments? Evidently the laws and customs, justifying the larger taxation of middle class consumption, must undergo a complete transformation. Accordingly, society set about accomplishing this by means of the utilization of income and inheritance taxes, as well as by the employment of the excess profits tax.

Prior to 1913, the United States experienced great difficulty in levying an income tax, because the Constitution required that direct taxes should be laid in proportion to the population. Such a tax laid during the Civil War was declared constitutional, but a later income tax law enacted during the last decade of the nineteenth century was declared unconstitutional by the United States Supreme Court. With the adoption of the constitutional amendment of 1913, however, the restriction laid upon the levying of direct taxes was removed, so that income tax laws are now as constitutional as those imposing tariff duties. It is needless to say that such laws are intended to take directly from the individual a certain share of his wealth which the coöperative processes of society have helped to produce. A portion of the social surplus is thus returned to society. This fund is used for the promotion of social welfare, while the consumption of the poorer classes is correspondingly relieved of a portion of the burden of taxation.

Another form of direct taxation is the inheritance tax. Social inequalities are exemplified in inherited fortunes as much as by slum environments. Inheritance taxes are usually graduated so that the larger inherited fortunes, when they pass into new hands, are taxed more heavily than smaller ones. Several European countries employ such a tax, while a few of our own states (New York, Pennsylvania and Wisconsin) also make use of this form of taxation. Of course this tax is designed to eliminate, rather than to accentuate, the glaring inequalities in individual incomes. In the course of time, the benefits of an invention go to society and are not forever confined to the family of the inventor. The advocate of the inheritance tax asks why a part of the social surplus should not be similarly enjoyed. For it must be remembered that the fruits of this taxation would, in normal times, be enjoyed by society in the form of better educational facilities, larger means of recreation, greater leisure time and in other phases of social welfare. In justice to the American industrial genius, it must here be said, however, that already a large part of the social surplus has been voluntarily relinquished from individual possession and is being socially enjoyed in the form of great educational foundations, large public libraries and fine charitable institutions.

Undoubtedly, war has hastened this process of socializa-

o

tion of wealth, and, when the period of conflict passes, its effects will still be felt in an increased socialization. Of course, the benefits of such changes in methods of taxation will, unfortunately, be required at first to repair the damage and misfortune brought about by the conflict. Society, therefore, may from this point of view be no better off than it was before the great conflict began. It will probably be worse off, because the enormous amount of capital that has been destroyed must be replaced. War has given rise also to the excess profits tax, which seeks to take from the artificially enriched industries the funds required for the conduct of the government and for the prosecution of hostilities. It has recently been estimated that, whereas formerly customs duties and excise taxes furnished nine-tenths of the revenue of the United States government, over one-half of our total revenue from taxation is now secured from the income and excess profits taxes (1918).

Another method that society is gradually employing to adapt itself to the condition brought about by the crea-

Through changes in distribution: *Why necessary.*

tion of a social surplus is reflected in various changes in the well-established system of wealth distribution. Of course, by distribution we mean the manner in which the wealth of society is distributed among the factors in production — land, labor and capital. The landlord receives rent, the laborer wages and the capitalist interest. The rise of the trust and of other great forms of organized capital has given birth to another factor in production, called managing ability, that receives for its labor and capital a new share in distribution called profits — a combination of wages and interest. Now, the nineteenth century brought about a condition whereby these shares in distribution — rent, interest, capital and profits — were very unevenly distributed. The growth of the social surplus was the main cause of this uneven distribution, because this socially created wealth went mainly to the landlord and to the industrial manager. Consequently, rent and profits increased enormously, while wages did not advance at the same rate. In comparison with labor conditions abroad, wages were high in the United States; but, as compared with the rise in rent and profits in this country, wages' rate of increase was slow. These inequalities are well illustrated by the estimate made several years ago that seven-eighths of the families in the United States owned but one-eighth of the national wealth. A later study made in 1915 estimated that sixty-five per cent of our population — the poor class, but not paupers — possessed no property; that fifteen per cent composed the lower middle class whose wealth was below $1000; that eighteen per cent made up the upper middle class whose wealth ranged from $2000 to $40,000; and that only two per cent of our total population were wealthy in the modern sense of the term. This two per cent owned three-fifths of the entire property of the United States. Hence arises the demand for a redistribution of the social surplus.

Perhaps the easiest method of readjustment is that known as profit-sharing. According to this plan, the employer, industrial manager or " captain of in- *Profit-* dustry " voluntarily gives up part of his profits *sharing.* to the worker. This may be accomplished through stock ownership, or through a system of deferred participation in profits, or by means of giving a cash bonus to the laborer in proportion to his wages. Naturally, the latter plan is most acceptable to the worker, whose returns would rise or fall in proportion to the degree of success in business undertakings. This plan has recently been inaugurated in an automobile industry where it has given great satisfaction. In addition to his regular wages, the laborer receives an extra cash bonus at the end of the year. Labor co-partnership or coöperation goes a step farther in this process and seeks to eliminate altogether the employer or entrepreneur. The working group subscribes or borrows its own capital and substitutes for the employer a committee of workmen, who direct the business undertaking for their mutual benefit. The best illustration of this experiment is found in the coöperative stores throughout Great Britain.

The Single Tax theory, first promulgated by Henry George in his " Progress and Poverty," is another method *The single* advocated for changing our system of wealth *tax.* distribution. Increased land values is an excellent example of socially created wealth. The holder of idle land, whether it be in an agricultural or urban section, waits upon the action of society for an increase in its value. A farm is enhanced in value by the settlement of the surrounding region, just as real estate values rise because of increased business or social improvements. In either case, society contributes to the rise in the value of the land. The Single Taxer calls this increased value, due to social and not individual action, the " unearned increment " which, under our present system, is appropriated by the landlord in the form of rent. He does not deny to the owner the value of any improvement he may make on the land; but he does believe that the extra value created by society should be taken by the community in the form of a heavy tax. In this manner, a part of the social surplus could be returned to society, which would be benefited by relief from other forms of taxation, by increased production, by greater social benefits and by decreased poverty. This principle has been applied in New Zealand, in European countries, in Vancouver and, in a modified form, in some of our own American states. While it is doubtful whether the Single Tax will accomplish all that its advocates claim, it is undoubtedly true that this principle offers society a splendid chance to secure a part of the social surplus. It is, therefore, more than likely that the future will see a greater utilization of this principle.

The most radical readjustment urged by social reformers is that embodied in the term Socialism. This system attempts to secure the social surplus for the worker by taking it from the landlord and the capitalist. *Socialism.* The Single Taxer aims to socialize land, but the Socialist would also socialize capital. That is, " the tools of production " are to be owned by society. Public ownership is to supersede private monopoly. Thus, wages will be increased by eliminating, to a large extent, profits, interest and rent. Labor is to have " the right to the full product," and the social surplus is to be divided among all laborers. Under this system, it is claimed that exploitation of labor would cease and that private monopoly for individual gain would no longer exist. In their place would arise equal opportunity for all and common coöperation for the public good. The evils of competition would be replaced by the advantages of monopoly, existing only for the public service. Through collective ownership of the means of production, the salvation of society would be attained. Such ideals are beautiful; but is society ready for this experiment? If we stake all, we may lose all. Unfortunately, self-interest, not the spirit of social service, is still the leading motive in human nature. Public morality is often low, while inefficiency and corruption are yet found in public life. While undoubtedly the functions of modern governments are rapidly expanding, it is still questionable whether the governmental structure could bear the additional strain imposed upon it by the complete adoption of such a system. Rather is a solution of the problem to be sought in a gradual absorption of so-called socialistic doctrines into the widening functions of modern government. Only indirectly will the true mission of socialism be fulfilled.

This discussion may make us question whether the problem of poverty is, or ever will be, capable of complete solution. Is it possible for society to make such changes in the social system as to secure complete adjustment between man and his environment? Is there something inherent in human nature that prevents this harmony from being attained? To answer these questions more fully we shall examine in detail the problem of poverty, the phenomenon of crime and the group of natural defectives.

## QUESTIONS FOR DISCUSSION

1. Give some examples of maladjustments.
2. Give meaning and examples of the process of adjustment.
3. When is it necessary for society to make adjustments?
4. Show the relation between progress and adjustment.
5. Mention some great adjustments made by society in the nineteenth century.
6. Explain the "social surplus."
7. How did the social surplus give rise to another problem of adjustment?

8. How did labor seek an adjustment?

9. How did the public?

10. Give several plans of profit-sharing.

11. What is the essential creed of socialism?

12. What is your opinion regarding the advantages and disadvantages of socialism?

13. Define what is meant by the "Single Tax."

14. What are its advantages and justification?

15. Where have income and inheritance taxes been tried?

16. What is their justification?

17. Should society permit the amassing of huge fortunes and their inheritance?

## TOPICS FOR SPECIAL REPORT

1. The effect of war upon the social surplus.

2. The coöperative stores of Great Britain.

3. The effect of war upon income and inheritance taxes in Europe and America.

4. The life and work of Henry George.

5. Single tax reforms in Australasia.

6. Karl Marx and the early socialists.

7. State socialism in Germany.

8. The present platform of the socialist party in America.

## REFERENCES

PATTEN, S. N. "New Basis of Civilization."

BURCH, H. R., and NEARING, S. "Elements of Economics." Chapters I, XXXII, XXXVIII–XLI (inclusive).

SEAGER, H. R. "Principles of Economics." Chapters XXVII–XXXIII (inclusive).

HAYES, E. C. "Introduction to Study of Sociology." Chapters VII–X (inclusive.)

KIRKUP, T. "History of Socialism."

WELLS, H. G. "New Worlds for Old."

GEORGE, HENRY. "Progress and Poverty."

NEARING, SCOTT. "Social Adjustment."

GILMAN, N. P. "Profit Sharing."

JENKS, J. W. "Government Action for Social Welfare."

# CHAPTER XVI

## The Problem of Poverty

I. Nature of poverty
  1. Definition of terms
  2. Extent of:
      a. Poverty
      b. Pauperism
  3. The point of view:
      a. Change of attitude
      b. Reformers' errors
      c. Theory of evolution
II. Causes of poverty
  1. Environmental:
      a. Physical environment
      b. Economic environment:
          (1) Low wages
          (2) Unemployment
          (3) Other causes
      c. Social environment
      d. Defects in government
      e. Defects in education
  2. Individual:
      a. Degeneracy
      b. Disease
      c. Intemperance
      d. Crime
      e. Desertion
      f. Death of main support
      g. Old age
      h. Defectives
      i. Indolence

**Nature of Poverty**. — In a discussion of poverty it is necessary at the outset to define several terms. That class in society with the lowest income is usually Definition referred to as the " poor." With the advance of of terms. civilization, the standards of living of both rich and poor have been raised. The well-to-do classes live in luxury unknown a few centuries ago to the corresponding group. The poor of to-day also possess more comforts than those enjoyed by a similar group in earlier society. The poor, however, in the sense of the lowest income class have persisted in society and must continue to exist in spite of all adjustments society may make. The rise of standards of living will go on in all classes, but in spite of this upward movement, the poor will necessarily remain so, unless society sweeps away all economic distinctions. / In sociology, however, the term " poor " is not used in this popular sense. The sociologist employs the special term poverty to mean the condition of that group only whose income, and therefore standard of living, is not high enough to maintain normal health and efficiency. It is in this sense, and to such a group, that the term poverty will be applied in this chapter. It may even be possible for the advance of civilization to eliminate such a group by raising its income to an amount required to maintain an " efficiency " standard of living. The pauper group is a part of the poverty class. Paupers are those individuals or families, in almshouses or in their own homes, who require economic help from various charity organizations. They belong to the group known as social debtors, for pauperism is essentially a state of dependency. Those individuals, however, who live in a condition of poverty, but who are too proud to receive outside help, should not be referred to as paupers.

The extent of poverty is difficult to determine, for social measurements cannot be made with absolute and undeviat- ing accuracy. Standards of health and ef- ficiency vary with the individual judgment of the observer. Again, the purchasing power of income fluctuates with the rise and fall of prices. Since poverty has an economic basis, its extent throughout the general population varies greatly with industrial prosperity and depression. Poverty is also much higher in the city than in rural communities. The extent of pauperism is almost equally difficult to determine. The almshouse shelters such different groups of dependents as the sick, the feeble-minded, the aged and the shiftless. Records are generally poorly kept and, unfortunately, many societies for long periods of time kept no records whatever./ Several individuals, however, have made special studies of the extent of poverty in a particular locality. Charles Booth made the first great investigation of its kind for London, and Rowntree undertook a similar study for the city of York. In these cities the estimated proportions of those living in poverty, that is, below an income required to maintain the normal standard of health and efficiency, were thirty and seven-tenths per cent and twenty-seven and eight-tenths per cent respectively. Robert Hunter, by similar investigations in our own country, estimated that the proportion of those living in poverty in our large cities and industrial centers rarely fell below twenty-five per cent. It is smaller of course in the rural sections but, for our country at large, the expression " the submerged tenth " is probably not an exaggeration. In 1904, in normal times of peace, Mr. Hunter estimated that about ten million inhabitants of the United States were most of the time underfed, poorly

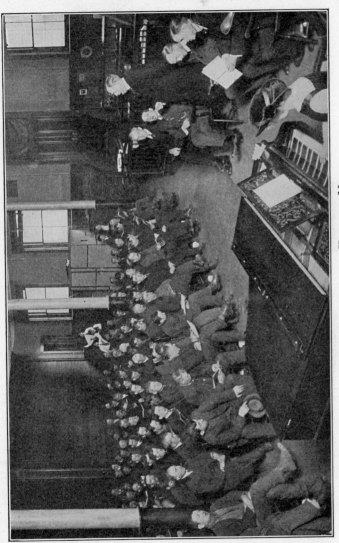

SUNRISE BREAKFAST FOR HOMELESS MEN.

housed and insufficiently clothed. On this basis the poverty group, excluding paupers, would seem to range from ten to twelve per cent of our total population.

The census of 1910 gave the number of dependents in our various institutions as 700,000. This estimate, how- *Pauperism.* ever, has little significance because most paupers are not in the almshouses but are cared for by what is known as the system of outdoor relief. The total number of dependents is probably between four and five millions. It is more likely to be nearer the upper than the lower figure because our population has increased nor- mally since 1904, and there is no indication that the per- centage of pauperism in normal times has materially de- clined. The support of this army of dependents requires annually about a half billion dollars. If we include the paupers with the poverty group, the total number of such persons will probably reach the fifteen million mark in ordinary times. The effects of the World War and new economic conditions remain to be seen in both Europe and America. The percentage of pauperism in our own country has been placed at five per cent. The following stray facts seem to bear out this estimate. In 1903, one twentieth of the population of the city of Boston were aided by public relief. In the same year, fourteen per cent of the families living in the borough of Manhattan were evicted from their homes for nonpayment of rent; and, in spite of the fear of a pauper's grave, ten per cent of those who died in the same borough were buried in potters' field.

The old attitude toward poverty was that it always had existed and always would continue to exist so long as the world endured. Almsgiving was regarded as a religious duty and an indication of the piety of the donor. The

monasteries of the Christian Church sheltered the poor and unfortunate of the Middle Ages. So, to-day, innumerable
*Point of view:* beggars in the Mohammedan countries of the
*Change of attitude.* world continually appeal to the traveler for "alms for the love of Allah." The modern viewpoint, however, is that poverty in its narrow sociological meaning is unnecessary. The same scientific spirit which has rooted out smallpox, yellow fever and other physical contagions is striving to cure the social disease of poverty. The remedy is not indiscriminate almsgiving, because that kind of charity only increases pauperism. The causes which produce this unfortunate condition must be eliminated by individuals and by society. Poverty will then diminish in the same way that the elimination of the mosquito has reduced the amount of yellow fever in the tropics.

A number of social reformers have made the error of assuming that poverty had but one cause. Thus, Malthus believed poverty was due to the pressure of population upon food supply. Karl Marx sought its explanation in
*Reformers' errors.* the ownership of the instruments of production by the capitalistic class. Socialism was therefore his remedy. To Henry George, poverty was the result of the rise in rent and only the "Single Tax" could remove it. Poverty, however, is a complex phenomenon and its causes are manifold. They are both objective and subjective. Not only environment, but heredity must be taken into account in analyzing the causes of poverty. Each case of dependency has its roots in a number of causes which lie both in the individual and in his environment.

Evolution in the field of biology may offer us a parallel.

Society may be regarded, for most individuals, as a form of the struggle for existence. Some environments are more favorable to survival than others. Again, *Theory of* variations exist between individuals; some are *evolution.* stronger, wiser and more efficient than others. We have seen that artificial handicaps may also exist, for there is not always an equality of opportunity. Artificial selection does not always eliminate the unfit, but merely places them in the lower or poverty group. Altruism in modern civilization expresses itself in the building of almshouses and in the organization of charity. Human society also differs from the animal world because of the existence of a directive intelligence, by means of which man may transform his environment and make purposive changes for his own betterment.

**Causes of Poverty.** — A people may suffer from poverty because of the barrenness of the physical environment due to poor soil or other natural restrictions. Mi- *Environ-* grations from poorer to richer regions then re- *mental:* sult in wars. Again, there may be unfavorable *Physical en-* climatic conditions, such as an excess of moisture *vironment.* or a lack of rainfall as found in swamp lands and deserts. Scientific agriculture, however, has done much for the productivity of such regions and has made them more capable of supporting a larger population. Natural forces may produce floods, earthquakes, storms or droughts and cause a given locality to suffer from temporary poverty or even pauperism. Illustrations of this fact are found in the Johnstown flood, in the San Francisco earthquake and in the storm at Galveston. Fires in our great cities have, by force of accident, reduced many families of means to actual want. Again, certain diseases, like malaria and hookworm, flourish in particular environments. Inhabitants of these regions are regarded as indolent and shiftless, whereas their constitutions are really undervitalized by environmental influences.

The minimum wage under which a normal standard of health and efficiency may be maintained has been va-
*Economic en-* riously estimated. For the normal family in
*vironment.* 1909 the annual sum of $700 or $650 was fixed as the minimum in certain places. For larger cities, like New York, Dr. Chapin estimated that a yearly income of less than $800 was not sufficient to maintain a normal standard of living for the average family of five persons. A similar sum was fixed upon after an investigation of the stockyard district of Chicago. There were, however, at that time five million industrial workers in the United States who were annually earning $600 or less. While a number of these were single men, found among the unskilled immigrant laborers, a considerable proportion of them were supporting families. In 1908, sixty-five per cent of the workers in the steel industry of Pittsburg, " the city of a thousand millionaires," were classified as unskilled laborers with wages ranging from $405 to $505 a year. A wage lower than the minimum required to maintain an " efficiency " standard of living seems to be the story of the New York tenements, of the stockyard district of Chicago, of the industrial towns of Pennsylvania and of the coal fields of West Virginia. Of recent years the problem has become more acute because of the great increase in the cost of living. Prices have increased enormously, while the rise in wages, except in the war industries, has not been proportional. Several years ago, four-fifths of the adult male wage earners in many industrial sections

of this country were receiving less than $750 a year, while a third received less than $500.

The World War, however, brought about an increase in wages unparalleled in many years. The reason for this was obvious. The usual relation between goods and labor was completely upset. For many years labor had been plentiful and the production of goods normal. The value of labor was, therefore, not high as compared with that of economic goods. But the outbreak of world-wide hostilities withdrew labor from production and thus decreased the normal output of commodities. Since goods were in demand and the Government needed them at all costs, prices advanced; and since the amount of labor employed in industrial production was greatly limited, wages also advanced. Every increase in price gave an additional impetus to a rise in wages. The cost of living increased so rapidly that wages often doubled and advanced to even a higher level. Workers who had previously received $600 and $700 per annum were receiving $1200 and $1500. At the close of the World War investigations conducted among shipworkers placed the minimum wage of a family of five at $1500 annually, and a report of the Bureau of Municipal Research of Philadelphia set the figure at $1800.

Unemployment, another phase of our economic environment, may be defined as involuntary idleness during normal working time. It applies only to the group of wage earners who are capable and willing to work, and not to the shiftless and indolent who avoid work at all hazards. This problem is social, as well as economic, in character. The Charity Organization Society of New York states that a half of all their applicants need work rather than material help. During the winter of 1914–1915 the unemployment problem became so acute in Philadelphia that a commission was appointed to investigate the problem. The report is most fruitful. During the winter, in a city of about one and a quarter million inhabitants, the number of unemployed in various occupations ranged from fifty to two hundred and fifty thousand. The amount of unemployment in normal times was found to be alarming. Lace weavers, for example, were found to have worked only three-fifths of their time in the last five years. One representative carpet mill never failed to lose twenty per cent of its time in any year during the last four years. It was estimated that dock hands did not work more than two days each week. It was found that every winter thousands of Italians returned to Philadelphia from the truck farms of South Jersey to render the city's unemployment problem more acute. Except in times of war or great prosperity there is probably a permanent excess of the supply of labor of the lowest grade. This situation partly explains why wages are so low, and why unemployment is so acute, among unskilled workers. Alternations of dull and busy seasons also throw many out of employment.

The problem of unemployment would be alleviated by the dovetailing of occupations, whereby an industry, located in an agricultural district, would furnish employment between the seasons of harvesting and planting. Seasonal trades are the source of much unemployment, but in some cases there is little excuse for their being seasonal. Better industrial organization in the form of labor exchanges or bureaus would help greatly in the solution of this problem. In times of panic and industrial depression the problem of unemployment becomes most acute. The local and federal governments should plan in advance their programs of public improvements, and as great a proportion as possible of this work should be deferred until labor crises arise. Public employment agencies should be established to furnish prompt and ready knowledge of the opportunities for labor.

The effects of unemployment are serious. In the first place this maladjustment represents a great waste of economic resources. It often means that the family of the unemployed worker becomes destitute and must be supported by the community. Charity may tide over the situation, but it is no solution of the real problem. Finally, unemployment often results in a deterioration of the worker. It may lead to family desertion or, by enforcing idle habits, it may pauperize the laborer himself.

That changes in industry may produce temporary hardship is well illustrated by the transition from the domestic to the factory system of industry. The amount of poverty is also greater during industrial crises and in periods of financial distress. Strikes and lockouts have a similar effect. Again, a bad system of land tenure, such as existed in England during the time of the " inclosures," produces much poverty. For many years the great Mississippi Valley furnished a supply of free land to those in our country who cared to move westward. The poverty problem in America may be said to date from the practical exhaustion of this supply of free land. Other economic causes of poverty may be found in various maladjustments brought about by changing economic conditions.

Social environment is another factor in the problem of poverty. Unsanitary living conditions may be as much the cause as the result of poverty. We have already spoken of bad housing conditions in *Social environment.* connection with the problem of the city. Such conditions

P

may produce sickness which often results in the death or unemployment of the wage earner. Thus, the family becomes dependent upon the charity of the community, a situation which might have been obviated by different living conditions. Sickness or death of the breadwinner may be merely the immediate and most obvious cause of poverty resulting from bad housing. Such distinctions are important, for in each case of poverty there are numerous contributory causes. Again, the associations that prevail in the congested districts of a great city may injure the morals as much as the health of those concerned. Idleness, shiftlessness or degeneracy in family life may thus result in poverty. The saloon, the immoral dance hall, vicious theaters and amusement places may lead to the dissipation of funds required for the necessities of life. Moreover, such pleasures inculcate ideas other than those of steady industry and produce a degenerating effect upon the health and morals of the worker. Again, unrestricted immigration may be as injurious to the immigrant himself as to the American worker whose wages and standards of living he lowers. Our study of immigration has shown how large a percentage of the recipients of charity were foreign born. Unwise philanthropy as a factor in poverty will be discussed in the following chapter. It will be sufficient to state in this connection that, so long as begging is more profitable than working, poverty will spread throughout society.

Political corruption often returns to power the legislator who fails to pass laws in favor of those who elect him. Be-
*Defects in government.* cause of inadequate legislation, monopoly prices take too large a share of the laborer's wages, child labor continues to harass his family and the building

inspector fails to report his landlord's condemned tenement. Legislation is no panacea for social ills, but wise laws and their proper enforcement will accomplish beneficial results. They are an essential part of any scheme of social reform. Again, bribery of the voter may result in the purchase of the necessities of life for some poverty-stricken individual. The ward "boss" may be to him a greater help in time of trouble than the local charity organization. Such a policy, however, is to say the least, shortsighted, because it does not eliminate the causes and conditions which give rise to poverty. The poor man's vote should compel beneficial legislation for social reform. The attitude toward government is changing and its sphere of activity widening. Like other institutions of society, government is being socialized. It must provide for the public health and recreation, as well as for the public safety. Bad housing conditions and unsanitary working conditions are a reproach to good government.

Among other ideals, education should aim to make the individual self-supporting. Lack of industrial training in our public schools has been one cause of de- *Defects in* pendency. Until recently, it often happened *education.* that a boy could not receive training in a trade at public expense unless he committed a crime and was sent to the industrial school or to the reformatory. Statistics also show that the proportion of illiteracy and ignorance among dependents is abnormally high.

Let us now inquire into those causes of poverty which are individual rather than environmental in nature. Pauperism is an acquired characteristic and consequently not hereditary. But a physical and mental degeneracy, causing poverty or pauperism, may be inherent in the germ cell

and therefore hereditary. This fact would seem to explain why pauperism may " run " in a given family and be
Individual causes: *Degeneracy.* regarded by the uninformed as hereditary. Such degeneracy may take various forms in the second generation. The offspring of a drunken parent may incline toward both drunkenness and pauperism. Neither characteristic is strictly speaking hereditary, as is the inherent weakness or degeneracy which produces it. The physical and mental stamina of certain stocks may be subnormal and their offspring, under force of circumstances, may drift into one of the various social debtor classes. They may also be regarded as inferior variations which cannot care for themselves in their struggle for existence. Certain studies of degenerate families seem to bear out this conclusion. For example, a study of the Juke family by Dugdale shows a long line of descendants traced in prison records, almshouses and drunkards' graves. The influence of the social environment of a particular family is also important, but must not be confused with its physical heredity. The only members of the Juke family who amounted to anything were those who left their old associations and started life afresh in some new community. Dr. Goddard finds his clew to degeneracy and pauperism in feeble-mindedness, and estimates that one-half of the inmates of almshouses are feeble-minded. As feeble-mindedness is hereditary, and not acquired, we are able to understand how many cases of pauperism may run in the same family. This is the theme of his most readable little story of the Kallikak family. Only segregation of the feeble-minded will prevent the propagation of their kind and the passing on to future generations of degeneracy and pauperism.

Disease is a most important cause of poverty. Dr. Devine states that seventy-five per cent of poverty is due to disease, not twenty-five per cent as is usually supposed. It is certain that from *Disease.* twenty-five to forty per cent of all cases applying for relief represent a temporary or permanent disability due to sickness. This is the individual expression of such objective causes as unsanitary living conditions, improper housing, bad working conditions and dangerous trades.

Although the importance of intemperance as a cause of poverty has perhaps been exaggerated, nearly one-fourth of all cases coming before charity organizations *Intemper-* were traced to the ravages of alcohol. The *ance.* Committee of Fifty who investigated this subject found that over forty-one per cent of the inmates of almshouses owed their condition directly or indirectly to alcoholic excess. Many families lived in want and squalor because the breadwinner persisted in spending his income in the saloon. As a destroyer of efficiency, alcohol was a frequent cause of unemployment. Intemperance is a subjective cause of poverty, but it has its roots in numerous objective causes such as pernicious social customs, long hours of work and poor facilities for recreation. Intemperance and the saloon must be regarded as results, as well as causes, of poverty. Immorality must also be mentioned, for Dugdale places it even ahead of intemperance as the cause of the degeneracy of the Juke family.

The imprisonment of the breadwinner is a frequent cause of poverty to his family. Society shelters, feeds and clothes the criminal, but permits *Crime.* innocent members of his family to suffer. To remedy this injustice some states have laws by which the products of convict labor are turned over to their families.

Desertion by the head of the family appears in from five to ten per cent of all cases of dependency in our large cities. *Desertion.* Children may be abandoned by their parents, or wives by their husbands. In the case of many destitute families relatives show a remarkable indifference to their condition. Charity workers find a surprising amount of neglect upon the part of near relatives and a failure to help in cases of dependency.

Death of the main support appears in from ten to twenty per cent of relief cases. Some form of social insurance for *Death of main support.* the poor or a sound life insurance system within their reach is earnestly advocated. Widows and orphans, however, have always appealed to human sympathy, and funds given by philanthropists have founded numerous institutions for the care of such persons. Charity workers find little difficulty in caring for orphans, for more funds are at their disposal for this group of destitutes than for any other.

Old age is frequently a cause of dependency and the almshouse is often the final home for the aged. Such a *Old age.* situation is cruelly unfair. Many old persons have been industrious workers and have reared large families. But, now, having outgrown their period of usefulness, they are incapacitated for further work. Old-age pensions would lift the stigma of the poorhouse from the aged, who have no means of support for their declining years. Society should at least provide separate and comfortable homes for the aged, where husband and wife will not be parted and where they will not come into contact with the feeble-minded, the degenerate and other subnormal groups found in the average alms-house.

Defectives are frequently public charges. The crippled and the blind constitute a large proportion of the beggars upon our streets. At present the almshouse is the general depository for most of these variant *Defectives.* groups. Special methods of treatment for each class of defectives will be discussed in a later chapter in which this group of social debtors will be carefully analyzed.

Shiftlessness and laziness are individual characteristics which may lead to poverty and pauperism. It is estimated that from ten to fifteen per cent of all cases of distress may be attributed to these individual *Indolence.* weaknesses. However, a number of so-called cases of laziness have been found, upon physical examination, to be due to an undervitalized health condition. For example, the shiftlessness of the " poor white trash " of the South was found in some cases to be due to hookworm. Malaria may play the same rôle, and poor health and malnutrition may often result in a lowered vitality. Again, retarded school children in slum districts have been found upon examination to be underfed and anæmic. Environment, however, will not explain every such case; for there are some individuals who are inherently lazy and shiftless. Again, many poor people are in a condition of poverty because of their own improvidence. A lack of judgment prevents their exercising a wise economy in applying their earnings to the purchase of food, clothing and other nec-essaries. Scarcity of funds necessitates buying in small quantities and only for immediate consumption. Hence the poor are often overcharged. For this reason, tactful settlement workers are carefully studying the manner in which the poor spend their small incomes and are seeking to advise them as to what constitutes wise economy.

## QUESTIONS FOR DISCUSSION

1. Define poverty in its sociological sense.
2. Distinguish between poverty and pauperism.
3. What is your opinion about the final elimination of poverty?
4. Give an estimate of the extent of poverty.
5. Give an estimate of the extent of pauperism.
6. How has our point of view regarding poverty changed?
7. Why is it important to study the causes of poverty?
8. What mistake did several reformers make?
9. Explain poverty from the standpoint of the theory of evolution.
10. Explain how the causes of poverty overlap.
11. Distinguish between the immediate and the remote, or the main and the contributory, causes of poverty.
12. What twofold classification do we make of the causes of poverty?
13. Explain the relation of the physical environment to poverty. Give illustrations. Give others not in the text.
14. Discuss the relation of wages to standards of living.
15. What is the meaning of a minimum standard of living?
16. Discuss the experiments made to express this in terms of income.
17. What has been the effect of the increased cost of living upon the relation between incomes and standards?
18. Discuss the percentages of the income of different groups spent for the necessities of life.
19. Discuss the causes, remedies, extent and effects of unemployment.
20. Give the economic causes of poverty.
21. Give the causes resident in the social environment. Name others besides those in the text.
22. Show how one factor may be both a cause and a result of poverty.

23. What defects in government and in our educational system increase poverty?

24. Explain the relation of degeneracy to pauperism.

25. Is pauperism hereditary when it seems to run in the same family in successive generations?

26. Name in order of importance the various causes of poverty resident in the individual.

27. Discuss each.

28. What is often the cause of laziness?

## TOPICS FOR SPECIAL REPORT

1. The amount of poverty in some great city (*e.g.* London or New York).

2. A minimum standard of living for your community (make detailed estimate of expenditures at present prices).

3. The causes of the poverty of the "X" family. (A study of some poor family with which you are acquainted. Distinguish between immediate and remote causes.)

4. The alleged improvidence of the poor as a cause of their poverty.

## REFERENCES

WARNER, A. G. "American Charities." Chapter II; also III, IV and V for supplementary reading.

DEVINE, E. T. "Misery and its Causes."

ELLWOOD, C. A. "Sociology and Modern Social Problems." Chapter XIII.

WILLITS, J. H. "Report upon the Unemployed in Philadelphia."

STREIGHTOFF. "The Standard of Living."

HENDERSON, C. R. "Dependents, Defectives and Delinquents." Chapters I, II, III, IV.

SMITH, S. G. "Social Pathology."

HUNTER, R. "Poverty."

DUGDALE, R. L. "The Jukes."

CHAPIN. "The Standard of Living in New York City."

BURCH, H. R., and NEARING, S. "Elements of Economics." Chapters IV, V.

# CHAPTER XVII

## Organization of Charity

I. History of charity
 1. Early times
 2. England — the poor law
 3. America — indoor and outdoor relief
 4. Germany — Elberfeld system
 5. The modern point of view
II. The almshouse
 1. Its characteristics
 2. Reforms and remedies
III. Outdoor relief
 1. The church
 2. Medical charities
 3. Private associations
 4. Charity organization societies
 5. Principles of relief
 6. Friendly visiting in the family
 7. Social settlements
 8. Care of dependent children

**History of Charity.** — Charity in its old sense of almsgiving is a very ancient practice often mentioned by
**Early times.** Hindu, Chinese and Egyptian philosophers. In
ancient Athens, a poor tax was regularly collected
and, in Judea, the synagogue was the center of relief for
the poor. Its successor, the Christian Church, attempted
in early times to socialize wealth through the process of
communism. One of the first officers in the primitive

church was the deacon, whose chief duty was to look after the poor of the congregation. Ancient Rome was said to have had asylums for abandoned children and for wounded soldiers. The poor may have sought shelter in the public baths of Rome, as they do at present in our own parks and public buildings. Trajan is reported to have cared for five thousand poor children. The most famous relief in Rome, however, was what was known as " Cæsar's bread." The poor Roman citizen could obtain food from the public granaries free or at a very low price. It has been estimated that, at the time of Julius Cæsar, three hundred and twenty thousand persons were registered for the free distribution of grain. Although intended as a social reform by Gracchus, its vicious and pauperizing influence upon the Roman people may be seen in the laziness and immorality of the later empire. It is the classical example of unwise philanthropy, which destroys independence, by removing the necessity for work.

In Rome, the support of the poor had back of it the political motive of securing the votes of the " populares." In the Middle Ages almsgiving was regarded as a method of securing the favor of heaven. The effect upon the giver seemed more important than the result upon the recipient. The medieval ascetic spirit founded numerous monasteries which served as inns for weary pilgrims and travelers. That riches were associated with sin, and poverty with saintly character, is well illustrated by St. Francis of Assisi and by the Order of Poor Friars. A monastery was often the center of almsgiving, and indiscreet charity frequently produced a great increase in the number of beggars who thronged the doors of the beautiful cathedrals. The church, however, was the only or-

ganized force in the Middle Ages which attempted to
alleviate distress by founding hospitals, asylums and
retreats for children and unfortunates.

With the break-up of serfdom, European nations began
to pass laws against vagrancy and wandering serfs. The
England —          dissolution of the monasteries by Henry VIII
the Poor          of England increased the amount of unrelieved
Law.          distress. It was not until the age of Elizabeth
that the state began to supersede the church as the dispensing agent of charity. Laws were passed which became
the foundations of the famous English Poor Law. The
parish was to make a list of its poor who were to be helped
by the compulsory contributions of the more prosperous.
The administration of these laws tended to increase pauperism and the consequent expenditure for relief. All the
needy were to receive help and, as almost all laborers were
needy, they were entitled to the stipend. This situation
was undermining the independence and manhood of the
English workman. Again, this condition was being exploited by employers who refused to raise wages because
of the state's supplement to labor's income. It has been
estimated that the amount spent for poor relief in 1818
reached 7,870,801 pounds, or almost forty million dollars,
for a population of only eleven million people. In 1832
a royal commission was appointed to investigate the matter
of state relief. It was found that a man was often economically better off when rated as a pauper than when rated
as an independent worker. In 1834 a new Poor Law Act
was passed. It provided for a central government board
and inspectors to examine the work of the local authorities.
No state relief was to be given to the destitute if able-
bodied. They must seek the workhouse to be built by

the union of parishes. The cessation of public outdoor relief was marked by a great decrease in the amount of pauperism. The workhouse now became the only institution of public charity. Its deadening character and maladministration have been criticized by many reports and pictured in many works of fiction. Its counterpart, the American almshouse, will be discussed in a later section.

By indoor relief is meant the institutional care of the poor supported in almshouses. Outdoor relief is the caring for this same dependent group in their own homes by gifts of money, provisions or other necessaries. Indoor relief is a recognized function of the modern state, for otherwise individuals might die upon the streets. Outdoor relief, however, as a state function, is still a matter of debate. The very helpless should be placed in institutions, but the care of those in slight need had perhaps best be left to private and individual charity. We have seen the history of public outdoor relief in England and know why it was stopped. In America there has been no consistent national policy. Public outdoor relief may exist in one community and be absent in another. Most of our large cities, like New York and Philadelphia, have abandoned this policy. When it was abandoned in Brooklyn, it was surprising to note how the appeals to private charitable organizations failed to show the increase that had been expected. The influence drawn from this fact is that much of the former public outdoor relief had not been needed or had been unwisely distributed. There are arguments both for and against public outdoor relief. In its favor may first be mentioned its apparent economy. It seems unnecessary to send an individual or his family to the poorhouse when

*America — indoor and outdoor relief.*

a slight financial aid will permit them to live at home. Again, since the disability of the breadwinner may be only temporary, outdoor relief often preserves the unity of the family. This system is also more flexible and may be varied according to the needs of the situation. Much of the economy, however, of public outdoor relief has not been a reality. English experience has shown how, like a contagion, the acceptance of relief may spread throughout a community. Again, giving to the poor requires great discrimination and an experience in social work not usually found in public officials. In many of our cities political corruption has vitiated its administration. The probability and amount of public relief has often been affected by the size of the pauper vote.

A number of German communities have handled the administration of public outdoor relief in a special manner.

Germany — Elberfeld system. The best known plan is the Elberfeld system. This is based upon the unpaid personal services of citizens acting in systematic coöperation with each other and under a salaried superintendent. There is a thorough examination of each individual dependent, a careful guardianship of him during his period of dependency and a consistent effort to help him regain economic independence. Four cases are usually assigned to each citizen almoner, who therefore knows thoroughly the needs of each dependent family. He is empowered to give relief according to a graduated scale prescribed by law.

Modern organized charity is the twentieth century development of what was known in earlier times as almsgiving. It differs from its early form as much as the modern locomotive differs from the prairie schooner. The scientific spirit has brought about as great a transformation in the methods of charity as in the methods of transportation. Poverty is no longer regarded as always necessary and saintly. It is viewed as a social disease re- The modern sulting either from a faulty social and economic point of environment or from individual delinquencies. view. The aim of organized charity is no longer the mere giving of alms to relieve an immediate distress which may shortly recur. The causes of poverty are investigated in the hope that many of them may be removed. A list of these causes has already been revealed in the previous chapter. On the physical side, the productivity of the natural environment is being increased and such phenomena as droughts and famines are becoming matters of scientific prevention. Maladjustments in the economic environment are being gradually eliminated, and experts in industrial management are attacking the problem of unemployment. Unfortunately, however, low wages inadequate for efficient living still stalk, like gaunt specters, a land of fabulous riches. The social environment must also be remodeled. Unsanitary housing conditions, the congestion of immigrants and the slums of our cities must disappear from the society of to-morrow. Defects in our governmental and educational systems must also be remedied. The feeble-minded and inherently degenerate must be so segregated that they cease to propagate their kind. Individual and social ideals of health and efficiency must be raised to a higher lever in order that shiftlessness and indolence may be reduced to a minimum. All this will not be accomplished by any sudden or quick reform, but only by the long, slow process of social evolution guided in a progressive manner by human intelligence. But while these are our ideals for the future of society, we must not neglect the practical problems of distress that confront us to-day and which require our immediate attention.

**The Almshouse.** — The poorhouse is the fundamental institution in American relief. It cares for the destitute not otherwise provided for and has been the sieve through which all forms of social derelicts, except the duly convicted criminal, have passed. The almshouse often contains the insane, the epileptic, the feeble-minded, the blind, the deaf, the crippled, the sick and those destitute of friends. Here mingle old folks and children, men and women, the honest and the dishonest. The first characteristic of the almshouse is therefore the heterogeneous character of its unclassified and unsegregated inmates. This may be clearly shown, for example, from the following table taken from Warner's " American Charities ":

| MISSOURI ALMSHOUSES 1903 | 89 COUNTIES (LESS THAN 200 PAUPERS) | ST. LOUIS | TOTAL | PER CENT |
|---|---|---|---|---|
| Males . . . . . . . | 1044 | 795 | 1839 | 54 |
| Females . . . . . . | 759 | 770 | 1529 | 46 |
| White . . . . . . | 1593 | 1463 | 3056 | |
| Colored . . . . . | 210 | 82 | 292 | 8.7 |
| Age above 60 . . . . | 669 | 593 | 1262 | 37.7 |
| From 18 to 60 . . . . | 1037 | 885 | 1922 | 57.7 |
| Under 18 . . . . . . | 87 | 67 | 154 | 4.6 |
| Between 2 and 14 . . . | 72 | 20 | 92 | |
| Defective classes : . . . | | | | 71.2 |
| Insane . . . . . . | 293 | 884 | 1177 | |
| Feeble-minded . . . | 504 | 47 | 551 | |
| Epileptic . . . . . | 96 | 85 | 181 | |
| Blind . . . . . . | 92 | 22 | 114 | |
| Crippled . . . . . | 187 | 76 | 263 | |
| Paralytic . . . . . | 67 | 31 | 98 | |
| Able to do some work | | | | 15 |

A second general characteristic of the almshouse is the fact that its inmates are often admitted and dismissed practically at their own option. A general *Its char-* exodus of the able-bodied from the almshouse *acteristics.* takes place in spring, but many return with the advent of cold weather. Since little work is done, except small jobs about the building, the very group which should be taught habits of steady labor is often given an excellent training in idleness. The institutional life is deadening to that very initiative which it should seek to kindle. The administration of the building has often been inefficient, because the remuneration of the superintendent is not always sufficient to attract an able man. As official requisites, affiliations with the political party in power are usually more important than executive ability or a knowledge of social problems and of scientific methods of charity. It was formerly common to pay no stated salary to the superintendent but to allow him the proceeds from the attached farm. This abominable practice led to innumerable abuses and to the exploitation of the inmates. The assistants were also frequently incapable, and the medical service, especially needed, was often of the lowest standard. If any system of inspection was required, it was administered in a most perfunctory, if not corrupt, fashion.

The very nature of these evils cries out for reform. The almshouse should not be the dumping ground for all the destitute classes of society. It should be *Reforms and* used merely as the temporary clearing house *remedies.* for various groups of defectives, to be assigned later to special institutions. The feeble-minded should be put under the permanent custody of a special institution, the

Q

blind (especially the young) should be sent to their own schools, and the tubercular inmates should be placed in sanitariums or in special hospital wards. The building of separate institutions requires great expenditures of public funds but it is imperatively needed. Children should never be permitted to grow up with such defectives, and old folks, likewise, are deserving of better treatment. Again, the almshouse should not be so easy of access and of departure. Paupers should be regarded as socially diseased and an attempt made to reëstablish in them a normal life and purpose. In only a few states are they deprived of the right to vote, with the result that at elections they go forth to swell the majority of the political organization in power. Women frequently use the almshouse as a maternity hospital in which are born the illegitimate and feeble-minded. Careful records of admission and discharge should be kept so that each case may be studied individually. At present few accounts are filed except those dealing with financial expenditures. The almshouse, which should provide a great amount of valuable clinical material, has little information of worth for the student of social conditions. Work of sound economic or educational value should be afforded those inmates that are physically or mentally capable of such labor. The administration must also be reformed and efficient government supervision provided. Private as well as public institutions which assume the responsibility for the lives of inmates, and which appeal to the public for support, should not be exempt from government inspection. Salaries should be adequate and competent officials appointed. An efficient corps of medical and social workers should be added according to the size and needs of the institution.

The best system of inspection seems to be that of a commission of responsible persons appointed by the governor without pay, but employing a salaried secretary and a body of paid inspectors. A separate salaried board might be charged with the centralized business administration of the various state institutions, whose activities must be closely correlated.

**Outdoor Relief.** — In general it would seem that institutional or indoor relief should be undertaken by the state. Many private and religious associations, however, maintain their own homes, asylums and other charitable institutions. Many also receive large state appropriations, although in most cases there is a legal proviso that the institutions so subsidized must be of nonsectarian character. It is sometimes argued that the state should cease these private appropriations and maintain its own charitable institutions. Whether these institutions be of a public or private character, it is evident that in each state there should be some system of government inspection and supervision.

Outdoor relief, on the other hand, has been left for the most part to private charitable associations. Many of these agencies for the relief of the poor in their own homes are administered in connection with **The church.** the activities of various church organizations. There are in America three main divisions, — the St. Vincent de Paul societies of the Roman Catholic Church, the United Hebrew Charities and, finally, the various societies of the different Protestant churches. There are also other independent religious organizations for philanthropic work, some of which are most estimable. Others, however, are fraudulent in nature, for they desecrate the religious garb they assume for securing funds. Again, much of the most sincere church charity is given in a very haphazard fashion. Professional beggars are known to have deliberately taken advantage of numerous church societies which sometimes make little investigation of the ultimate effects of their donations. In the third place, different sects should coöperate, rather than discriminate, in their charitable activities. The unfortunate man who meets with an accident upon the street is driven to the nearest hospital, Jewish or Gentile, and no questions are asked regarding his creed. More of the same spirit in charity work is needed. At present, however, it would seem that distinct charity organizations based upon religious sects have certain inherent advantages. Each religious organization understands better, and meets more effectively, the needs of its own group. It is also natural for dependents to seek help first from members of their own religious sect.

The most direct aim of medical charities is the relief of the physical distress of the poor. The gain is social **Medical** as well as individual; for the community is **charities.** thereby spared the support of an otherwise dependent member of society. Missionaries have found that medical assistance is the quickest way to reach the hearts and minds of those among whom they work. Social workers in our own slums have found this fact to be equally true. Many of our large city hospitals have a social service department, whereby the social workers supplement the work of the surgeon and nurse, by following up the cases discharged from the hospital as cured. Medical charity is also a means of diffusing information regarding health, hygiene and sanitation. Organized medical charity protects the public health. A municipal hospital is primarily designed to care for contagious diseases, and similarly adequate provision should be made for tubercular patients. Maternity hospitals or wards have been established for the poor, and orthopedic hospitals correct the deformities of growing children. It is also possible for the poor to have the eyes examined free and thus to correct faulty vision. Finally, there are free dispensaries for the dressing of wounds and for the care of other physical ills, as well as free wards for undergoing surgical operations and for treatment during serious illness. Although medical charities have been taken advantage of by many individuals who are able to pay for medical aid, their benefits far outweigh any well-founded objections charged against them.

Private charitable associations are especially needed when experiments are to be tried and pioneer work attempted. Much of the charitable work, which is now done by government institutions, was first undertaken by a group of individuals who proved, by practical examples, what could be done along certain lines. All kinds of philanthropic work are carried on by private associations. There are homes for orphans, for crippled children and for the aged, founded by benevolent individuals. There are also private asylums for certain classes of defectives for whom the state has made no adequate provision. There is an infinite number of large and small associations for the relief of the poor in their own homes. Free employment bureaus, housing commissions and settlement houses in poverty-stricken quarters have been founded by private philanthropy. All honor should be accorded such public-spirited citizens and the spirit of altruism which impelled them. Such institutions represent one of the noblest characteristics of modern civilization. Private charities, however, have their own peculiar dangers. They are so easily formed that there is a temptation to multiply them. It therefore happens that some fields are over-crowded, while others are neglected. Again, the funds of a small association are often inadequate to carry on the work proposed but would be sufficient for a stronger organization doing similar work. Among these numerous good societies it is easy for fraudulent ones to flourish and to collect money for supposedly benevolent purposes. Again, money may be spent sincerely, but foolishly, according to the eccentricity of the donor. Public-spirited individuals who wish to make bequests would do well to consult some official in the local society for organized charity. In this manner a good perspective of the field would be obtained, as well as expert advice from a professionally trained social worker.

Charity organization societies — or similar associations known by slightly different names — exist in most of the

**Charity organization societies.** large cities of Great Britain and the United States. The pioneer American organization in this field is the Society for Charity Organization, established in 1877, in the city of Buffalo. Its purpose may be regarded as that of a central clearing house for all forms of outdoor relief. Its aim is not so much to furnish material aid to the destitute as to help restore them to economic independence. The causes of poverty are studied in order that conditions in the environment may be improved. Cases requiring immediate need are referred to a particular charity to care for them. Thus, the central organization acts as a directive agency rather than a means of distribution of material help. If an individual is out of work, employment is sought at one ɔf the employment agencies; if sick or diseased, admission is secured to a free ward in a hospital or in a special asylum. If a family seems in need of help, the society sends a trained worker to make a careful study of the case, which is duly recorded in a card index system. Recommendations are made to benevolent societies likely to give aid, or the aid of the former employer, of relatives and of friends, is solicited in order to help the unfortunate to regain his economic independence. The Society for Organizing Charity is sometimes criticized because so small a proportion of its funds is spent for actual relief and so large a proportion for " red tape." Again, some object to its alleged sense of superiority which seeks to direct the activities of other societies. Answers to these objections are unnecessary. In the matter of social service there can be no such thing as a caste of superiority. The need of organization and investigation is so great as to call for a central society for that particular purpose. Its case records are open to other charity societies, which seek to give aid, but which have neither the time nor ability for investigation. The so-called " red tape " prevents the success of impostors. Hence, all benevolent individuals, or private associations for the dispensing of charity, will do well to seek this central society for information as to the relative needs of their various applicants. The Society for Organizing Charity seeks to prevent overlapping and waste of energy. If all the charities of a city would report to this one central clearing house all that they are doing, they could easily learn from how many sources the applicant is receiving help. Beggars upon the streets should be referred to this society, and solicitors for funds should produce its written endorsement before receiving favorable consideration.

The first principle of relief would seem to be the securing of adequate knowledge before giving aid to the applicant. Principles Is the family in actual need or is it seeking to of relief. live as a parasite upon the community? What kind of aid and what amount is needed? The habit of indiscriminate almsgiving upon the street is a most pernicious practice. Many beggars are impostors, and others should be placed in special institutions for defectives. It is wise to remember that indiscriminate help may injure rather than aid the recipient. The " nickel " given from the impulse of generosity may find its way, not to the home, but to the saloon. In the second place, the aim of relief should be to secure as far as possible the economic independence of the needy. Thus the remote cause of poverty must be removed, not merely the immediate distress. The terms " worthy and unworthy " should be replaced by " needy and not needy." No relief should be given to those who are capable of supporting themselves. In some cases discipline of the applicant is needed, rather than any relief. Legal measures must also be taken in such cases as that of the husband who deliberately deserts his wife and children. A third principle of relief is to teach the helpless how to help themselves, rather than actually to help them in the most direct manner. A fourth principle of scientific relief is the careful supervision of the recipient of charity. This is well done by what is known as " friendly visiting," a principle to which separate consideration will be given. In conclusion, let it be stated that scientific charity does not seek to do less but more for the poor. It might seem from what has been said that organized relief tends to suppress the impulse of generosity. Nothing, however, could be farther from the

SAVING THE BOY FROM THE EVILS OF THE STREET.

truth; for scientific charity simply seeks to make relief more effective by a better direction of its usefulness. Thus there arises a science of philanthropy which emphasizes service rather than mere almsgiving.

In order to investigate the cases, and to supervise the work of organized charity, a corps of social workers is necessary. These are known as " friendly visi- **Friendly** tors." They do more than merely supply food **visiting in** and clothing. Their aim is the rehabilitation **the family.** of family life and the restoration of normal standards of health, efficiency and morality. This new profession of social service requires infinite tact, sound judgment, common sense, an attractive personality and a considerable knowledge in a particular field. A knowledge of local means of medical relief, of laws of landlord and tenant, of hygiene and of food values is essential to the success of such work. The friendly visitor must become personally acquainted with the individuals in the family and must not pose as the agent of a charity organization. Personal supervision of the dependent and his family has been the distinct characteristic of the Elberfeld system.

Friendly visiting has been an essential part of the work of settlement houses established in the slum districts of various cities. Hull House in Chicago, for **Social settle-** example, has been a center of ennobling influences **ments.** which have radiated throughout a very dark section of the city. Open house is maintained and various forms of recreation and games appeal to the young and old. The spirit is fraternal and the inhabitants of the section are not dealt with in a patronizing manner. Higher ideals of morality, of family life, of industrial efficiency and of personal health and cleanliness are continually upheld.

Advice is not superimposed, but given incidentally where-ever possible. Such a social settlement ministers to a much larger group than paupers and dependents; for many independent and self-respecting people of the poorer class are helped by such means to higher standards of living. The social settlement not only acts as an antidote to the dangers of the big city, but also offsets the baneful influence of the streets. Police magistrates and the juvenile courts have recognized the value to the delinquent child of such institutions.

No child should be permitted to remain for any length of time in the poorhouse. Unfortunately, many or-phanages are but little better; for the institu-tional atmosphere of such places is deadening to the growing child. The cottage system, con-sisting of a number of small houses each under a house mother, is immeasurably superior to the institutional plan. The securing of homes in real families is undoubtedly the best plan of treatment, although it requires great care in selection. Since it is fairly easy to secure, some method of visitation should be maintained after adop-tion. The child of the depraved home presents a more complex problem than does the orphan. Where great cruelty is practiced, or where the parents are immoral or habitually intoxicated, the courts may take the child out of the home and place it elsewhere. This is only done in extreme cases, because one important principle of relief is to keep the family intact and the child under the in-fluence of its mother. For that reason, the state of Illi-nois inaugurated the system of pensioning widows with children. Under such a system, the poverty-stricken mother is not compelled to part with her child whose sup-

*Care of dependent children.*

port might otherwise have been problematical. The opponents of this law maintain that it cannot be administered without abuses. Day nurseries have been established in some districts, where poverty compels mothers to work for long hours in factory, shop or domestic service. While this plan is a dangerous invitation to many to shift the care of their children from the home to the nursery, the only other alternatives are to confine the little ones in the close rooms of the tenement or to allow them to roam the neighboring streets and alleys.

## QUESTIONS FOR DISCUSSION

1. Tell of the effects of the free distribution of grain in Rome.
2. What was the medieval attitude toward charity? Explain the work of the church.
3. Explain the effects of the English Poor Law.
4. Give the arguments, for and against, public outdoor relief in America.
5. What has been its history in this country?
6. Why do you think it has succeeded in some German cities?
7. Describe the Elberfeld system.
8. How does the modern point of view regarding poverty and charity compare with the older?
9. What is the outlook for the future?
10. What are four characteristics of the almshouse?
11. What reforms can you suggest?
12. Discuss the strong and weak points of church charities.
13. What charitable work does your church do?
14. Do you think it is scientifically done and what improvements do you suggest?
15. What charitable associations have you ever seen at work?
16. Justify medical charities as a community function.
17. What are some dangers of numerous private charitable associations?
18. What is the purpose of the Charity Organization Society?

19. Show its relation to other charitable organizations.
20. Has your locality any such organization?
21. What are some principles of a sound relief policy?
22. Why is the work of a "friendly visitor" difficult?
23. Why is it necessary to investigate cases and why does the dependent family need supervision?
24. When is it necessary to remove children from their homes? Is this a usual policy?
25. What should be your attitude toward beggars upon the street?

## TOPICS FOR SPECIAL REPORT

1. The charitable work of the medieval monks.
2. The history of the English Poor Law.
3. Friendly visiting.
4. The work of your nearest society for organizing charity.
5. The work of a settlement house near you.
6. The inmates of an almshouse. (Information to be secured by a personal visit or from the published reports of some institution.)
7. The work of some orphanage. (In your description indicate whether it has the institutional atmosphere.)
8. How a group of students might coöperate in some form of organized social work.

## REFERENCES

DEVINE, E. T. " Principles of Relief."
WARNER, A. G. "American Charities."
HENDERSON, C. R. "Dependents, Defectives and Delinquents." Part II. Chapters I to X.
MANGOLD, G. B. "Child Problems." Book V. Chapters I to X.
ADDAMS, JANE. " Twenty Years at Hull House."
WALD, L. D. " The House on Henry Street."
HENDERSON, C. R. "Modern Methods of Charity."
RICHMOND, M. E. "Friendly Visiting."
DEVINE, E. T. "The Spirit of Social Work."
SMITH, S. G. "Social Pathology." Chapters on The Church and Charity, The State and Charity, Private Charity and Poverty.
DEVINE, E. T. "The Family and Social Work."

# CHAPTER XVIII

## The Problem of Crime

**General Considerations.** — The advance of civilization has been marked by greater security of life and property. The function of the state in whatever form it existed was always to protect the members of the group, Progress not only from outside invasion, but also from un-attained. social individuals within. The growth of association has branded as criminals those who refuse to coöperate in preserving the social order. The " King's Peace " was one of the first expressions of the growing police power of the state. Early conditions, in comparison with modern, presented a greater amount of turmoil and confusion. In ancient Rome, gangs of cutthroats and freed gladiators were hired for the work of assassination. The cities of medieval and modern Europe were notoriously unsafe. The carrying of rapiers became a social custom founded upon necessity. As late as the reign of Queen Anne, the narrow, unlighted streets of London were harassed by foot-pads and " gentlemen " who played " pranks " upon their victims. Outlaws, like the fabled Robin Hood, were so numerous in the rural districts as to make traveling un-safe. Not only were piracy and smuggling common, but the government itself resorted to the press gang in order to recruit naval enlistments. Modern society has been made much safer by the repression of such disorders, so that in the course of centuries there has been a great de-crease in the number of brutal and serious crimes. While numerous individual cases of cruel crime still exist, they are not nearly so common and flagrant in character. Modern society, however, has a new type of unsocial in-dividual in its midst, more polished and less brutal, but equally dangerous. Professor Ross well describes him in " Sin and Society." The complexity and organization of twentieth century society permit him to work at long range and with less fear of detection. Instead of running a dagger through his victim, the modern criminal may supply impure milk or adulterated food with the same deadly result. Or, rather than loot a house and carry off the goods, he may wreck financial undertakings and rob innocent stockholders. Although the old brutal crimes are therefore not so numerous, a new type of refined criminal has sprung into existence. Hence, the development of commerce and industry has made necessary the enactment of new criminal laws.

The simplest definition of crime is that of violation of the law. Crimes are wrongful acts against society, or against individuals, punishable by legal penalty. **Crime and** At one time, crime was regarded simply as an **the law.** offense against the individual affected. The aggrieved man or his family sought vengeance against the offender without the intervention of the group as a whole. Gradually, however, the idea grew up that crimes were offenses not only against individuals, but also against society. The newly established social order was regarded as being threatened by such unsocial individuals. Therefore, the political unit, whether in the form of the patriarchal family, the tribe, the feudal group or the nation, was forced to meet its own problem of social control. The group, not the individual, came to punish crime. To this day, however, torts require the initial action of the individual, rather than the state, for their redress. In order to define and punish crime it was found necessary to formulate a body of laws, written or unwritten, explaining what should constitute deviations from the normal standard of conduct. A good idea of the civilization of a people, or of an age, may be obtained from its code of laws. A comparison of the Twelve Tables of early Rome with the elaborate code of Justinian illustrates one phase of the social progress attained during the intervening period. The legal code reflects not only the degree but also the type of civilization. Each society punishes severely those crimes which threaten its particular type of social organization. In a theocracy, blasphemy and, in an absolute monarchy, *lèse majesté* are great crimes against the state. In an industrial society new crimes, like the falsification of records and the forging of checks, must be defined in the legal code.

As civilization has advanced, the normal standard of conduct has risen. Crime will always be present in society, since there will always be those who fail to meet the constantly rising standards of conduct. Like poverty, crime is somewhat relative in character. Laws, as the legal expression of the group standard of morality, must reflect the popular will. Statute books must therefore be kept abreast of the changing social conscience. It is unfortunate to have obsolete laws upon the statute books, and so-called blue laws should either be enforced or repealed. Again, new laws should be passed to express new social standards of public opinion. Otherwise, individuals may be held morally guilty by the community, but their actions may be entirely within the law. The social conscience may see little difference between unregulated child labor and slavery, or between certain dangerous trades and murder; but this subjective estimate of individual action is not sufficient, for public opinion must express itself in laws and, to secure the enforcement of these laws, the social conscience must be educated to the new standard. This process of education should precede the legal enactments which, otherwise, will remain unenforced. Prohibition, for example, will fail if it does not reflect the sentiment of the community.

The extent of crime is difficult to determine, for the number of prisoners convicted and sentenced represents but a fraction of the total number of criminals. **Extent of** Many are not even apprehended, while others **crime.** are acquitted because of a lack of convincing evidence. Our estimates, however, can be based only upon the number of sentences rendered or upon the number of persons actually in confinement in a given year. The number of foreign-born criminals is not in excess of its proportion to the general number of males of criminal age in our total population. We have seen, however, that the children of the foreign born show a decided criminal tendency. It often happens that about one-third of our prison population is negro — a proportion far in excess of the proportion of the colored to the total population. That the number of the two sexes in society at large is fairly equal is a familiar biological fact. The male population in prisons, however, is about ten times that of the female. In 1910 there were 479,763 persons committed to penal institutions. This number is not unusual and the number of annual commitments approximates the half million mark. The number of convictions is never equal to the number of crimes committed. The special prison census of 1904 reported for that year a little over two thousand convictions for homicide, while the actual number of such crimes committed was several times that figure. Indeed, the annual homicide rate in the United States, for the opening years of the twentieth century, has been between six and ten thousand. England, on the other hand, has averaged between three and four hundred such cases.

R

In the year 1900, Eugene Smith estimated that in the United States there were 250,000 persons who made **Cost of crime.** their living wholly or partially by crime. To maintain these criminals it cost the country $400,000,000 annually, while another annual expenditure of $200,000,000 was necessary for their trial and conviction. This total of $600,000,000 was about the equivalent of the annual sum spent for public education in the United States. This estimate of the cost of crime would probably be conservative for the present time.

The alleged increase of crime in recent years is difficult to determine because standards of conduct have not re-**Alleged increase.** mained constant. New laws have been added and new offenses created, which did not exist previously. Moreover, the number of commitments and the number of crimes are not identical. Again, an apparent increase of crime may mean merely that the law is being more strictly enforced. There also exists a great discrepancy between the laws of the different states. It would seem, however, to some writers that there has been an increase of crime in the United States. This assertion is based upon the fact that the prison population has increased proportionately more rapidly than the total population. The statistics of certain states collected between 1907 and 1910 indicate an increase of serious crime, while the increase of minor offenses is generally admitted. Other writers, however, take a different view of the matter. European statistics do not show any decided increase of crime within the last few years. If anything, a slight decrease has been noted in some countries of continental Europe. England, whose criminal procedure is excellent, shows a considerable decrease in the number of crimes committed.

**Causes of Crime**. — Both in number and character the causes of crime resemble those of poverty. The same set of circumstances, which may make one individual a pauper, makes another a criminal. The causes of crime lie both in the environment and in the individual.

There seems to be a generally accepted opinion that crimes against person are more common in southern countries and crimes against property are more prevalent in northern lands. Similarly, in the same country, crimes against property, such as burglary, increase in winter, while those against *Environmental: Physical environment.* persons, like murder and assault, show an increase in spring and summer. Curves of the increase and decrease of crime, which have been plotted graphically, show this variation according to climate and season. Weather influences also have a decided influence upon conduct, as all individuals in charge of large groups have noticed. Wardens in prisons and asylums note a decided difference in the conduct of the inmates upon clear crisp windy days and upon damp days with high humidity.

The economic causes of crime are similar to those of poverty. Individuals react differently to the same set of causes. Unemployment may drive one man to steal and another to beg. Inadequate wages *Economic environment.* may reduce one woman to a standard of living below the poverty line, while another of weaker will becomes a moral delinquent. The student should review the economic causes of poverty and observe how they are applicable to crime.

Conditions in large cities are conducive to crime, for here social ills and economic maladjustments are intensified. Glaring contrasts between poverty and riches are

temptations to illicit gains.   Here bad associations are easily
formed, for the criminal as well as the pauper group gravi-
*Social*          tates toward the city.   Gangs of thieves make
*environment.*   their quarters in congested districts, like those
depicted in Dickens' story of Oliver Twist, and in similar
tales of to-day.   After long monotonous hours of toil,
immoral amusement places are sought for relaxation as
an escape from crowded tenement houses.   The city
must, therefore, furnish wholesome recreation centers
which may compete with the vicious theaters and dance
halls.   Motion pictures, too, should be censored so that
wrongful ideals may no longer be upheld before their
audiences.   All these conditions are typical of the city
which represents a great density of population.   At the
other extreme are isolated and sparsely settled communities, which are also characterized by increased criminality.
Note, for example, the lawlessness of frontier life.   The
regions between these two extremes of density of population are freest of crime.

The family should be the chief agent in the socialization of the individual.   Demoralized homes, which cannot
perform this function, furnish an undue proportion of
criminals.   Illegitimate and even dependent children seem
inclined toward criminal careers.   Eighty-five to ninety
per cent of delinquent children in reform schools come
from bad homes.   On the other hand, a healthy stable
family life is antagonistic to crime.   The proportion of
unmarried to married men is also greater in the prisons
than in the general population.

We have seen that the criminality of the negro is from
three to four times as high as that of the whites.   Again,
children of the foreign born, rather than the immigrants

themselves, show a greater proportion of criminality. The South Italian, however, is often prone toward serious crimes and the Irishman toward minor offenses.

Social drinking in the form of " treating " is a bad social custom and was often, directly or indirectly, responsible for crime. The saloon, for many weak persons, was the door to the jail as well as to the almshouse. The carrying of concealed weapons is also a vicious custom, and the elaborate display of wealth is a suggestion to crime. The moral attitude of the community toward crime is extremely important. When the standard of conduct is high and public opinion severe, there is relatively a small amount of crime. A rigid enforcement of the law, rather than heavy penalties, will result in a diminution in the number of crimes committed.

Defects in law and government will increase the amount of crime. If the police are lax or criminal in the performance of duty, crime will flourish, and the crim- *Defects in* inals will be given political protection by the very *government.* officers whose duty it is to enforce the law against them. This is the story of numerous vice commission reports. The legislature and the courts should coöperate to make justice swift and certain. In England, crime has been reduced by this method. A faulty prison system, under which first offenders mingle with hardened criminals, is also productive of crime.

Defects in our educational system may indirectly be the cause of crime, just as they are of poverty. Illiteracy is high in the jails as well as in the almshouses, *Defects in* and lack of industrial training is equally appar- *education.* ent. The teaching of a trade in early years might well have afforded idle hands an opportunity for honest work.

The causes of crime residing in the individual may be hereditary or acquired. Crime is no more hereditary

Individual causes:

*Hereditary traits.*

than is pauperism, although the physical or mental degeneracy back of it may be inherent. This degeneracy may be transmissible and thereby cause certain families to show bad criminal records. We do not believe, however, that there is a fixed criminal type, but that criminality is often the evidence and result of inferior biological stock. Investigations of criminologists show that criminals in general present a greater number of physical abnormalities than the average man. Imbeciles, the insane and epileptics constitute an undue proportion of the criminal class. Judges have found it difficult to distinguish between crime and insanity, and have confessed doubt as to whether the criminal should be committed to the penitentiary or to the asylum. Mental degeneracy, like feeble-mindedness, may " run " in families, producing criminals, paupers, drunkards and imbeciles. The criminal who is inherently degenerate will have offspring likely to follow in his footsteps. But the criminal who becomes such because of his environment will be apt to have normal offspring.

However, if these children are surrounded by bad influences in early childhood, it is easy for them to become

*Acquired traits.*

criminals. The cause lies, not in heredity, but in the bad social environment from which they should have been freed. Acquired traits are the effects upon the individual of the social and economic environment. These are usually not transmissible. Just as normal conditions produce normal men, so an abnormal and unhealthy environment may produce the criminal. Intemperance, for example, is an abnormality brought about by the evils of environment. The Committee of Fifty found that alcohol was the chief cause of crime in thirty-one and eighteen-hundredths per cent of cases and a contributory cause in forty-nine and ninety-five-hundredths per cent. Bad company and evil associations also loom large in many criminal careers.

Other individual factors affecting crime are age and sex. Practically all crime falls within the active period of life, between the ages of twenty-one and forty. The *Age and sex.* average age of men in penitentiaries is often between twenty-seven and twenty-eight years. Sex is also important, for the prison population is largely made up of males. Easily nine-tenths of those sentenced to imprisonment are men.

In order to reduce the amount of crime in society the environment must be improved by the removal as far as possible of its causes. Since the reformation **Some conclusions.** of the criminal is difficult, the actual prevention of crime should be the aim of society. Three conditions are necessary. In the first place, the evils in the environment must be corrected. Furthermore, each child should be afforded proper development through the normal process of education and socialization in the midst of healthy surroundings. A third condition is also necessary. There must be enough control exercised by society over heredity to eliminate, by practical eugenic measures, the inherently degenerate in society.

**Classification of Crimes and Criminals**. — Serious crimes are known as felonies, but the less important, like vagrancy, are called misdemeanors. A great difference **Classes of** in criminal laws exists among the several states. **crimes.** The legal codes of the different states have varying degrees of punishment for the same offense. This condition frequently works injustice, as well as confusion, in the administration of criminal laws. Another distinction should be made. Vice is an act which injures the individual himself, but not necessarily society, which crime does affect. Our present social organization is so complex, however, that this distinction is of little real value. Drunkenness may become as much a crime as a vice. Sin is distinctive as an offense against God's law rather than man's. A most fundamental distinction in classifying crimes is that between crimes against persons and crimes against property. Another type of modern offense represents crimes against the social order, for civilized society seeks to supervise numerous actions — from the regulation of transportation to the issuance of marriage licenses. Crimes may be classified subjectively as well as objectively. Thus, there may be (1) crimes by accident; (2) those of passion; (3) those of premeditation.

There are numerous classifications of criminals, but the most useful is the simple division of criminals into three Classes of classes: (1) the born; (2) the habitual; and criminals. (3) the occasional. The born or instinctive criminal is the individual of bad heredity and of degenerate stock. He may be insane, feeble-minded or afflicted with other hereditary handicaps. The habitual criminal has a normal heredity but has been perverted by an evil environment. Hence his criminality is acquired. With the development of bad habits and a vicious point of view, it is almost as difficult for him, as for the born criminal, to lead an upright life. Both these types are repeaters before the bar of justice. The occasional criminal is rather the single offender. He has committed a crime in passion, or under the force of circumstances, and is most capable of future reformation.

The great Italian criminologist, Cæsar Lombroso, expounded the theory of a certain definite criminal type. To this type belonged most of the individuals **An old** who had committed serious crimes against so- **theory.** ciety. It could be recognized by physical characteristics such as skull and jaw formation. According to this theory, certain signs of mental degeneracy, such as insensibility to the sufferings of others, were supposed to be present. This class was indifferent to social approval or disapproval and the fact of guilt created no sense of shame. This degenerate criminal class was regarded as resulting from atavism or reversion to type. A primitive man had been born into modern civilized society.

## QUESTIONS FOR DISCUSSION

1. Why have our criminal laws increased in number?
2. What acts are now regarded as criminal which were not so regarded in the past?
3. Name some offenses which were formerly regarded as criminal but are no longer so regarded.
4. How do the crimes of the unsocial individual of to-day differ from those of the past?
5. Define crime.
6. Who punished crime in early society?
7. Why does crime persist with the advance of civilization?
8. Explain how law is the legal expression of the group standard of conduct. Is it fixed or variable?
9. Why is the extent of crime difficult to determine?
10. Give an estimate of the size of the prison population of the United States.
11. What racial groups are conspicuous?
12. Estimate the cost of crime in the United States.

13. Is crime increasing?

14. How are the causes of crime similar to those of poverty?

15. What influences in the physical environment affect conduct and how?

16. Why is crime prevalent in the city?

17. What practical municipal reforms can you suggest?

18. How is a healthy family life preventive of crime?

19. Name some vicious social customs.

20. Show how defects in government and political corruption increase crime.

21. Show the relation between crime and hereditary degeneracy.

22. Show the relation between crime and age, and crime and sex.

23. What should be the three aims of preventive measures?

24. Distinguish between several kinds of crime.

25. Give a simple classification of criminals.


## TOPICS FOR SPECIAL REPORT

1. The new type of criminal.   (See "Sin and Society," by Ross.)
2. Crime and city life.
3. Crime and the negro.
4. Crime and the immigrant.
5. The Italian school of criminologists represented by Lombroso.
6. The effect of climate and the seasons upon crime.


## REFERENCES

Ross, E. A.   "Sin and Society."

Ellis, H.   "The Criminal."

Hayes, E. C.   "Introduction to the Study of Sociology."   Chapter XXXII.

Ellwood, C. A.   "Sociology and the Modern Social Problems." Chapter XIV.

Henderson, C. R.   "Dependents, Defectives and Delinquents." Part IV.   Chapters I, II and V.

Smith, S. G.   "Social Pathology."   Chapters on The Nature of Crime, Economics and Crime, Psychology of Crime.

# CHAPTER XIX

## TREATMENT OF CRIME

I. Criminal procedure
  1. Historical development:
      a. Private warfare
      b. Medieval trials
      c. King's court
      d. Jury trial
      e. A body of law
  2. Modern problems:
      a. The legal machinery
      b. Defects in system
II. Punishment of crime
  1. The point of view:
      a. Vengeance
      b. Prevention
      c. Reformation
  2. Early treatment:
      a. Former cruelty
      b. Prison reform
  3. The present prison system:
      a. The county jail
      b. Mass treatment inadequate
      c. Need of special institutions
      d. Administration
      e. Prison labor
  4. Advocated reforms:
      a. Indeterminate sentence
      b. Parole
      c. Substitutes for imprisonment
      d. Abolition of capital punishment

5. Delinquent children:
   a. Juvenile courts
   b. Reform schools

**Criminal Procedure**. — In the patriarchal, tribal and feudal stages of society the aggrieved man's cause was *Historical development:* *Private warfare.* championed by his family, tribe or feudal lord. This method of settlement caused endless blood feuds like those which existed between the Arabian tribes or the clans of the Scotch highlanders. The injury was avenged with interest by the perpetration of a similar wrong upon the aggressor himself or his group. Thus, the strife and confusion continued in the well-known feudal warfare of medieval Europe. Such was also the condition in ancient Israel, where Moses instituted cities of refuge, in which homicides were temporarily safe from the avenger. The altars of ancient temples and of medieval cathedrals were protecting sanctuaries. Gradually, the power of the central government increased and took into its own hands the restoration of order and the punishment of crime. In time, the injury came to be measured in terms of money value. This was known as *wergeld* (worth money) among the Anglo-Saxons, and the code of King Alfred regulated minutely how much was to be paid for the loss of an eye, a hand or a finger.

A famous method of trial in the Middle Ages was that by ordeal. The religious faith of the period was respon- *Medieval trials.* sible for the belief that God would declare in some miraculous way the innocence or guilt of the accused person, who was required to place his hand in boiling water, or to walk over red-hot plowshares. If, after three days, the wound was regarded as healing, the accused was considered innocent. Otherwise, he was guilty, for God had refused to protect him. A more rational method was that of compurgation. The accused might bring his friends to swear that they believed his oath. If the number of compurgators was not sufficient, he must undergo the ordeal. The word of a noble was equal to that of several thanes, whose testimony in turn outweighed that of ordinary freemen. William the Conqueror introduced into England from the continent the wager of battle. Each party, like Rebecca in Scott's "Ivanhoe," chose a champion and the two warriors fought out the cause in the presence of God and man.

In the Middle Ages there were three kinds of courts — those of the nobles, those of the church and those of the king. The church tried all sins such as heresy, *The king's* and the condemned were handed over to the *court.* state for execution. Many other matters, like those pertaining to marriage and divorce, fell within her jurisdiction. Each noble lord also maintained his own court and possessed dungeons in his castle for those vassals who refused to obey his law. As feudalism declined, most cases came gradually into the king's court. The accused received a fairer trial from the royal justices upon the circuit than from the feudal courts. As the fines and penalties constituted a considerable source of income, the jurisdiction of the king's peace became gradually extended. The baronial courts came to be things of the past. Certain streets, houses, individuals, days and other such circumstances were declared to be under the king's peace, and all cases thus arising were to come before the king's courts.

There are two kinds of juries — the petty and the grand. The former tries the criminals whom the latter has previously indicted or held for court. The king's court in

England developed trial by jury as a more suitable method of administering justice than the old medieval customs

*Jury trial.* just described. The traveling royal justice, who was to sit upon the case, issued an order for a number of men to investigate the offense and render a sworn verdict. In a criminal case, they were to state whether they thought the man guilty or not and, in a civil case, they were to designate which of the two parties had the better claim. Gradually a distinction was made between those who knew the facts, and came to be regarded as witnesses, and those who were unacquainted with the facts. The latter were apt to be more impartial and were called to pass judgment upon the case. These constituted the germ of the petty jury. The grand jury, as well as the petty jury, is associated with the reign of Henry II of England. At that time there had been a great increase in the number of crimes, and the criminals had not been apprehended. Hence, Henry II provided that, when the king's justices came to a county, a number of men should be selected and required to give upon oath the number of crimes committed in that locality and the names of those suspected. The state, and not the aggrieved individual, thus came to be the prosecuting party, and the grand jury came into existence for the indictment of criminals. The sheriff of each county was required to raise the " hue and cry " against the offender and could demand the assistance of all good citizens in securing the arrest of the supposed criminal.

The justices sitting as a combined body, or the individual members upon the circuit, kept a record of the cases settled and the decisions rendered. These may be regarded as the formal legal expression of the unwritten customs and moral ideas of the community. They were generally logical, consistent, conformable to custom and came to be known as the "common law." This body of law *A body of* was centuries in formation and, to-day, lies at *law.* the bottom of English jurisprudence and its American offspring. In addition to the common law there is also statutory law. This is made up of numerous formal enactments passed, in England, by Parliament and, in our own country, by the national Congress and state legislatures.

Although the federal courts punish offenders against national laws, the great volume of criminal cases, as well as civil, come before the state courts. Each state is divided into judicial districts which *Modern problems:* correspond, more or less, with county lines. *The legal machinery.* The state judiciary is organized into courts of common pleas for civil cases, and courts of quarter sessions for the trial of criminals. Since every citizen has the right to be protected from arbitrary seizure, a warrant is generally required for his arrest, unless the offense has been committed in the presence of the constable or policeman. The sheriff is the supreme county official charged with the duty of arrest, custody or execution of the criminal. The coroner is the county official who investigates the causes of deaths in an effort to prevent and punish crime. Cases may be brought before a magistrate, in the city, or a justice of the peace, in the country. Trivial cases are within their jurisdiction and they may discharge the prisoner or assign a light penalty in the form of fine or imprisonment. If the offense is serious, the prisoner is sent to jail to await trial by the county court, or set free upon the payment of bail given in proportion to the seriousness of the offense. The accusation is tested before the grand jury and a bill of indictment is filed or the accused is released because of insufficiency of evidence against him. If not released, the prisoner is finally arraigned before the bar of justice when his case is called before the court. The charge is read and he may plead innocent or guilty. He may employ his own lawyer or, if he is unable to pay for such service, the state provides an attorney for him. The district attorney, or one of his assistants, represents the state by the prosecution of the criminal. Witnesses who testify are forced to appear in court by the serving of subpœnas. A jury of twelve men renders a verdict of guilty or not guilty, and the judge fixes the sentence. The jury decides upon the evidence in the case — true or false — and the judge upon its legal significance.

The jury system is rightly regarded as one of the greatest results of English political development. The prisoner *Defects in* who is given every opportunity for defending *the system.* himself is regarded as innocent until proved guilty. Like all social institutions, trial by jury, however, has its defects. Under this system a large number of the guilty escape, for it is agreed that it is better for nine guilty persons to escape than for one innocent man to suffer. A unanimous verdict of the twelve jurors is generally necessary for conviction and, if any one of the numerous rules of procedure is broken, a new trial may be secured. In this country the work of the courts is notoriously slow, whereas justice should be swift and certain in order to be effective. In the third place, those serving upon juries are often relatively uneducated. Intelligent individuals who should perform this civic duty often seek to escape such work in order to engage in their own more profitable occupations. Others plead conscientious objections to serving. Again, the jury is apt to be swayed by the skill and eloquence of lawyers who gain their ends by sentimental use of the pathetic prisoner or of the dramatic witness. Some writers upon jurisprudence would substitute for the jury a bench of three judges. Many regard this, however, as too radical an innovation.

Undoubtedly some changes should be made in legal procedure. For example, the state should employ social experts in criminology as well as those versed in the law. These should be trained to distinguish between the different classes of criminals and to pass upon questions of insanity and abnormality. Their special training in psychology would also enable them to evaluate testimony. In the next place, a great discrepancy exists in the administration of the law. Not only do the legal codes of the different states vary greatly in penalties inflicted for the same crime, but within a given state there is a great variation in the severity of the decisions of the different judges. This situation is difficult to avoid because the human equation is ever present.

The last objection to our criminal system, however, is most fundamental. We are still seeking to make the punishment fit the crime and not the criminal. Retribution is usually the aim of punishment and its character and amount are fixed according to the gravity of the crime. However, if reformation is the desired end, the punishment should be made to fit the needs of the criminal, rather than the nature of the crime. Such a policy would mean that different offenders would receive different sentences for the same offense. The single offender or occasional criminal might be treated with leniency because he is not likely to repeat his wrongdoing. The habitual criminal, however,

s

might be sentenced for the same offense to the permanent custody of the penitentiary, and the instinctive criminal assigned to one of the institutions for defectives. It must be said, however, that judges do make distinctions between first offenders and hardened criminals. They are also sentencing a greater proportion of prisoners to specialized institutions where more individual treatment may be secured.

**Punishment of Crime.** — The first point of view in regard to punishment for crime was that of revenge. This attitude was most conspicuous in the early days of private warfare, when the aggrieved individual or his group vented his wrath upon the offender, whose entire family was often made to suffer. If the offender himself could not be secured, substitutes taken as hostages might suffer the fate intended for the original wrongdoer. " An eye for an eye and a tooth for a tooth," was the spirit of that age.

*Point of view: Vengeance.*

Somewhat of the same spirit continued long after crime came to be looked upon as a social rather than an individual offense which the state itself undertook to punish. In order to deter others from a similar course, an attempt was made at intimidation through torture and death by the most cruel means. Executions were public and the heads of criminals and political victims were placed upon long poles and exhibited from the walls and towers of the town. This was a common sight upon London Tower.

*Prevention.*

Curiously enough, the severity of the penalty has been found to have a less direct relation to the repetition of the crime than was at first supposed. Torture and barbaric punishments have lowered the public morality, and driven toward crime as many as have been

*Reformation.*

deterred from it by fear of cruel penalties. The modern point of view toward the whole criminal problem is that of reformation or improvement, both in the criminal himself and in his environment. Prevention of crime through the improvement of the social environment is most fundamental. Regarding the individual criminal, the reformatory rather than the punitive attitude should be taken. Like the pauper, he should be viewed as one who is socially diseased. In rendering sentence society, through its instrument the judge, should prescribe for him in the rôle of social physician.

Formerly, many crimes were punishable by death administered in various ways according to social sanction. Burning was common for slaves and heretics but, with the advance of civilization, beheading became popular. In England, the block and, in France, the guillotine took the place of the stake. Hanging has been a common fate for modern criminals and only recently has it given way to the more humane method of electrocution. Until recent times torture was frequently practiced. The victim might be drawn and quartered, or broken upon the wheel, and in ancient times crucifixion was common. The death penalty was not only cruel but frequent. In the first quarter of the sixteenth century the public executioner at Nuremberg put to death eleven hundred and fifty-nine persons, and seventy thousand executions took place during the reign of Henry VIII of England. As late as the last century, the death penalty was inflicted upon children and those guilty of minor offenses such as stealing. Branding and flogging were also common. Unfortunates sentenced to sit in the pillory were pelted by jeering crowds, while the public

*Early treatment:*

*Former cruelty.*

hangings at Tyburn prison in London were regarded as holiday amusements. In revolutionary France the women, while knitting, enjoyed the ghastly guillotine.

The prisons of ancient times defy description. Prisoners languished in filthy underground dungeons until *Prison re-* death put an end to their misery. Often they *form.* were political offenders against whom no just legal charge could be brought. Such was the situation in the famous Bastille. To prevent this arbitrary imprisonment, the English parliament had passed a " Habeas Corpus Act." Debtors, however, continued to suffer imprisonment until very recent times. Prison conditions were unspeakable. The sick and diseased spread their contagions, while often the two sexes mingled promiscuously. In some jails so little food was provided that many prisoners were forced to beg from their more fortunate brethren. The jailors were generally brutal characters who exacted fees on the slightest pretext. The warden of the Marshalsea, pictured in Dickens' story, had at one time an income of £3000 a year derived from such sources. Modern prison reform may be said to date from the time of the Italian, Beccaria, and the Englishman, John Howard. Beccaria was a student who published a book against torture and advocated a reform of the criminal law. John Howard (1726–1790) was one of the greatest reformers of all times. As sheriff of Bedford, he was placed in charge of the prison where a century before John Bunyan had written " Pilgrim's Progress." By personal experience he became acquainted with the jail conditions which he pictured before the House of Commons. A great traveler, he visited the prisons of many leading European countries and studied their wretched conditions. He called attention to the most glaring evils and inaugurated a movement for their reform.

The greatest evil in our present prison system is the county jail. This is regarded by experts as a most efficient school for crime. Here prisoners are committed thirty or ninety days for minor offenses. In the jail are confined those guilty of misdemeanors, while the more serious felons are sent to the penitentiary. Old and young mingle freely, and the vicious hardened criminal narrates his deeds to the young offender, who thus acquires criminal knowledge and bad habits. The tramp, the outcast, the drunkard and the disorderly are kept here along with those who are merely awaiting trial. In most counties there is not sufficient need or enough funds to warrant the building of larger and better jails. When such is the case, however, several counties should unite in the building of a district jail which can provide proper separation of prisoners, adequate discipline, regular industry and effective reformatory measures.

*The present prison system: The county jail.*

Difference in types of criminals makes the need of individualized treatment imperative. In other words, distinctive institutions for different criminal classes are needed. The instinctive criminal, often feeble-minded or otherwise defective, cannot be reformed and is dangerous at large in society. This small group should be kept in permanent custody. The habitual criminal is difficult of reformation and is apt to commit further crime. He should be placed in a state penitentiary, under an indeterminate sentence, and should be kept there until there is adequate proof that he is no longer a menace to society. The single offender should be separated from the

*Mass treatment.*

hardened criminal. In some cases he may well be dealt with outside the prison walls by a system of probation. Young offenders need very careful treatment because they present the possibility of reform. Reform schools are therefore needed for juvenile offenders.

In order to avoid mass treatment and to individualize the prison systems for the various groups of offenders, Pro-

*Need of special institutions.*

fessor Ellwood suggests that each state should have at least the following separate types of institutions: (1) county and city jails, which should be used only for the temporary detention of prisoners awaiting trial. One evil of our present system, as we have seen, has been the use of the county jail or the city " lock-up " as the place of imprisonment for all the different groups of prisoners serving petty sentences. (2) Reform schools for all children under sixteen years of age, or at least under the compulsory school age. (3) Reformatories for first offenders, particularly for the young. This group would thus be separated from habitual criminals, and in the treatment of this class industrial training should be emphasized. (4) State penitentiaries for all habitual criminals. (5) Special reformatories for vagrants, inebriates and like characters. (6) Hospital prisons for the criminally insane. Other defectives, wherever found, should receive specialized treatment.

The administration of institutions dealing with charities and corrections is generally under a board of managers

*Administration.*

or a commission. The responsible head of the prison, however, is the warden or superintendent. In order to secure efficient administration this officer should be empowered to appoint subordinates, but under a civil service system. There should be a competent medical staff in addition to the force of clerks, guards and house-keepers. Industrial training is important because, if the prisoner is to become a useful member of society, he must have some means of livelihood when discharged from prison. Trade schools should be established for the young, while the older men are given employment in the shops or in work around the institution. In the past, prisoners have been forced to perform unprofitable occupations or those of little practical value in after life. In some penitentiaries, classes are conducted where illiterate convicts are taught to read and write.

Formerly, prison discipline has been very severe and the lock step method in vogue. Warden McKenty, of the Eastern Penitentiary in Pennsylvania, has found that a more liberal spirit is not only advantageous to the man himself in the process of reformation, but is also a factor for good throughout the entire institution. The same spirit characterized the work of Superintendent Osborne at Sing Sing. Instead of the brutal punishments, the deprivation of special privileges may be used with greater power for effective discipline. Under this system prisoners are graded and each grade has greater privileges than the one below. Marks and demerits may be given, so that the prisoner with a good record may be able to advance to the highest grade. There may also be the possibility of shortening the sentence by good behavior. In some hardened cases it is found necessary to resort to a system of solitary confinement, combined with restricted diet, or even to corporal punishment. In earlier days, a controversy existed between the advocates of what was known as the solitary or separate system of confinement and its opponents. They have been known as the Pennsylvania and Auburn systems respectively. The former method guards against corruption due to evil associations, but the lack of human contact may result in insanity or some lesser form of mental abnormality.

It may be said of the administration of prisons, as well as of almshouses, that more complete records should be kept. There should be some central clearing house for the records of prisoners, many of whom have been found to be repeaters under assumed names. There is a system of measuring each individual criminal known as the Bertillon system. The lengths of the bones are recorded, for these do not grow after physical maturity is reached. A front and side photograph of the prisoner is also taken for the " rogues' gallery." The print of the thumb is a further mark of identification, for no two of these are alike.

Prisoners were employed in earlier days at most severe labor. In the last century convicts, like Jean Valjean in *Prison labor.* Victor Hugo's story, were sent to the galleys. Convict labor upon the roads is still common and may be beneficial, if properly regulated and supervised. It was formerly the custom to lease a gang of convicts to some contractor who was responsible for their care. They were often poorly treated, however; for profit, not reformation, was the aim of the contractor. The evil of this system became so apparent that the state was forced to keep control of its prisoners when they were turned over to an outside employer. Prisoners should be made to work because idleness is physically, mentally and morally pernicious. The work, however, should have some kind of educational value, and enable the convict to earn an honest living. In the past, prisoners have been taught a trade only to find,

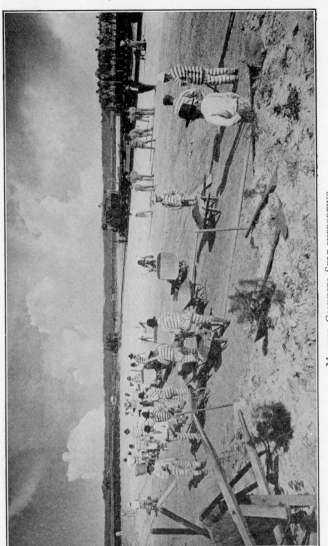

MAKING CONVICTS SELF-SUPPORTING.

when discharged, that it possessed little practical economic value. Organized labor has opposed convict labor as injurious to the wages of the free workman. Some states either prohibit or place a limit upon the prison output. Under the law of 1897, in Pennsylvania, not more than thirty-five per cent of the inmates of a penal institution may be employed in the production of goods for sale, nor may any power machinery be used. The "state use" system attempts to overcome this objection of the labor unions by producing articles needed in various state institutions. Farms are also being purchased by the state, because outdoor work is physically most beneficial to the prisoner. Convicts are also at work upon roads and other public improvements.

It is impossible to know in advance just how long it will be necessary to keep an individual a prisoner before he is sufficiently disciplined to be set at large. Hence many advocate the indeterminate sentence which does not state exactly the length of imprisonment. The convict must furnish evidence by his conduct, self-control, obedience and habits of steady work, that he is capable of making an honest living. Students of law fear that this system would be a temptation to prison officials to keep certain prisoners longer in jail than would be just to them. On the other hand, an individual convicted of some serious crime might be released too soon. The occasional criminal would profit, and the habitual criminal suffer, by its adoption. It is true that the indeterminate sentence places an enormous responsibility in the hands of the wardens of the penitentiaries. It also necessitates an entire change in our point of view toward the criminal. Punishment must no longer be unalterably fixed according

*Advocated reforms:*
*Indeterminate sentence.*

to the nature of the crime, but must be adjusted to the nature of the man who commits the crime.

The indeterminate sentence presents the objection that it is impossible for prison officials to predict how a man will *Parole.* use his newly obtained freedom. His conduct within prison walls may be sufficiently excellent to win the approval of the officials, but when restraint is removed he may again become morally deficient. Hence, some writers have argued that the prisoner should not be permanently discharged, but only conditionally freed under the system of parole. He is not to be released until employment has been found for him, and he must break loose from his former evil associations. He must return to the penitentiary occasionally with a report from his employer and, perhaps, from another reputable citizen. At the end of his term of sentence, he is relieved of this supervision, which has been a good preparation for absolute freedom. If, on the other hand, he violates his parole or again falls into evil ways, he is returned to jail. The parole system has many good features but, like other prison reforms, it is difficult of administration. Clever criminals have been known to forge reports and meanwhile resort to their old practices. The administrator should always hesitate about furnishing parole to the habitual criminal.

Instead of being sentenced to the county jail for a misdemeanor, the offender, unless a dangerous character, might *Substitutes for imprisonment.* be put upon probation by the judge. When work has been secured, he should be regularly visited by the probation officer. For the first offender, the fear of imprisonment may be a great deterrent. But if, on the other hand, he were imprisoned, he might lose all hope of an honest future. In certain cases fines may be substituted for imprisonment, but some method should be devised whereby poor offenders may be able to discharge their indebtedness in installments and thus avoid jail. Fines, however, have little reformative value to the criminal and frequently work great hardship to his poverty-stricken family. Reparation to the injured party should be required as the condition necessary to suspend a sentence of hard labor. This is not only just to the injured party, but also of disciplinary value to the offender. Transportation of criminals has sometimes been used as a substitute for imprisonment, but the results have not always been beneficial. Australia was originally used as a penal colony, but the practice was finally stopped after numerous appeals from the colonists. For vagrants, feeble-minded and certain other classes of delinquents, agricultural colonies under strict supervision have been advocated. Such colonies, however, must be kept isolated.

The abolition of capital punishment has been urged by some writers, who question the right of society to take the life of an individual, while admitting its right *Abolition* to put the offender in permanent custody in *of capital* order to prevent a recurrence of similar out- *punishment.* rages. Others regard the death penalty for murder as just, and plead the old argument of retribution expressed in the rule of " an eye for an eye and a tooth for a tooth." Others fear that the abolition of capital punishment would lead to a great increase in the number of serious crimes committed. We have seen, however, that the fear of cruel punishment does not always work as a deterrent to crime. At present, the death penalty prevents many juries from condemning criminals whose guilt is practically assured. The abolition of capital punishment would thus result in a greater number of convictions for the serious crimes.

Juvenile courts were first established in our large cities. Certain states have since authorized all judges, in districts

*Delinquent children: Juvenile courts.*

where there is no special juvenile court, to suspend ordinary rules of procedure in dealing with criminals under eighteen years of age. The object aimed at in such cases is to prescribe reformatory treatment for those young persons who seem to be starting upon a criminal career. In conjunction with the court there is a probation officer to investigate the case and to supervise the young delinquent. He is not sentenced to imprisonment, but is allowed to return home upon probation. The court officer watches over his conduct and environment. School attendance or, if beyond school age, the character of employment is especially important in these cases. Home conditions should be good and association with evil companions avoided. No publicity is given these juvenile offenders who, under such circumstances, might be tempted to regard themselves as of some importance.

Special institutions are needed for youths who have committed crimes serious enough to send an adult to the peni-

*Reform schools.*

tentiary. A rural environment and the occupation of agriculture are often found to be beneficial, while trade instruction is necessary for those who return to city life. The cottage system of administration in such cases is more effective than mass treatment in dormitories. Individualization and personal contact are essential in the education and reformation of youthful offenders. The aim of all such treatment is the quickening of the moral sense, and the development of self-reliance in the form of ability to acquire economic independence.

## QUESTIONS FOR DISCUSSION

1. How was crime originally punished?
2. Describe the various kinds of trial used in the Middle Ages.
3. Trace the origin of trial by jury in England.
4. Follow the trial of a criminal from his arrest to his conviction. Show the duties of the various judicial bodies and officers.
5. Show the strength and weakness of our present criminal procedure.
6. What reforms are advocated?
7. How was the point of view toward the criminal changed? Discuss the three stages.
8. Discuss early prison reform and reformers.
9. Discuss the evils of the present county jail.
10. Show the dangers of mass treatment.
11. What different types of institutions are needed in any adequate prison system?
12. What improvements have been made in penal administration?
13. Discuss the opposition to convict labor.
14. What should be the the aim of convict labor?
15. Show the evils of the contract system.
16. Give the arguments in favor of and against the indeterminate sentence.
17. Explain the parole system.
18. What substitutes for imprisonment have been tried?
19. Give the arguments for and against capital punishment.
20. What is your opinion?
21. How do the juvenile courts differ from the others?
22. What are the functions of a probation officer?

## TOPICS FOR SPECIAL REPORT

1. Trial by ordeal and compurgation.
2. The judicial system of Henry II.
3. The criminal code of England a century ago.
4. The life of John Howard.
5. Early prisons and their occupants.
6. The model penitentiary.

7. Trade unions and convict labor.
8. The reform school and the boy criminal.
9. The penal institutions of your own state.

## REFERENCES

HAYES, E. C. "Introduction to a Study of Sociology." Chapter XXXIII.

HENDERSON, C. R. "Dependents, Defectives, and Delinquents." Part IV, Chapters III, IV, VI.

MANGOLD, G. B. "Child Problems." Book IV.

WINES, F. H. "Reformation and Punishment."

SMITH, S. G. "Social Pathology." Chapter on Treatment of Crime.

Reports of the National Conference of Charities and Corrections.

State Prison Association Reports.

ELLIS, H. "The Criminal."

HENDERSON, C. R. "Preventive Agencies and Methods."

TAYLOR, W. L. "The Man Behind the Bars."

# CHAPTER XX

## Defectives in Society

**Physical Defectives.** — The census of 1900, as originally reported, placed the number of blind in the United States at a hundred and one thousand, but a revision by experts led the Census Bureau to reduce this number to sixty-five **The blind:** thousand. The census of 1910 showed a further *Extent.* reduction by reporting 57,272 blind people in our population. The difficulty in estimating the number of blind lies in classifying the partially blind who constitute about half the total number. The proportion of males among the blind is higher than that of females, because many men lose their vision in explosions and other industrial accidents. Almost half the blind are reported as being sixty years of age or over. It is therefore evident that blindness is associated with advancing age and with the decline of physical vigor. For the good of future generations it is imperatively necessary that eyesight be properly safeguarded. Greater precautions must be taken in the school, in the home, in the factory and in other places of employment. The correction of errors of vision by the use of glasses may be preventive of future blindness and is becoming viewed as a matter of social as well as individual concern.

Blindness from infancy is not uncommon. A large proportion of this physical defect is due to a disease known *Causes of* as ophthalmia, an infant blindness, which has *blindness.* been estimated to cause about one-tenth of all cases of blindness. It often occurs in cases where the parent is diseased, but it may be prevented in almost every case by washing the eyes of the newly born babe in a very weak solution of silver nitrate. This preventive measure is rarely practiced by the ignorant midwives who officiate at the births of many infants in our poorer and immigrant homes. Hence the plea for the presence of a physician at each birth, and the use of the maternity hospital for those too poor to pay for proper medical attendance. While conditions of modern civilization are especially severe on the eyes, the advance of medical science may counteract the tendency toward defective vision. It is by reason of this fact that the proportion of blind of school age is not increasing, but actually decreasing, in comparison with the general increase of blindness in the total population.

According to the census of 1910 there are forty-four schools for the blind in the United States. At present there are about five thousand students. Schools *Treatment* for the blind were first established through pri- *of blind.* vate funds in Boston, New York and Philadelphia; but various states are now making special provision at public expense for the education of this group of unfortunates. The course includes the usual elementary branches and special instruction in reading and writing and industrial training. The first system of printing devised for the blind was by means of raised letters. The system of Louis Braille, devised first in 1829, does not use the actual letters but employs dots, a plan which possesses many advantages over the earlier system. In a number of public schools in our larger cities special classes for the blind are maintained. This arrangement does not necessitate their leaving home permanently to live in a distant institution. It is necessary that parents educate their blind children, for the Census reported that nearly one-half of the blind were not in attendance at any school. It is surprising to learn how much can be done by scientific educational training to make blind children, who are still in the formative period, independent and self-reliant. Other faculties can be trained to do a large part of the work

T

ordinarily done by the eyes. When blindness occurs, the sense of touch becomes highly developed.

The treatment of the blind is rendered difficult by the fact that a large proportion of them suffer from other defects as well. A study at the Pennsylvania Institution for the Blind revealed, for example, that forty-five per cent of the girls and thirty-six per cent of the boys had indications of curvature of the spine. In weight, height and lung capacity they were also below the normal. Physical exercise, especially of a corrective nature, is imperatively needed. Industrial education must also be emphasized. Manual training is taught the blind, as well as handicrafts, like chair-caning, broom-making and carpet-weaving. Employment is necessary to keep the blind from dwelling upon their misfortune and from becoming morbid and melancholy. A second and equally important reason for occupation is the necessity for securing economic independence. The blind beggar upon the street is not only a pathetic figure, but often a cause of misdirected charity, injurious to himself as well as to the community.

The number of blind engaged in gainful occupations is increasing and the state should deliberately foster the movement. Several states have established special workshops for the blind, where they can find certain types of work adapted to their abilities. Special employment agencies also are on the lookout for positions which can be filled by the blind. The adult who becomes blind in mature years, through accident or loss of physical vigor, is the most unfortunate of this entire group, for a complete readjustment is necessary in his case. New York City has adopted a system of giving pensions to the adult blind, as a subsidy to those who are trying to become self-supporting.

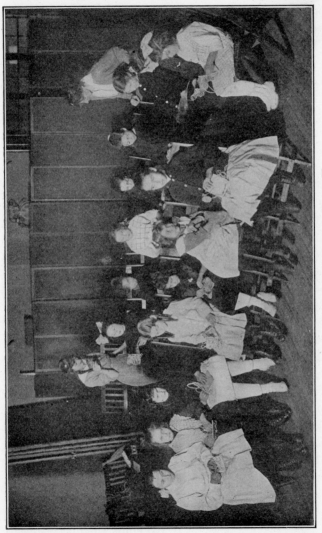

TEACHING THE BLIND TO SEE WITH THEIR HANDS.

In addition to the blind, the deaf and the dumb constitute two other classes of physical defectives. Some unfortunates, like the celebrated Miss Helen Keller, **The deaf:**
possess all three defects. The inability to speak, *Extent.*
however, has been found in a number of cases not to be
due to any defect in the brain or speech organs. Deaf
mutes are often unable to speak, or are forced to speak
imperfectly, because of their inability to hear. Many
have never learned to talk merely because of a lack of
opportunity to hear themselves and others speak. About
five per cent of the deaf are also feeble-minded and should
be placed in institutions for the latter rather than for the
former. A national census in 1906 recorded the number
of deaf as 86,515. There are, therefore, apparently more
deaf than blind in the United States. There are so many
degrees of deafness that it is even harder to estimate exactly
the number of deaf than to approximate the number of
the blind. In round numbers, it is somewhere near one
hundred thousand and does not seem to be decreasing in
proportion to the total population as does the number of
blind. Of the total number, about one-fourth are reported
as being totally devoid of the power of speech. What
proportion of these are really dumb or have simply never
learned to speak because of their deafness cannot be ascertained.

There are numerous causes of deafness, but the most
common are, perhaps, accident and disease. *Causes of*
Adults are often attacked by catarrhal colds and *deafness.*
diseases of the ear. In the young, scarlet fever, meningitis
and adenoids stand out conspicuously as causes of deafness. A third cause may be found in geographical environment. The mountainous country of Switzerland has a

high deaf rate, while the low country of the Netherlands has a lower one. This may, however, be due to other than geographical causes. Blindness is also higher in bright desert lands where the rays of the sun are intense. The multitude of blind beggars in the Orient may, however, also be due to the lack of medical knowledge and of scientific treatment. A fourth cause of deafness is heredity, although the exact part played by this factor is difficult to ascertain. The marriage of deaf people, with whom deafness is inherent and not merely acquired, will often result in deaf children. About one-fifth of all the deaf are born deaf and a large proportion of these come from totally or partially deaf parents. A fifth cause may lie in consanguineous marriage, that is, in marriage between near relatives. Thus the Jews, who permit the marriage of cousins, have an unusually high rate of deafness. It has been stated that four per cent of the deaf are the offspring of consanguineous marriages. Near relatives are apt to possess a somewhat similar heredity. If defective hearing should exist in both parents, this physical handicap will be intensified in the child who draws his heredity from both. There is little, however, to prove that consanguineous marriage is in itself a cause of deafness, provided the defect does not exist in parental heredity.

The education of the deaf is highly important because, as we have seen, many present the possibility of being *Treatment of* taught to speak. When the speech organs or *the deaf.* brain centers are defective, the sign language may readily be utilized as a method of communication. For those who are merely deaf and have the ability to speak, the reading of the lips of the speaker will enable the conversation to be followed. The ability to understand what is being said by watching the lips of the speaker is now being taught, and the facility of the deaf in this respect is sometimes marvelous. It is naturally easier for the deaf to pursue higher education than for the blind, and for this reason Columbia Institute at Washington offers them collegiate work. There is a special agency for collecting and diffusing knowledge concerning the deaf in America. It is known as the Volta Bureau and was endowed by Dr. Alexander Graham Bell with the money awarded him by the French Government for the invention of the telephone. Certain large cities have day classes for the deaf in addition to the state institutions. Like similar classes for the blind, they possess the advantage of allowing the children to live in their homes and to mingle with other normal children. Industrial training is important for their economic independence. The number of occupations open to the deaf is far in excess of those open to the blind and, as a result, most of the former become entirely or partially self-supporting.

Certain physical deformities exist from birth due to hereditary causes. A large number, perhaps, are caused by accidents. In the case of industrial accidents, the crippled should be beneficiaries of some type *The crippled.* of social insurance. Often they can become self-supporting. As with the two other groups of physical defectives, special preference should be shown them in filling positions within their capabilities. Railroads, for example, often give such positions as flagman to men crippled in their service. The aim should be to prevent the crippled from becoming beggars upon the streets. Frequently, they evade the law by becoming venders of small articles, which the " purchaser" seldom takes. Crippled peddlers should not be allowed to trade upon their misfortunes. This is as demoralizing to themselves as to the community. It may also lead to the feigning of injuries to excite the pity and generosity of the passer-by. Personal interest, not merely a financial contribution, will accomplish the best social results. The local charity agent will strive to find honorable positions for such unfortunates and will look after them until they become self-supporting. In cases of very serious injury, when they have no income or relatives capable of supporting them, the crippled should become inmates of a special home for incurables.

**Mental Defectives**. — It has been estimated that there are about a half million mental defectives in the United The insane: States. Of these, about two hundred thousand *Extent.* fall within the various groups included under the general term insane. This is a conservative estimate, for the census of 1910 reported 187,791 persons in institutions for the insane. In addition to this number, there are many insane in almshouses, jails and in their own private homes. The annual cost of the care of the insane has been estimated to equal the annual sum expended on the construction of the Panama Canal. It seems to be increasing both in Europe and America. This increase in the amount and cost of insanity must, however, be somewhat discounted because many cases of insanity, formerly concealed, are now being disclosed and cared for in public institutions. Again, since the lives of the insane are being preserved by modern medical science, there is a natural increase in the total number of insane patients. The cases show a slight excess of males over females and a decided excess of adults over the young.

Among the various interrelated causes of insanity, hereditary predisposition may first be mentioned. Although
insanity may seem to run in families, its rela- *Causes of*
tion to heredity is not so clearly established as is *insanity.*
that of feeble-mindedness. It would seem that insanity
is often more an acquired characteristic than an inherent
one. A mental weakness or instability may be inherent
in certain family stocks and, under pressure of circumstances, an individual of such ancestry is more apt to
become insane than one who has inherited a sounder
and stronger mental constitution. We have said that
tuberculosis was not hereditary but that weak lungs were.
Similarly, it is the neurotic taint or the predisposition toward mental disorder that may result in insanity, epilepsy
or some other mental disease. A second cause of insanity
is immorality, which produces terrible diseases leading to
insanity. Children of parents suffering from such diseases
are more likely to be mental defectives than those of healthy
parentage. Again, immorality and its resultant diseases
may produce mental disorders in the individual himself.
Softening of the brain and insanity often follow in later
life as a result of physical excesses. Alcoholism is another
important cause of insanity, which may appear either in
the individual guilty of such excess or in his offspring.
Again, fracture of the skull, bone pressure, blood clots
and lesions of the brain may result in insanity. Finally,
bad mental habits may be the cause of an unbalanced
mind. Worry, shock, fright, overwork, severe mental
strain and anxiety are frequent causes of insanity, particularly when the mind is not naturally strong.

In ancient times the insane were regarded as possessed
by devils. Their incoherent statements were sometimes

considered prophetic utterances, and their wild actions ascribed to supernatural influences. In recent times, and *Treatment of* upon American soil, mental defectives have occa-*the insane.* sionally been burned or hung as witches. Lunatics have often been put in prison and in chains for safekeeping. Modern science, however, insists upon medical treatment for the insane, in addition to detention. If such cases are treated as soon as signs of mental disorder manifest themselves, it is sometimes possible to effect a cure. Insanity may take such diverse forms as melancholia, paranoia or hysteria. The monomaniac is the individual whose mind is unbalanced in one direction, while the maniac is one whose mind does not function properly upon any subject. Many asylums group their patients according to ease of administration. The noisy patients, the filthy and the orderly are the usual distinctions. The insane of wealthy families may secure proper treatment in numerous private asylums, but insane paupers generally receive inadequate care. Many are kept in the almshouse in special cells and little attempt is made at curative treatment. Some insane are still confined in jails and prisons. A good working classification of insane patients is that of acute and chronic cases. For the chronic cases kindly custodial care is needed, but for the acute cases medical treatment may result in considerable improvement. Persons afflicted with a mental malady will often recover, if at all, within the first year. Hence the need of haste and the necessity for individual and personal attention. There is little definite knowledge of permanent cures for these obscure mental maladies, but much has been accomplished by the use of massage, baths of various kinds, electricity, varied diets, and general mental and physical rehabilitation.

Epileptics must be treated as a special class of mental defectives. Epilepsy itself is a little understood malady, the causes of which are very obscure. The ordinary manifestations of the disease are convulsions, of greater or less severity, at varying intervals. The lives of many otherwise intelligent and useful people are overshadowed by a dread of these terrible attacks. Many feeble-minded, however, are also epileptic, and epilepsy is a common trait of criminals. About half the children of epileptic parents are epileptic, and nearly all the other half show serious defects of different kinds. It is, therefore, the duty of society to discourage the propagation of such people. Special provisions should be made for their custody; for the public care of epileptics in America is most deficient. They are either left at large or are placed in almshouses and insane asylums, in neither of which institutions are they properly cared for. Special colonies should be founded for epileptics, who need a quiet outdoor life, a careful diet, and mental and physical occupation in agreeable surroundings.

*Epileptics.*

Feeble-mindedness must be distinguished from insanity. The insane suffer from a cessation of the normal working of the mind; the feeble-minded from an undeveloped mentality. The brain of the insane represents a broken or impaired mental machinery, while that of the feeble-minded has been imperfect from childhood. An adult whose intelligence has been normal may become insane in later life, but the feeble-minded are generally such from birth. They have inherited a low-grade mentality. Again, an insane person may have all his faculties, but they have ceased to work in unison. On the other hand, the feeble-minded individual has been born

**The feeble-minded:**
*Definition and extent.*

with some faculties lacking. The number of the feeble-minded is alarmingly great. Conservative estimates made in Great Britain and in the United States fix a proportion of one feeble-minded to every three hundred of the population. The grades of mentality shade so gradually from the normal to the subnormal, that it is difficult to estimate even approximately the number of feeble-minded. It is certain, however, that there are more feeble-minded than insane persons. Dr. Goddard places the number in the United States at three or four hundred thousand.

An attempt has been made to fix the standard of intelligence for each year of mental development in the life of *The three* the average child by the system of Binet tests. *classes.* This provides a long series of questions for each year of childhood. Their character is practical and the subjects are chosen from the child's everyday experiences. They become more difficult and require more thought for each advancing year. On the basis of satisfactory answers to the majority of the questions in each series, a child's mentality is classified as, for example, that of a normal eight year old or that of a ten year old. Since psychological or mental experiments are never so exact as those of physical science, the results of the Binet tests of mentality cannot be regarded as absolute. By such a general scheme, however, the feeble-minded are classified according to their mental age irrespective of their actual age. Of these, there are three groups: idiots, imbeciles and " morons." A mentality equal to that of a normal child of two years belongs to the idiot class. These cannot care for themselves, nor learn to speak, and many are physically deformed and misshapen. Since they are generally short-lived and cannot reproduce, this class is not self-perpetuating. The group whose mentality may advance further, but is limited to that of a normal eight year old child, constitutes the imbecile class. Members of this group may live to maturity, but their mentality, actions and conduct will be those of a young child. The "moron" represents the mental ability of normal children between eight and twelve years of age. This is the most dangerous group because it so nearly approximates the normal. The "morons" mingle with the rest of the world unnoticed by the casual observer. The dangers arising from these child-adults in society will be discussed later.

Although vice and alcoholism sometimes produce feeble-mindedness, the condition itself is generally due to heredi-tary causes. While it is true that this taint may *Its hereditary* pass over certain individuals and even genera- *character.* tions, feeble-mindedness nevertheless runs in families. A law of heredity, known from its discoverer as Mendel's law, throws light upon the proportion of feeble-minded offspring born of the union of a normal person with one who is feeble-minded. The mating of two feeble-minded persons seems certain to produce feeble-minded offspring. It would thus appear that feeble-mindedness is not usually an acquired trait, but is generally inherent in the germ cell. The hereditary character of feeble-mindedness may be clearly shown by a study of various families like the Kallikaks, the Pineys, the Ishmaelites and the Smoky Pil-grims. Here it is seen to persist in particular families, and to be widespread in certain isolated localities where these defectives have propagated their kind. From such studies it is evident that considerably over half the number of cases of feeble-mindedness are hereditary. It must be said, however, that some feeble-mindedness, like the "Mongolian" type, has appeared in families whose heredity fails to furnish any feeble-minded ancestry.

A very small proportion of the feeble-minded are confined in institutions. The vast majority of these physical adults, with childish minds, are at large in society and a constant menace to its welfare. They react easily to suggestion, for inhibition or restraint is a characteristic of the adult mind. The feeble-minded naturally find it difficult to compete with those of normal intelligence, and a larger number are the recipients of charity or find their way into the poorhouse. Possessing the physical strength of adults, they become, through their mental deficiency, a constant source of crime. Indeed many are moral imbeciles incapable of distinguishing right from wrong. Out of six hundred children appearing before a Chicago Juvenile Court, twenty-six per cent were feeble-minded. A large proportion of the inmates of reformatories and prisons also belongs to this class. Dr. Goddard places the proportion of feeble-minded in our almshouses at about one-half and gives the same ratio for the criminal class. Again, it has been estimated that from twenty-five per cent to fifty per cent of the immorality among women is due to feeble-mindedness. The cost to the state in crime and pauperism of the feeble-minded would justify the expenditure of a large sum of money for their custodial care. If they are permitted at large, they will continue to reproduce their kind and to lower the average level of intelligence throughout society. This is the great danger of the moron group, who closely approximate the physical normal, but who transmit the hereditary taint of feeble-mindedness to their offspring.

*The dangers.*

The need of custodial care for the feeble-minded is imperative, if society ever expects to reduce the number of these defectives. They must be segregated *Need of in-* and prevented from mating. This course is best *stitutions.* suited to their own real happiness because they delight in the amusements and toys of childhood. They take pleasure in playing with other children of the same mental age. In this manner, they would no longer be exploited or tempted by those of mature intelligence. Little hope, however, can be held out for their ultimate advancement. Feeble-mindedness is apparently incurable. Nothing can be done for idiots except to satisfy their physical wants. The imbecile group does not need so much attention and they may be taught to care for themselves. The morons, however, are capable of receiving an education equivalent to that of children of corresponding mental age. Manual training may teach them to use their hands productively. Few states have met the problem of the feeble-minded by providing for their permanent custodial care in special institutions. Indeed, there are not nearly enough such institutions to care for this defective group. The institution for the feeble-minded at Vineland, New Jersey, is deserving of special mention, for here Dr. Goddard has carried on his valuable investigations.

**Conclusion**. — The last five chapters have dealt with social groups for whom adjustment is imperatively needed. They are all subnormal. All act as a hindrance *Social debtor* to social progress and constitute a large part of *classes.* the general problem of social adjustment. They are conveniently designated the social debtor classes and comprise the dependents, the delinquents and the defectives in society. The causes of their deficiency have been seen to lie both in social environment and in individual character. In order to eliminate maladjustments, the environment — both economic and social — must be transformed to meet the needs of the individual. Adverse environing conditions must be so changed that individual abnormality may be removed wherever possible. "An ounce of prevention is worth a pound of cure" is as true of social ills as of bodily ailments. Poverty and crime must be prevented rather than cured, and conditions giving rise to defectives must be as largely as possible eliminated.

In considering the future of these unfortunates, individual heredity must be regarded as well as the social
**The future.** environment. Society has already begun the work of adjustment. Charity is being organized, almshouses improved and prison systems reformed. But what is being done to improve the race biologically? The solution of many social problems depends not only upon the progress of ideas, the psychological factor, but also upon the physical improvement of man, the biological factor. From this point of view, a sound physical heredity is as important as a good social environment. Eugenics may be defined as the science of the biological improvement of the race. Because man in the past has grown up haphazardly, is there no reason for supposing that conscious measures may not be taken for his deliberate biological improvement? To be sure, extremists have brought this idea into disrepute by their radical suggestions. But all students of society agree that a rational application of eugenic principles will not only result in race improvement, but that such application is imperatively needed for certain classes in society. For example, it is undoubtedly the duty of society to prevent the propagation of inherently

degenerate biological stocks, like the feeble-minded, whose deficiency is hereditary. As society advances, it is hoped that its eugenic standards will be raised.

## QUESTIONS FOR DISCUSSION

1. How may infant blindness be treated?
2. Give the extent of blindness in the United States. Is it increasing?
3. Describe any school for the blind that you have seen. Name any in your community.
4. What lines of training are especially needed?
5. Give the extent and causes of deafness.
6. Explain the rôle of heredity in producing deafness.
7. Why is the inability to speak so common in the deaf?
8. What should be society's attitude toward, and treatment of, its crippled members?
9. What should you, as an individual, do for the crippled beggar upon the street?
10. Discuss the extent and increase of insanity.
11. Discuss the causes of insanity.
12. Is insanity hereditary?
13. How were the insane regarded and treated in former times?
14. What improvements are needed to-day?
15. What should society do for the group of epileptics?
16. Distinguish between feeble-mindedness and insanity.
17. Discuss the extent of feeble-mindedness in the United States.
18. Discuss the three groups of the feeble-minded.
19. Show its hereditary character.
20. What are the dangers arising from the feeble-minded being at large in society?
21. Can feeble-mindedness be cured?
22. To what extent may they be taught?
23. What is the duty of society regarding the feeble-minded?
24. What are the three groups of social debtors?
25. What should be the attitude of society toward the individual social debtor?

26. What should be the keynote of reform?
27. What is "eugenics"?
28. What may the future hope for in this direction?

## TOPICS FOR SPECIAL REPORT

1. Ophthalmia, or infant blindness.
2. Industrial training for the blind.
3. Teaching the deaf and dumb to speak.
4. Civilization and increased insanity.
5. The provision made for the care of the feeble-minded by the laws of your state.
6. The work of some school for feeble-minded children.

## REFERENCES

SMITH, S. G. "Social Pathology," Chapters on Nature of Insanity, Care of the Insane, The Feeble-minded, Provision for the Blind, Treatment of the Deaf.

HENDERSON, C. R. "Dependents, Defectives, and Delinquents." Part III.

United States Census. Special Reports on Blind and Deaf.

United States Census of 1910. "Insane and Feeble-Minded."

GODDARD, H. H. "Feeble-Mindedness."

GODDARD, H. H. "Kallikak Family."

DAVENPORT, C. B. " Heredity in Relation to Eugenics."

# CHAPTER XXI

## The Problem of Prohibition

I. Historical survey
 1. Attitude of the past
 2. Temperance movements in America
II. Alcohol and society
 1. Consumption of liquor
 2. The economic aspect:
  *a.* Size of liquor industry
  *b.* A source of government revenue
  *c.* Impaired industrial efficiency
 3. The social aspect:
  *a.* Report of Committee of Fifty
  *b.* Poverty and pauperism
  *c.* Crime and alcohol
  *d.* Family life
  *e.* The public health
  *f.* Alcohol and heredity
  *g.* The race problem
  *h.* The social cost of drink
 4. Regulation of the traffic:
  *a.* Prohibition
  *b.* Local option
  *c.* License system
  *d.* Gothenburg system
  *e.* The limitations
 5. The saloon:
  *a.* Common features
  *b.* Substitutes
  *c.* Substitutes

SINCE society is constantly undergoing adjustment, new problems are always calling for solution. Social morality varies from age to age in accordance with changes in social thought and customs. What is regarded as legitimate in one period is considered, in another, as subversive of society's best interests. The old individualistic attitude toward conduct is giving way to that of social welfare. Hence society is beginning to regulate man's consumption and to direct it, wherever possible, into productive channels. Perhaps the most important of these new problems of adjustment is that of prohibition which, from small beginnings, has steadily advanced to a position of great magnitude.

**Historical Survey**. — The use of fermented liquors seems known to all races and all ages. The ancient Hebrews cultivated the vine and, in the Bible, frequent references are made to wine and the wine press. Indeed a total abstainers' society existed long before the Christian era in a sect of Israelites who drank no wine. The classical peoples of Greece and Rome were also wine drinkers, and festivals were held in honor of Bacchus, the god of conviviality. The Koran, however, forbids the use of intoxicants, and Mohammedan lands have been free from alcoholic excess. This is likewise true of the followers of Buddha and Brahma, and of most Oriental nations. The Chinese empire has been supposedly under prohibition for 2400 years, as an imperial edict forbidding the use of intoxicants was issued in 459 B.C. European civilization, however, has unfortunately carried strong drink to various " unenlightened " nations of the earth. " Fire water " has often had the same effect upon the black tribes of Africa as upon the red men of America.

*Attitude of the past.*

However, European nations have long been accustomed to the use of alcoholic beverages. The countries of North Europe have shown the same fondness for their national beers and ales, made from grains, as the Mediterranean lands have shown for the fermented juice of the grape. The Anglo-Saxon, like other Germanic races, evinced a great desire centuries ago for eating, drinking and fighting. Their mead halls are famous in song and story. In fact, the " flowing bowl " was in almost universal use throughout the Middle Ages, and in general use until comparatively recent times. Indeed, certain cordials bear the names of the monastic orders which made them, for their manufacture was considered altogether legitimate. In the nineteenth century, drunkenness upon the streets was a common sight in England as well as in the United States. For centuries the national drink of Russia was vodka, a kind of potato whisky. At the beginning of the World War its sale was forbidden by an imperial decree, but it is almost too early to state the social result of this sweeping prohibition. In fact, the titanic conflict called serious attention everywhere to the prohibition problem and gave it a general impetus never before attained.

Many of the early colonists brought to America the taste for alcohol and the desire for conviviality. In the early days social drinking was universal and the clergy drank in the homes of their parishioners. Strong drink was considered essential to barn raisings **Temperance movements in America.** and husking bees. It was served upon all special occasions, and weddings and funerals alike were characterized by the consumption of liquors. Before the Civil War, however, great temperance movements were inaugurated. Societies were formed whose members pledged themselves not to use distilled liquors.  Later were formed total abstainers' societies which proscribed the use of all alcoholic beverages.  The first permanent prohibition law was passed by Maine in 1851, and a national prohibition party was later organized.  Religious denominations also began to take a stand against the consumption of liquor, and certain church organizations, like the Catholic Total Abstinence Society, were organized.  One of the earliest independent temperance societies was the Order of Good Templars.  In 1883 the Women's Christian Temperance Union, under the leadership of Frances E. Willard, was made a world-wide organization.  It has undertaken a campaign of education to keep young people from the use of alcohol.  An Anti-Saloon League of the various states has also been federated into a strong national organization.  It has agitated for legislation toward prohibition or local option and has insisted upon the enforcement of all existing laws against the saloon and the illegal sale of intoxicants.

**Alcohol and Society.**—The number of habitual and even occasional users of alcoholic liquors has steadily declined. The total abstainer was formerly rarely to be found, but gradually a large area of our country passed under either prohibition or local option laws.  In spite of these facts the consumption of alcoholic beverages steadily increased.  In order to understand this increase we should divide alcoholic liquors into their natural groups.  In the first place, there are the malt liquors such as beer and ale.  The percentage of alcohol in the average American beer was three or four per cent.  The second group includes the different varieties of wines.  Here the percentage of alcohol varies from about eight to fifteen per cent.  Distilled liquors such as whisky and gin, constitut-

*Consumption of liquor.*

ing the next class, contain as high as thirty-five or forty-five per cent of alcohol. The consumption of distilled liquors in America remained fairly constant, amounting annually to about one and one-half gallons per capita. Of wines we drank little, as compared with their enormous consumption in France, Italy and other European countries. Our per capita consumption varied from one-third to two-thirds of a gallon. The consumption of malt liquor was much larger than was ordinarily supposed. This fact was alleged by some to further the cause of temperance, because these liquors contain so small a percentage of alcohol. The increased consumption of malt liquors, however, was not accompanied by a decreased consumption of distilled liquors. In 1910 the per capita consumption of malt liquors had reached twenty gallons and, in 1914, twenty and one-half gallons, but in 1915 it fell (as did that of other kinds of liquor) to eighteen and one-quarter gallons. The total annual consumption of beer in the United States was greater than that of any other country in the world. Our national drink bill was almost two billion dollars a year, or twenty dollars per capita. This is almost double the annual expenditures of the federal government in normal times and is over three times the entire sum spent for education in the United States.

The amount and cost of liquor consumption in the United States indicate the economic importance of this industry. In the last forty years of the nineteenth century The the industries of our country grew in productive economic capacity about sevenfold. The United States *Size of liquor* Brewers' Association pointed to the United *industry.* States Census to show that our brewing industries in the period increased twentyfold. There were about fifty thousand employees in the brewing industry. Here wages were relatively high, while the number employed in proportion to the capital invested was low. The United States Census for 1910 found that in this business there were about sixty-eight thousand retail dealers with one hundred thousand employees. The total capital invested in the liquor business is hard to approximate. In 1905 the United States Manufacturers' Census capitalized the malt liquor industries at over a half billion dollars. Indeed, they ranked sixth among our leading industries. Our annual consumption of sixty million barrels of beer required every year one hundred million dollars' worth of farm products. This citation of the magnitude of the brewing and liquor industries must not be taken as an argument in their favor, but rather as evidence of the pressing need of a comprehensive solution of the whole question.

However, it is an economic fact that a great industry cannot suddenly be legislated out of existence without temporary maladjustment, although the final result may be entirely beneficial to society. Both the labor and the capital involved in the enterprise are obliged to seek other industries and in certain cases the individual loss is great. Of course, the farm products which entered into the production of liquors will eventually be used in the manufacture of breadstuffs. The government's attitude on this question in war time was expressed in a federal law which became effective September, 1917. In order to conserve the food supply of the nation, this act forbade in time of war the use of grains for purposes of alcoholic distillation. In this manner, it was hoped more fully to utilize the food value of grain, and at the same time gradually to change individual consumption from unproductive to productive channels.

This war measure paved the way for the federal prohibition amendment.

From the very beginning of our national history the liquor industry has been heavily taxed. An internal excise tax, as well as a tariff upon foreign imports, was part of Alexander Hamilton's comprehensive plan of providing for the finances of the new republic. Both these taxes have always fallen heavily upon alcohol. In fact, before 1917, the federal income derived from all liquor taxation was about a quarter of a billion dollars annually. Before the World War the internal revenue taxes came second to the custom receipts as a source of national income. The three branches of internal revenue in order of importance were: (1) the tax upon distilled liquor which, because of its higher rate, yielded two or three times the amount of (2) the tax upon fermented liquors, such as beer and other malt liquors and (3) the tax upon tobacco. The states, and particularly the local government, also received a large income from the taxation of alcohol through licenses to sell. Indeed, we may state, in conclusion, that about one-fifth of our annual drink bill went to the government. But when we consider the relation of alcohol to crime, to the almshouse, and to lowered economic efficiency, we shall see that the liquor industry was but a false and delusive source of income.

*A source of government revenue.*

The spread of the prohibition movement has been largely due to industrial causes. While some phases of the problem are still open to discussion, the economic basis of prohibition is the solid ground upon which the whole movement rests. Alcohol and industrial efficiency are essentially antagonistic. Formerly, work was often irregular and performed by the laborer

*Impaired industrial efficiency.*

in his own home and at his own convenience. Now, production is based upon the factory system, and work is done by coöperative effort. Definite working hours make the tipsy employee undesirable, no matter how skillful he may be when sober. Again, the use of machinery, now universal, requires a steady hand and a clear head. An employee addicted to alcohol may therefore imperil the lives of others as well as the safety of himself. Indeed, alcohol has been a potent cause of industrial accidents. Sobriety is an essential element in the " Safety First" movement, and many railroads are requiring total abstinence as a condition of employment. Organized labor, which formerly resented the idea that the " workman should have a keeper," is now beginning to see in alcohol a foe to its best interests. During strikes, the government has forbidden the local sale of intoxicants, in order to prevent the drunken disorder which so frequently accompanies them. Even in times of regular industry, the distress caused by alcoholic excess is apparent. Many employers have therefore advocated prohibition on purely economic grounds. But the South went "dry" in order effectively to insure the economic reliability of the negro. We may state in conclusion, therefore, that alcohol represents a great loss of efficiency to the employee, and a waste of material, time and effort to the employer.

Thus far we have discussed the economic side of the prohibition problem and have indicated the importance

The social aspect:
*Report of Committee of Fifty.*

of alcohol in terms of labor and capital. It is now our purpose to show the reverse of this picture, in order to see how large a proportion of the destruction of both material and immaterial wealth is caused by this same agency. It is well known, for example, that a direct relation exists between the use of alcohol and the spread of crime and pauperism. The basis of our discussion is a special investigation upon this subject by a sub-committee of the so-called " Committee of Fifty." This committee was made up of a number of prominent and trained men, who undertook a sociological investigation of the liquor problem in its various aspects. It has been criticized for spending so much time and effort upon obvious causal relationships. The Committee, however, very properly wished to present carefully collected and absolutely definite statistical facts of scientific value. It spent a long period investigating thousands of individual case records and visited hundreds of almshouses and state penitentiaries. The spirit of prejudice is absent from this report, and no causes are ascribed to alcohol unless the relationship is definitely established. While the report of this committee appeared more than a decade ago, it is nevertheless one of the best and most comprehensive investigations of its kind.

We have seen that the causes of poverty are numerous and that an individual may be both lazy and intemperate. In the report of the Committee of Fifty intem- *Poverty and* perance is not regarded as a cause of poverty *pauperism.* " unless it was found to be so important that without it poverty would not have existed and unless it was the principal and determining cause." This investigation concluded that about twenty-five per cent of the poverty which comes under the view of charity organization societies may be traced directly or indirectly to alcohol. Of the cases studied, eighteen per cent fell into poverty through personal intemperance, and nine per cent through the intemperance of parents or others. Of the cases in almshouses, thirty-seven per cent may be traced to alcohol. In the case of destitute children not less than forty-five per cent of the dependency was found to be due to the intemperance of parents, guardians or others. While admitting that there are other important causes of poverty and that poverty itself may be a cause as well as a result of intemperance, it is impossible to escape the conclusion that alcohol increases the sum total of poverty in a community.

It is also impossible to trace crime to a single cause, and we are often forced to speak of first, second and even *Crime and* third causes of crime. The statistics collected *alcohol.* by the Committee of Fifty relate only to convicts in state prisons and reformatories. Since they do not include the ordinary county jails, which hold persons sentenced for mere misdemeanors, such as drunkenness, the estimate of the rôle of alcohol is less significant than would otherwise appear. The investigation covered 13,402 convicts in seventeen prisons and reformatories scattered throughout twelve different states. It was conducted with the utmost care and exactness. Of the total number of cases investigated, intemperance appeared as one of the causes in nearly fifty per cent. It was, however, a first cause of crime in only thirty-one per cent and the sole cause in but sixteen per cent. Other investigations confirm the importance of intemperance as a cause of crime.

Intemperance is often the cause of a disrupted family life. The importance of the family as a social institution *Family life.* and the necessity of a wholesome family life for the socialization of children cannot be too strongly emphasized. The immoderate consumption of alcohol, resulting in the intemperance of husband or wife, is often fraught with fearful consequences to the development of happy childhood and to the economic independence of the family. Alcohol, as we have seen, is a frequent cause of poverty and often results in the destitution of children. Intemperance may also put the breadwinner in jail. Drunkenness is a frequent cause of desertion and in some of our states a legal basis of divorce proceedings.

The habitual use of alcohol weakens the physical power of resistance to disease and, thereby, results in many curable maladies proving fatal. Again, alcoholic *The public* excess is the direct cause, in many instances, of *health.* certain diseases of the heart, liver, kidneys and nervous system. Finally, there is alcoholism itself, a specific disease named directly after its cause. How many men annually fill drunkards' graves cannot be accurately estimated, for alcoholism itself is not recorded by the coroner when friends of the deceased are able to designate any other cause. We have also seen that intemperance is a cause of insanity. Dr. Billings, representing the Committee of Fifty, found, from a recent compilation of reports of numerous insane asylums, that not more than from fourteen to thirty-nine per cent of the inmates were total abstainers. The average showed that twenty-four per cent of all the insanity was attributed by the authorities of these institutions to alcohol. In cases of feeble-mindedness, however, alcoholism may represent the effect rather than the cause.

Is the taste for alcohol inherited? It is often popularly stated that the alcoholic appetite is inherited and that the son follows in the father's footsteps, not from *Alcohol and* choice, but from compulsion. However, we *heredity.* know that acquired characteristics are not inherited. If they were, each generation would begin where the preceding generation ended. Racial progress or racial degeneration would be quick and cumulative. Biology teaches the doctrine of the " continuity of the germ plasm," that is, that only those characteristics inherent in the germ cell are transmissible to the offspring. By the nontransmissible character of acquired traits, nature protects itself and gives a fresh start to each generation. However, a physical degeneracy may be characteristic of the germ cell, and this inherited weakness may make resistance to alcohol extremely difficult. For example, a deranged nervous system may be inherited, and this in turn may develop a taste for alcohol. The second generation of alcohol users may be of an inferior physical stock, and alcoholism itself may be a manifestation of a defective biological inheritance. Moreover, it must be borne in mind that the germ cell is contained in the body cell and dependent upon the latter for nourishment. Hence, the germ cell may be indirectly affected by malnutrition or by the poison of alcohol or by disease toxins.

An overindulgence in alcoholic liquors is primarily the white man's vice and from him the negro and Indian have

*The race problem.* learned it. Long ago, however, precautions were taken to safeguard the negro in this respect. The country negro of the South found it difficult to secure alcohol because of prohibition laws. Even in the towns where the saloon evil existed, his poverty acted as a check in this direction. Although the use of alcohol by the negro has not been so great, yet it has been a source of considerable race friction and the cause of much prohibition sentiment in the South. It has been an effective agent for crime by arousing the worst passions of the negro. On the other hand, many lynchings and race riots have been instigated by the white man's craving for alcohol. Alcohol is therefore conducive to the mob spirit as well as to crime.

We have spoken of the cost of liquor in the United States and of our large annual drink bill. This, however, represents only the first cost. A second and greater *The social* cost may be read in poverty, crime and shortened *cost of drink.* lives. Those who die from alcoholism are enumerated in the census report as less than one per cent, but we have seen why this estimate is lower than the actual number. Investigations of medical men have shown that at least three per cent should be so classified. Moreover, this estimate does not take into account the loss of life due to murders and suicides, in which alcohol plays a sinister rôle. Nor does it include those killed or injured in accidents caused by intemperance. It is also impossible to estimate the enormous economic loss from impaired industrial efficiency due to alcohol. Attempts have been made to estimate in dollars and cents the public cost of liquor in the form of government expenditures for the support of paupers and criminals. The following estimate was made by Professor Collins of the annual expense attributable to alcohol in poor relief cases:

| | |
|---|---:|
| Hospitals (40% due to liquor) . . . . . . . . | $4,000,000 |
| Insane Asylums (35% due to liquor) . . . . . . | 5,500,000 |
| Feeble-minded institutions (45% due to liquor) . . . | 5,400,000 |
| Almshouses (37% due to liquor) . . . . . . . | 3,200,000 |
| Public Orphan Homes (46% due to liquor) . . . . | 4,100,000 |
| Outdoor Relief (30.5% due to liquor) . . . . . . | 12,000,000 |
| Private Charity (30.5% due to liquor) . . . . . . | 30,500,000 |
| | $64,700,000 |

If fifty per cent of crime was chargeable to liquor (as estimated by the Committee of Fifty and the Massachusetts Labor Bureau Investigations), we might attribute to alcohol one-half of the cost of police, of criminal courts and of jails and penitentiaries. The sum has been found to be about $40,000,000 annually.

The social evils due to alcoholic excess make necessary some kind of government regulation of the liquor traffic. **Regulation of the traffic:** The old individualistic theory of "personal liberty" is not applicable to present-day conditions. It is true that sumptuary laws may be carried to excess and that the individual's consumption of economic goods may be over-regulated. This criticism, however, cannot be justly applied to the regulation of the alcoholic appetite. The spirit of the twentieth century is against the anti-social element in society; it does not tolerate the development of anti-social tendencies. Society has long recognized the right of the state, through its police power, to restrict individual action for the sake of public welfare, when such unrestrained action interferes with the health, safety or morals of the community. From the financial standpoint alone, it is evident that, when public taxation is charged with the support of jails and almshouses filled with alcoholics, the community must have the right to regulate the consumption of alcohol.

The regulation of the liquor traffic, like many other social problems in the United States, was for a long time under the control of the several states. Unlike federal problems, this question was, during the nineteenth century and almost two decades of the twentieth, referred to each state for settlement. Many states had passed prohibition measures, and the geographical area of the "dry" territory had widened. For a long time the Supreme Court upheld the legality of shipping liquor into "dry" territory from other states. Congress, therefore, under its authority to regulate inter-state commerce, passed the Webb-Kenyon Act, which prohibited such shipments. While the World War was in progress a special wartime prohibition act was passed. Meanwhile, the friends of prohibition had been active and *Prohibition.* had secured the ratification of the Eighteenth Amendment, which legalized permanent federal prohibition through constitutional amendment, and which went into effect, January 16, 1920. Its wording was purposely vague, but it empowered Congress to pass a law not only to enforce the new amendment, but also to define what constituted an intoxicant. Accordingly Congress passed the Volstead Act defining the alcoholic content of intoxicating beverages. Possibly a later Congress may make a new definition increasing or decreasing this alcoholic content. It is too early to pass judgment upon this law. Its advocates claim that the social and economic effects resulting from its enactment have already been great and that they will increase. Its opponents stress the difficulty of its enforcement and point for proof to the illicit traffic in intoxicants.

Prohibition is now, therefore, the law of the land, but before leaving the subject we may consider briefly from the theoretical viewpoint other forms of regulation which prevailed more or less before the prohibition amendment was enacted.

In order to be effective, prohibition requires the support of public sentiment throughout the state. Of course it is more difficult to receive undivided *Local option.* support from a large area than from a smaller one. The system of local option attempts to meet the situation by permitting each community within the state to pass upon the liquor question. A locality opposed to prohibition would not, therefore, under local option have prohibition imposed upon it. A county which deliberately votes itself dry is much more apt to have sufficient public sentiment against liquor to make the law effective. While local option lessens the likelihood of open contempt or defiance of the law, it still has the problem of the "speak easy," or the secret evasion of the law. It also makes the liquor question omnipresent in local politics. The exact method by which the power of local option was exercised varied according to legal usage in different states. In some communities a vote was taken annually; in others, once in several years, and in still others a vote on the question might be taken at any time upon the petition of a sufficient number of voters.

Several states were without any provision for local option and were under what is known as the license system. This *The license* is often referred to as the high license system, *system.* for frequently the sum required to obtain a license is so great as to reduce to a minimum the number of license holders. The inverse proportion of the amount of the license fee to the number of liquor dealers afforded an easy system of regulating the traffic. Not only did the high license system lessen the number of saloons, but it helped to drive out of existence those of the worst character. However, costly improvements and capitalistic investments are no indications of moral respectability. But it may be said that the high license system is more apt to result in a closer obedience of the law, since the holders have much to lose if their licenses are not renewed. Many object to the license system because of the government recognition and implied sanction of the business. Again, its administration is difficult because of political interests. Generally the licensing power is vested in the county courts, the judges of which have the right to determine how many taverns may exist in a community. The license system is a source of considerable revenue to the community. In fact, one objection urged against its abolition was the necessity of increasing the tax rate in order to make up a resulting loss of revenue.

The Gothenburg system originated in Scandinavia. The aim of this system is the elimination of the motive to private gain in the liquor traffic. So long as *The Gothen-* large profits accrue to individuals or corpora- *burg system.* tions interested in the sale of intoxicants, the saloon will be made an attractive place for private gain. Under the dispensary or state account system, as the plan is also called, the sale of some or of all classes of liquors is conducted by the government itself. As originally worked out in Scandinavia, a sharp distinction is made between the mild malt liquors and the distilled spirits. The first group is not regarded as sufficiently pernicious to come within the regulations of the system. The retail traffic in spirits, however, is placed in the hands of public corporations, the profits of which, after deducting five per cent on the capital invested, go to public purposes. Thus the motive to private gain is removed. The public spirit shops are relatively few and comparatively unattractive. They lack the entertaining features which sometimes make the tavern a center of sociability. Desiring to imitate the good features of this system, South Carolina at one time proposed to create a complete state monopoly of the liquor traffic, and to appropriate to the public treasury all the profits

x

accruing therefrom. The trial of the foreign system, however, proved rather unsuccessful in this country and South Carolina abandoned it for local option and, later, for prohibition.

Social reform by restrictive legislation is always difficult. If men could be legislated into goodness, the millennium would be easily attainable. It is far easier to pass prohibition laws than to change the habits and desires of mankind. This must not for a moment be considered a reflection upon prohibition; it is a mere statement of fact. Always we must bear in mind that the underlying principle of social reform is the development of character. Prohibition is merely a means to an end and must always be regarded as such by the student of society. It is a valuable instrument of economic and social reform because it makes more difficult the satisfaction of unworthy desires. It hedges the individual with restrictions upon anti-social actions. It is thus a prop and moral support to right conduct. It is not, however, an end in itself. Furthermore, we must remember that prohibition must rest upon a solid foundation of favorable public sentiment. Without this element, it may become an incentive to the violation of law.

*The limitations.*

Unfortunately, for many years, the American saloon presented one of the most acute social problems of urban life. It performed the twofold function of satisfying the physical appetite and of gratifying the social desire for comradeship. In fact, many social writers characterize the saloon as " the poor man's club." Here, in the cold winter months, were warmth, food and drink. Newspapers were also provided and the wage earner, possessing the spirit of democracy, was

*The saloon: Common features.*

attracted by the atmosphere of social freedom. Frequently, the saloon was a center of political activity and the rendezvous of local politicians. This attracted the voters and gave them a feeling of importance. Not infrequently, too, the saloon performed the function of an employment bureau.

It is a sad commentary upon American social conditions that, in the past, American workmen in large cities should have been so largely dependent upon the saloon for social life and comradeship. Substitutes for *Substitutes.* the saloon must be found. One of these lies in the formation of workingmen's clubs. The Young Men's Christian Association has done splendid work in encouraging the physical and moral growth of American manhood by providing gymnasiums and wholesome amusement centers, as well as reading rooms, and the means of educational advancement. The Young Women's Christian Association is doing a similar work for girls and young women. Municipal clubhouses might well be established where proper dancing and other healthful amusements could be enjoyed. Community centers for musical celebrations and other entertainments are well worth the financial outlay involved. Germany has its low-priced opera and France the beginning of a municipal theater. Experiments have also been made in coffee houses, tea houses and temperance taverns, where amusement features and social attractions are provided. The motion picture house also made great inroads on the saloon. In fact, time may prove this form of amusement to be the most successful successor of the saloon. From another point of view the tendency in American life toward outdoor sport may prove a most potent factor in counteracting the desire for artificial stimulants. Outdoor life must take the place of indoor relaxation. Finally let us remember that, above everything else, the best antidote to the saloon is a happy family life.

### ARTICLE XVIII
#### Liquor Prohibition Amendment

1. After one year from the ratification of this article the manufacture, sale, or transportation of intoxicating liquors within, the importation thereof into, or the exportation thereof from the United States and all territory subject to the jurisdiction thereof for beverage purposes is hereby prohibited.

2. The Congress and the several States shall have concurrent power to enforce this article by appropriate legislation.

3. This article shall be inoperative unless it shall have been ratified as an amendment to the Constitution by the Legislatures of the several States, as provided in the Constitution within seven years from the date of the submission hereof to the States by the Congress.

## QUESTIONS FOR DISCUSSION

1. Give the history of temperance sentiment and societies in America.

2. Find out what you can about the present organizations against liquor.

3. Discuss the consumption of different liquors in the United States before the enactment of the prohibition amendment.

4. What was our annual drink bill?

5. Show the economic importance of the liquor industry.

6. Discuss liquor as a source of federal revenue.

7. How is the modern organization of industry particularly injured by the consumption of alcohol?

8. Show the relation between intemperance and poverty.

9. What is the relation between intemperance and crime?

10. Can a "taste for liquor run in the family?"

11. Name the four methods of dealing with the liquor traffic.

12. What was the Webb-Kenyon Law?

13. Discuss the advantages of prohibition.

14. Discuss the high license system as a means of regulating the liquor traffic.

15. Discuss the aim and salient features of the dispensary system.

16. How did your state handle the liquor problem?

17. What seems to be the present outlook for prohibition?

18. What legal restrictions now limit the sale of alcohol?

19. Why is a substitute for the saloon necessary?

20. What experiments have been urged along this line?

21. What semi-philanthropic organizations have done efficient social service in competing with the saloon?

## TOPICS FOR SPECIAL REPORT

1. The effect of the World War upon the legal status of the liquor traffic in the different nations.

2. The liquor problem in the United States and in England.

3. The eighteenth amendment to the federal Constitution.

4. The opinion of life insurance companies regarding the use of alcohol.

5. The evils of fraudulent patent medicines.

6. The work of the Women's Christian Temperance Union and of the Anti-Saloon League.

## REFERENCES

Committee of Fifty Reports on the
        Liquor Problem — Summary of Investigations.
        Liquor Problem — Economic Aspects.
        Liquor Problem — Legislative Aspects
        Liquor Problem — Physiological Aspects.
        Liquor Problem — Substitutes for the Saloon.
BARKER. "The Saloon Problem and Social Reform."
WARNER, H. S. "Social Welfare and the Liquor Problem."
BEMAN, L. T. "Prohibition of the Liquor Traffic."
Year Book of United States Brewers' Association.
Anti-Saloon Year Book.

# CHAPTER XXII

## THE PROBLEM OF DIVORCE

I. Marriage relations
1. Early peoples
2. The Romans
3. Marriage a sacrament
4. Marriage a civil contract
II. Divorce in the United States
1. Marriage laws in the United States
2. The rapid increase of divorce
3. Comparison with Europe
4. Distribution of divorce:
   a. Geographical
   b. Urban influence
   c. Race
   d. Nativity
   e. Religious belief
   f. Other facts
5. Legal grounds for divorce
III. Causes of the increase of divorce
1. Economic changes:
   a. Modern industrialism
   b. Economic emancipation of woman
   c. Higher standards of living
   d. City life
2. Social progress:
   a. Rise of individualism
   b. The woman's movement
   c. Popularization of education and law
   d. Moral and religious changes

IV. The outlook
 1. National Congress on Uniform Divorce Laws
 2. Work of religious bodies
 3. Remedies:
  *a.* Legal
  *b.* Educational
 4. A problem of adjustment

THE family is rightly regarded as the most fundamental institution of society, and yet, even this institution is, to-day, undergoing important changes. In fact, not only the family but the school and the church are affected by the general process of social readjustment taking place throughout the world. Accordingly, in the remaining chapters, we shall discuss first, the instability of modern family life; secondly, the evolution of the school and, finally, the present tendencies in moral and religious development.

**Marriage Relations**. — Not only are the beginnings of the present monogamic family found among the most primitive peoples, but its rudimentary germs Early may even be traced back to the simple pairing peoples. system of the higher animals. Thus, the present form of the family rests upon thousands of years of evolution, and its ultimate stability will not be endangered by one short period of transitional development. Nevertheless, even among primitive peoples, we find numerous deviations from the permanent monogamic form of marriage. Here the duration of the marriage relation varies from a very transitory state, among a few groups, to lifelong union among others. Indeed, the character and permanency of family life is one indication of the degree of civilization attained by a particular society. Sometimes the relation is so temporary as to scarcely deserve the name of marriage.

With the development of group life, loose marriage relationships become more definite, and some sort of ritual or symbolic ceremony grows up to celebrate the union. Divorce in the sense of breaking up this marriage relationship is very old. Among early peoples, the right to a dissolution of the bond was generally given to the man and not to the woman. This was true in polygynous lands, but not where polyandry prevailed. Among all civilized peoples, from the earliest times, the ideal marriage has been that of lifelong union. The ancient law code of Hammurabi, ruler of the earlier Babylonian kingdom, mentions causes of divorce, punishments for the woman who violates the marriage relationship and regulations for the disposal of the property or for the transfer of the dowry of divorced parties. In ancient Jewish society, where the patriarchal system prevailed, family life was stable and authoritative. But even here, the right of the husband to put away his wife was conceded in the Mosaic code.

The family of the early Romans was not only patriarchal, but also characterized by ancestor worship. The **The Romans** marriage ceremony was of a religious nature, in which the bride's father freed her from the worship of her own household gods, whereupon she accepted the ancestor worship of her husband's family. Divorce and polygyny were practically unknown among the early Romans, whose family life was pure and stable. Adoption was frequently resorted to by the Roman family when the line of descent was jeopardized by the lack of natural offspring. With the decay of ancestor worship, however, the patriarchal family declined. The decadence of family life was also hastened by the growth of a skeptical philosophy, and by the numerous political and social changes of the later Republic. In the days of the Empire, marriage came to be regarded as a private contract and the old idea of the religious nature of marriage, prevalent in the early Republic, gradually disappeared. The great law system of Rome also began to grow in complexity and to include the legal rights of women and children. Divorce, which was formerly almost unknown, became more and more frequent. The right of divorce was opened to wives, as well as to husbands. Among certain classes, in the decadent period of Roman history, divorce was so common and so easy to obtain that a stable family life ceased to exist. Vice was rampant and played a sinister part in the downfall of the Empire. Rome at this time is the classical illustration of the apparently direct relationship between unstable family life and national disintegration.

The Christian ideal of the Middle Ages was ascetic. The early church fathers regarded both woman and the institution of marriage as obstacles in the path of saintly living. Celibacy was the rule for the Marriage a sacrament. clergy. Whereas the early church had exercised but little jurisdiction over marriage, the ceremony later became religious and was performed by the priest in the parish church. Marriage was finally enumerated as one of the sacraments of the church and the whole subject placed under ecclesiastical jurisdiction. This point of view, known as the sacramental theory, regards marriage as indissoluble. The wide jurisdiction of the ecclesiastical courts of the Middle Ages included not only religious matters, but also questions regarding marriage. The church courts not only possessed the power to try heretics, but also the authority to pass upon the validity of marriages. A marriage might therefore be annulled because of some fault impairing its validity, but divorce itself was not granted. The Roman Catholic Church to-day still regards marriage as a sacrament and refuses to recognize any right of divorce.

The Protestant Reformation, weakening the authority of the church, served to strengthen the authority of the

**Marriage a civil contract.** state. This resulted finally in the civil authority taking over many powers formerly exercised by the church. The Renaissance had attacked the ascetic ideals of the medieval church and the Protestant Reformation permitted the marriage of its clergy. The trend of modern times has been consistently toward a separation of church and state, and this movement has reflected itself in a changing attitude toward marriage. A civil marriage act was passed by the England of Cromwell. On the continent, this development was largely a result of the French Revolution, and the nineteenth century witnessed the triumph of the idea throughout Europe. Although the laws regarding divorce had long remained practically undisturbed, the principle involved in the new theory began to produce its results later. Ecclesiastical courts, like those of the feudal nobles, had long lost all power, for their jurisdiction had been usurped by the state courts. When divorce was finally recognized, the civil courts were the only proper legal agencies to grant the right. In the marriage ceremony of to-day the religious, as well as the civil idea, persists. An entirely civil marriage, however, is possible and the ceremony may be performed by a magistrate or by a justice of the peace. It is usually necessary to procure a license from the state authorities before any ceremony can be performed by a clergyman. Some European countries require a civil marriage, but it may be followed, if desired, by the religious ceremony.

**Divorce in the United States.** — In the United States, the whole question of marriage and divorce lies within the jurisdiction of the several states. The federal government has no authority in the matter. Hence, great discrepancies exist within the several states in both marriage and divorce laws. For example, there is no uniformity regarding the legal age of marriage, nor agreement concerning the degree of relationship within which marriage is forbidden. Certain states forbid the intermarriage of whites with negroes, others of whites with Indians, and still others of whites with Chinese. Again, some states are lax in the enforcement of marriage laws and in requiring the registration of all marriages. This registration is either not done at all or so poorly done in some sections as to be of no real value. In general, we may say that the marriage laws of the United States are entirely too lax, and that hasty marriages often result in divorce. Not only should the applicant for a marriage license be required to live a given time in the district, but it has also been proposed that a certain time should elapse between the issuance of the license and the performance of the marriage ceremony. Laws have been recently passed in some states prohibiting the marriage of certain degenerate classes, like the feeble-minded and those possessing hereditary defects. Other eugenic measures have also been proposed to improve the physical stock of the race. Some of these are excellent, but others are too radical in the physical tests required for the marriage certificate.

*Marriage laws in United States.*

In 1887 the Commissioner of Labor was authorized by Congress to collect and report the statistics of marriage

Rapid in-<br>crease of<br>divorce. and divorce throughout the country. This report covered the twenty years from 1867 to 1887.

In South Carolina no marriages were recorded, and in other districts the registration was far from complete. Divorce statistics for this period, unlike those for marriage, were fairly complete and sufficiently accurate for purposes of scientific study. In 1905 the Director of the Census was authorized to make a similar investigation for the next twenty years, namely from 1887 to 1906 inclusive. This was published several years later and made possible a study of the divorce movement in the United States over a continuous period of forty years. Unfortunately, we have no complete and authoritative figures for the years following 1906 to enable us to bring the investigation up to the present time. It was found from this census study that, in the decade between 1867 and 1876, one hundred and twenty-two thousand divorces were granted; between 1877 and 1886, two hundred and six thousand; between 1887 and 1896, three hundred and fifty-two thousand and between 1897 and 1906, five hundred and ninety-three thousand. The chart on the opposite page shows the steady annual increase in the number of divorces.

This chart also shows that, in the last twenty years, almost a million divorces have been granted in the United States. This increase of divorce should be compared with the increase of population. In this way we "refine" our "crude" statistics of divorce. This may also be accomplished by comparing the number of divorces with the number of marriages. Whereas the population in 1905 was little more than double that of 1870, divorces were six times as numerous. Thus we may say that the increase of divorce has been three times as rapid as the increase of population. Whereas the married population a little more than doubled between 1870 and 1900, the number of divorces increased fivefold. Whether this threefold velocity of divorce will continue constant, be accelerated or be diminished, is a matter of conjecture. A projection

| 1867 | 9,937 | 1877 | 15,687 | 1887 | 27,919 | 1897 | 44,699 |
|------|-------|------|--------|------|--------|------|--------|
| 1868 | 10,150 | 1878 | 16,089 | 1888 | 28,669 | 1898 | 47,849 |
| 1869 | 10,939 | 1879 | 17,083 | 1889 | 31,735 | 1899 | 51,437 |
| 1870 | 10,962 | 1880 | 19,663 | 1890 | 33,461 | 1900 | 55,751 |
| 1871 | 11,586 | 1881 | 20,762 | 1891 | 35,540 | 1901 | 60,984 |
| 1872 | 12,390 | 1882 | 22,112 | 1892 | 36,579 | 1902 | 61,480 |
| 1873 | 13,156 | 1883 | 23,198 | 1893 | 37,468 | 1903 | 64,925 |
| 1874 | 13,989 | 1884 | 22,994 | 1894 | 37,568 | 1904 | 66,199 |
| 1875 | 14,212 | 1885 | 23,472 | 1895 | 40,387 | 1905 | 67,976 |
| 1876 | 14,800 | 1886 | 25,535 | 1896 | 42,937 | 1906 | 72,062 |
| Total | | Total | | Total | | Total | |
| 1867– | | 1877– | | 1887– | | 1897– | |
| 1876 | 122,121 | 1886 | 206,595 | 1896 | 352,263 | 1906 | 593,362 |

of the same rate to the end of the present century would mean that half of the marriages, then contracted, would end in divorce. Such a situation would not be unlike that prevailing in the days of the declining Roman Empire. The Census of 1910 reported 156,176 men, or three-tenths per cent of the entire male population, as divorced, and 185,101 women, or four-tenths per cent of the female population. These figures, however, did not include any divorced persons who had remarried. Thus the number was smaller than the actual number of divorce cases.

The United States has the unenviable reputation of leading the civilized world in divorce. Professor Willcox, Comparison in his book upon the divorce problem, gave the with Europe. following divorce figures for 1885 and showed that the United States, at that time, had more cases of divorce than all the leading nations of Christendom combined:

| | | | |
|---|---|---|---|
| United States . . | 23,472 | Russia . . . . . . . . | 1,789 |
| France . . . . | 6,245 | Austria . . . . . . . . | 1,718 |
| Germany . . . | 6,161 | Great Britain and Ireland . . | 508 |

In the same year Australia granted a hundred divorces and Canada but twelve. Professor Ellwood gives the following figures for 1905, just twenty years later:

| | | | |
|---|---|---|---|
| United States . . | 67,976 | Austro-Hungary . . . . . | 5,785 |
| Germany . . . | 11,147 | Great Britain and Ireland . . | 821 |
| France . . . . | 10,860 | Australia . . . . . . . | 339 |
| | Canada . . . . . . . | 33 | |

While this table shows the United States still far in the lead, it is also important, incidentally, to note how rapidly the divorce rate increased in the European countries. But although the increase in the number of divorces is not a national but an international phenomenon, characteristic of modern civilization, our own country is the most conspicuous example of this evil. In 1905 we had about one divorce to every twelve marriages, while in France the ratio was one to thirty; in Germany one to forty-four and in England one to four hundred. In a few of the states the ratio ranged from one to eight, one to seven, one to six, and in Oregon, Washington and Montana, there was one divorce to every five marriages. The infrequency of divorce, however, does not necessarily indicate, as will be shown later, a better or higher family life in those states or nations possessing a lower divorce rate. Customs, laws or religious beliefs may keep the family intact even when family life is disintegrating. Where divorce is difficult or impossible to obtain, there may be many disrupted families who cannot register their disruption in the divorce statistics of the courts. The " Report on Marriage and Divorce " by the United States Census Bureau already mentioned shows that our divorce rate is higher than that of any other western nation. It is about three times that of France, five times that of Germany, and thirty times that of Great Britain.

We have already seen that a great difference exists between the divorce laws and, consequently, the divorce rates of the different states. In general, the Distribution: divorce rate is greater in the Northern and *Geographical.* Western states than in those to the South and East. Divorce has been compared to a great cloud lowering from the Northwest. There are three great geographical centers of divorce: (1) New England, (2) the states of the Central West, and (3) the Rocky Mountain and Pacific Coast states. The Middle Atlantic and Southern groups of states show the lowest proportion of divorce. Recently, however, the divorce rate has shown a rapid increase in some Southern states and also in the city of Philadelphia. The Census Report (1909) showed that the divorce rate in the North Central states was two and one-half times that of the North Atlantic states, while the divorce rate of the Western division was four times as great.

In Europe, divorce was regarded as a phenomenon of city life, because the rate was so much higher in the urban *Urban in-* than in the rural districts. The census inves-
*fluence.* tigation, however, found that this difference was not so strikingly significant in the United States. Although great variations exist, it is nevertheless true that in our own country the divorce rate is higher in the urban than in the rural districts.

Court records in the South often do not give information concerning the color of the litigants. Consequently, *Race.* it is impossible to establish any definite fact in regard to the comparative proportion of divorce between the two races. Again, many of the negroes live so near the poverty line that legal divorce through the courts is too expensive. Simple desertion, often by mutual consent and without due process of law, is comparatively more common.

The rôle of the immigrant in the divorce problem is not so uncertain. The divorce rate is much higher among *Nativity.* the native born than among the foreign element of our population. Many immigrants come from lands where both tradition and religion are so strong that these forces persist in the new country and operate against the divorce evil.

Because of the uncompromising attitude of the Roman Catholic Church against this evil, divorce is much more *Religious* common in Protestant than in Catholic com-
*belief.* munities. In Switzerland, for example, the divorce rate is higher in the Protestant than in the Roman Catholic cantons. Some observers claim that the divorce rate is highest among those of no religious profession.

The divorce rate is about four times as high among

childless couples as among those having children. Of the million divorces granted between 1887 and 1906, no children were reported in about sixty per cent of the families affected. Thus, children would *Other facts.* seem to be an important factor in about two cases out of five. Regarding the party to whom the divorce is granted, we find that twice as many women receive divorces as men. Thus, about two-thirds of all divorces are granted upon the plea of the wife, and about one-third upon the plea of the husband. Regarding the duration of married life, the census report showed that, in one-quarter of all the marriages terminated by divorce, the separation took place within two years, and, in one-half of the cases, within five years after marriage.

The legal grounds for divorce vary as much among the different states as do the actual rates of divorce. South Carolina refuses to grant divorce. New York *Legal* has but one cause, while in other states there *grounds for* are many legal grounds upon which divorce may *divorce.* be granted. The three leading ones are desertion, cruelty and adultery. Often the legal grounds upon which divorce is granted reveal little information as to the real cause of the disrupted family life. To the student of social problems, the causes underlying the broken family are of more importance than the actual divorce, which merely legalizes the disruption already accomplished. Furthermore, desertion, for which reason two-fifths of all divorces are granted, is a " blanket " term. It is used in many cases as the legal ground for granting the divorce, but the real cause of the disrupted family is not disclosed. Although there is but one legal ground for divorce in New York, many divorces are granted under that name but for other causes.

Y

Variation between the states in the strictness of divorce laws often results in a certain amount of migration from state to state for divorce seekers. Hence, a change in our constitutional system, whereby a uniform federal divorce law may be enacted, is earnestly advocated by many students of the divorce problem.

**Causes of the Increase of Divorce**. — The rise of the factory system marked the passing of the economic func-

Economic changes: *Modern industrialism*. tion of the family. Production went from the home to the factory. In earlier days, the father farmed, the wife spun and within the family circle were produced most of the necessities of life. To-day, even articles of food, like bread and soup, are more often prepared in the factory than in the home. Although division of labor and the use of machinery have made goods cheaper and more plentiful, these forces have broken up the economic interdependence of family life. Great industrial centers have developed where not only fathers, but also mothers and children, find employment. The factory system has lessened the work to be done at home, but has offered to women and children employment in the factory. Different members of the family become employed in different places and occupations. Interests vary and the home sometimes becomes merely a place in which to eat and sleep. Such a situation often results in the production of unsocialized children, because high ideals of family life are lacking. Again, the neglect of practical training in the duties of motherhood may bear fruit in the unhappy homes of a future generation. That the school is taking over some of the old home duties may be seen by the new vocational courses and the courses in domestiç science. Mothers, employed long hours in factories, have little time to teach or to illustrate by example the art of happy home-making to daughters often similarly employed. In some cases, nervous or physical exhaustion makes them unfit for their own duties of wife and mother. The severe struggle for existence may also take the charm from married life. An equally grave situation is met in the homes of another class where the opposite situation prevails. Modern industrialism has lessened the amount of work to be done in the home, particularly in the cities. Therefore, women of the wealthy class often live at idle ease. It is this group of " idle rich," where the birth rate is low, that furnishes so many divorce scandals. Leisure time, unprofitably or unwholesomely employed, saps the moral fiber far more than a hard-pressed or overworked existence. In conclusion, we may say that the industrial revolution has broken the economic unity of the family and placed the industrial work of woman outside the home. It has brought an increasing amount of wealth unevenly distributed. Unfortunately, not only leisure time and the size of the family seem inversely proportional, but social classes at opposite extremes often present, for far different reasons, a like problem of disrupted family life.

The entrance of woman into industry has been marked by various economic as well as social consequences. While the movement will undoubtedly be ultimately advantageous to society, it nevertheless produces in the period of transition certain undesirable social consequences. Until very recent *Economic emancipation of women.* times, woman, rightly or wrongly, has always been regarded as economically dependent upon man. This view has obtained in spite of the fact that woman has always performed a large part of the industrial labor of society. Her work, however, has been less noticeable than that of man, because it has been confined to the home. Matrimony, therefore, was regarded as a means of support for women. But, now, the employments opened to woman have so widened that matrimony is no longer regarded as a necessary means of support. Divorce offers a way out of an unhappy married life, while industry furnishes the means of support. Woman is now in industry as an independent competitor, receiving definite wages for services rendered. This growing economic independence of woman may be read in the laws establishing the property rights of married women. Not only divorce but late marriages, as well as spinsterhood, are frequent manifestations of the economic emancipation of woman.

With the advance of industrial civilization, has come a rise in standards of living which, of course, has been accompanied by an increase in the cost of living. *Higher standards of living.* Wants and desires have increased faster than incomes. The luxuries of yesterday have become the necessities of to-day. Higher standards of living are socially desirable, but when they exceed wholesome limits the results are often disastrous. Each group desires to imitate the standards set by the next higher economic class. This is the cause of much domestic unhappiness, which reflects itself in increasing divorce. Luxurious living and the increased cost of living are thus partly responsible for the later age of marriage and for the increase of divorce. Professional men of to-day are often, financially, unable to undertake the responsibilities of married life until they attain the larger income that comes with later years. But at this later age, the habits of the individual are relatively more fixed and harder to change. Thus, the adjustment necessitated by marriage is more difficult in later than in early life. On the other hand, it may be said that mature years bring judgment and discretion, while early marriages, rashly contracted by impetuous youth, often result in marital disasters. It is true that a rising divorce rate in this country has accompanied the advancing age of marriage, but the latter may not be the direct cause of the former.

Our new industrial system has resulted in an enormous growth of cities. As we have seen, the divorce rate is higher in urban than in rural communities. *City life* Here are most apparent the differences in standards of living. Again, vice and immorality are often associated with city life. Slums constitute a difficult environment for a wholesome family life, while a normal happy family life is hard to attain even among those living in the fairly congested districts.

The rise of individualism, as we have seen, took place in the period following the Renaissance. It expressed itself in the Protestant Reformation and in the French and American Revolutions. As a further *progress:* result of this liberalizing movement, marriage *Rise of individualism.* came to be regarded more as a civil contract than as a sacrament. The old authoritative type of the family reached its extreme development in patriarchal days, when woman was regarded as the property of the husband. For many centuries, traces of that spirit lingered in family life but, to-day, they have been entirely obliterated by the spread of individualism. Again, social institutions are not now regarded as existing for themselves but rather for the benefit of those who create them. Thus, the family as an institution is not always considered inherently sacred.

The rise of individualism has reflected itself in what is generally known as the " Woman's Movement." We have *The Woman's Movement.* spoken of the economic emancipation of woman and now pass to a consideration of the intellectual and legal aspects of the problem. The inferior position of woman, due to her economic dependence upon man, no longer exists. Under the old system, the wife had little redress for wrongs suffered. She often accepted her fate stoically, but with the acquisition of new rights and a new point of view, woman has chosen to obtain relief from conditions to which she formerly submitted. The rising divorce rate — unfortunate though it be — does reflect the growing freedom of American women and does not necessarily indicate that conditions of family life are worse than they were before the movement began.

The decrease of illiteracy shows that education is no longer the prerogative of the few. Public schools, free *Popularization of education and law.* libraries, and daily newspapers disseminate knowledge which brings emancipation from tradition. Knowledge and progress always produce social unrest. To this principle the institution of marriage is no exception. Existing injustices are more keenly felt, and an escape is sought from a condition which formerly was endured. Law, as well as education, has been popularized. Ordinary legal knowledge is now within the reach of every one, and the courts are open to all. Individuals who formerly knew little of divorce now know how and why it may be obtained.

History bears witness to the fact that no stable family life has endured without a religious basis. In Rome, the decay of religion was followed by the increase of divorce. At present, we are witnessing the passing of the dogmatic age of religious history. With the change in the point of view goes an increase of divorce. *Moral and religious changes.* Although dogma to-day does not occupy a position of supreme importance, it is true that character and service are becoming more important. New ethical concepts of right and wrong are being formed. Formerly, it was regarded as pious to continue the sacred marriage relationship in spite of all differences, and to endure any suffering that might arise. At present, however, the modern attitude seems to be that marriage, like the Sabbath, was made for man and not man for marriage. Again, an increase of divorce does not necessarily mean an increase of immorality. It may mean that our moral standards are higher and that fewer wives will permit infidelity or brutality. Thus, the new situation may really be an indication of higher ideals of family happiness, and of the fact that women are no longer compelled to tolerate a dual standard of morality.

**The Outlook.** — In response to the invitation of the governor of Pennsylvania, a commission of over one hundred representatives from almost all the states of the Union met at Washington, in February, 1906. This meeting was known as the National Congress on Uniform Divorce Laws. *National Congress on Uniform Divorce Laws.* No federal divorce law was regarded as feasible because it would require the passage of a constitutional amendment. It was desirable, however, that all states coöperate in order to secure uniform divorce legislation. It was agreed that all applicants for divorce should be *bona fide* residents of the state in which the suit is filed, and that, to secure a decree of absolute divorce, the applicant should reside two years in the state. The congress desired to see the number of causes of divorce reduced and to standardize the whole divorce question. It was thought that a decree, dissolving the marriage tie and permitting the remarriage of either party, should not become operative until after the lapse of a reasonable time. The Wisconsin, Illinois and California rule of one year was recommended. It was also recommended that each state collect and publish annually statistics upon marriage and divorce. While uniform divorce laws would be of great advantage, it must not be imagined, however, that mere uniformity of legislation would prevent the increase of divorce, the causes of which are deep-seated and complex.

The attitude of the Roman Catholic Church upon divorce has already been mentioned. The Protestant **Work of religious bodies.** churches have also been alarmed at the rapid increase of divorce and, at various meetings of the governing bodies of the different denominations, action has been taken upon the subject. Slight discrepancies exist in the resolutions of the different bodies, but a consistent effort has been made to lessen the number of causes of divorce. Infidelity is usually regarded as the sole scriptural ground for the granting of divorce. The indiscriminate marriage of divorced people has also been condemned.

The desirability of uniform marriage and divorce laws is apparent, but uniformity in administration is also **Remedies: *Legal.*** needed. Not only a decrease in the number of causes for absolute divorce, but also a legal prohibition of the marriage of divorced people, is often recommended. This latter restriction, however, is re·

garded by some writers as both dangerous and undesirable. Better, perhaps, would be the recommendation of the National Congress on Uniform Divorce that a certain time must elapse after the granting of divorce before remarriage is permitted. This is sometimes done by a *nisi* or conditional clause, which prevents the divorce from becoming operative until after the lapse of a year or two. This condition affords the possibility of a reconciliation, while it lessens the likelihood of fraud or scandal. Some communities have established special Courts of Domestic Relations. Under this system, all applications for divorce first come before a special tribunal which carefully investigates the case in order to determine whether, for the good of society, the dissolution of the family tie is warranted. Reconciliation is generally the aim of the court, but unfortunately, it is often too late to accomplish this end. Regarding all remedies for divorce, it is well to remember that divorce itself is merely the legalization of the disruption of family life already accomplished. Real reform has its roots in premarital conditions and in family life itself, rather than in restrictions on divorce. Bad marriages are essentially the cause of divorce. These include, in the words of Professor Howard, "frivolous, mercenary, ignorant and physiologically vicious unions." Again, the various causes resident in the environment, which hinder a wholesome family life, should be carefully considered in any comprehensive attempt to solve the divorce problem.

In seeking to remove the divorce evil, the proper education of the young is as necessary as the legal remedies. Education, in its broadest sense, is designed to *Educational.* fit the child for his proper place in society. It is more than formal instruction in a course of study. It should therefore emphasize the basic position of the family, the sanctity of the marriage relationship and the necessity for high family ideals. To do this the church, the school and the home should coöperate, each having the same aim but pursuing different methods. The importance of the family, not only to the individuals concerned but to society itself, should be emphasized. Attention therefore must be given, not only to moral education, but to careful training in the actual duties of the home. From the standpoint of the family, the modern course in domestic science is a most important factor in promoting social welfare.

It would seem that the family, like other social institutions, is in a process of transition. The economic bonds

A problem of adjustment. which formerly held the family together are weakening, while at the same time the patriarchal ideal of family life is gradually disappearing. The family of the future must depend solely upon mutual love, consideration and forbearance. It will, therefore, be stronger and of a higher type. Again, the unfortunate increase of divorce is one indication of social progress, which is always a costly process. Enlightenment illuminates injustices and maladjustments. The older type of family was more stable because it rested upon an authoritative basis. A more democratic type must be evolved in harmony with the higher ethical standards of the age. Of the monogamic family we need not despair. The single pairing family will persist. After the process of adjustment is completed, the ideal of lifelong union will once more triumph. The new type of family will be founded upon the principle of mutual attraction and consideration, while the spirit of dominance and subordination will disappear.

## QUESTIONS FOR DISCUSSION

1. Is the permanent monogamic family an old social institution? Discuss from the life of primitive peoples.

2. Compare the family life of early and later Roman history.

3. Discuss the institution of marriage in the Middle Ages.

4. Explain the sacramental theory of marriage.

5. Show how marriage came to be regarded as a civil contract.

6. Name some proposed reforms regarding our marriage laws.

7. Show the rapid increase of divorce in the United States.

8. What do you mean by "refining" statistics?

9. Illustrate in the case of divorce.

10. How does our divorce rate compare with that of Europe?

11. Show the geographical distribution of divorce in the United States.

12. Compare the urban and rural rates. Give reasons for the difference.

13. Show the influence upon our divorce rate of race, nativity and religious belief.

14. What are the most important legal grounds of divorce? Discuss their general significance to the student.

15. Outline the causes of the increase of divorce.

16. Discuss the effects of the industrial revolution upon the home and family life.

17. How does the opening of numerous occupations to women affect the divorce rate and why?

18. Show the rôle played by the higher standards and increased cost of living.

19. Explain the rise of individualism and its effect upon divorce.

20. Discuss the effect of the popularization of law and education.

21. How has the moral and religious sentiment in regard to marriage altered?

22. Discuss the proposed legal remedies for the divorce problem and their limitations.

23. Explain another remedy.

24. Show how the increase of divorce presents a problem of social adjustment.

25. Explain both the pessimistic and the optimistic side of the phenomenon of increased divorce.

## TOPICS FOR SPECIAL REPORT

1. The position of women in ancient Athens and Rome.
2. The cost of social progress.
3. City life and divorce.
4. The problem of desertion.
5. Migration for divorce.
6. The remarriage of divorced people.
7. The divorce laws of your state.

## REFERENCES

Ellwood, C. A. "Sociology and Social Problems." Chapter VIII.

Lichtenberger, J. P. "Divorce — a Study in Social Causation."

Goodsell, W. "The Family as a Social and Educational Institution."

Willcox, W. F. "The Divorce Problem: A Study in Statistics."

Howard, G. E. "History of Matrimonial Institutions." (Reference.)

Adler, F. "Marriage and Divorce."

Report on Marriage and Divorce — U. S. Census 1909.

Blackmar, F. W., and Gillin. "Outlines of Sociology." Chapter X.

# CHAPTER XXIII

## The Evolution of the School

THE school, another important institution of society, has slowly evolved from humble beginnings. Its present form should, therefore, be studied in the light of its past history. Like the institution of the family, it is now undergoing great changes due to the process of gradual readjustment to new conditions.

**Historical Survey.** — Among primitive peoples there is no separate institution known as the school, and, often, Primitive not even a specialized class of teachers. The peoples. family is the earliest school, and the home the chief place of instruction. The aim of the training is to fit the child for his physical and social environment. Practical training in the means of obtaining food, clothing and shelter is obtained more by unconscious imitation than by formal instruction. The teaching of the folkways and customs of the group is carried on either by the parents or by the elders of the tribe. Initiation ceremonies are found among nearly all primitive people and have special educational significance. By this means the boy who has reached manhood is officially admitted to the tribe. The main purpose of the test is to measure endurance and courage, which are the most highly esteemed virtues among primitive peoples. The youth may even be beaten and subjected to mutilation, which may leave identification marks throughout life. Some Australian tribes, for example, knock out one of the front teeth in the ceremony of initiation.

With the advance of civilization, we find the beginning of a specialized class of teachers. These, at first, are the elders and the medicine men, who later develop into the priestly caste. They form the earliest teachers to pass down the learned lore and sacred traditions of the group. Thus, the priests of ancient Egypt and Chaldea possessed a monopoly of the knowledge and learning of that day and gave instruction in religious ceremonies. But among early peoples the school, as a separate institution, did not exist, and the education of the masses was confined to the practical training of the home.

Since the method of primitive education was largely that of imitation, conformity to group standards was sought rather than independent thinking. Al- Greeks and though the school as a separate institution had Romans. developed among the Chinese and Hindus, education with them consisted largely of mere memorization of sacred texts. It is among the ancient Greeks that we first find evidences of a more liberal spirit in education. Here was given the opportunity for individual development, a fact which explains their progress in civilization. The ideal of a well-rounded education was fostered. The body of the youth was trained by gymnastics and the mind by music, literature and philosophy. Aristotle expressed the aim of life as " living happily and beautifully." A familiarly modern note lay in the fact that the Greeks regarded education as a means of fitting the individual for citizenship. The Romans were a more practical people than the artistic and intellectual Greeks whom they sought to imitate. In the earlier days of Rome, the home was the chief educational center, and here were taught the simple virtues and plain rules of conduct. The later period of Roman history witnessed the establishment of an elaborate system of schools. Numerous libraries and several universities were founded. As among the Greeks, education was merely for the higher classes and did not touch the great masses of the population, a large proportion of whom were merely slaves.

Under Constantine, Christianity became the official religion of the Roman Empire and later, through an edict of Justinian, the secular schools and universities The Middle were closed. Education was henceforth domi- Ages. nated by the church. The pagan learning fell into disrepute and the old culture declined. The ideal was no longer that of complete living, but rather that of religious asceticism. The only schools were those of the monasteries, which sought to prepare their inmates for the clergy. In spite of the general ignorance, the monasteries were seats of learning where the monks laboriously copied, and thus preserved, the old manuscripts. Scholasticism must here be mentioned as a peculiarly characteristic feature of the intellectual life of the Middle Ages. The syllogism was used in an academic attempt to systematize knowledge and to support various theological dogmas. Under these influences, universities arose with faculties of theology, law, medicine and philosophy. Large assemblies of students gathered, in the various university towns, to listen to Abelard and other great teachers of that day. These turbulent centers of the intellectual life of the Middle Ages prophesied the dawning of a brighter day.

The Renaissance has been characterized as an outburst of individualism. This characteristic was, perhaps, most **The Renaissance.** marked in its intellectual and artistic aspect. The joy of living succeeded the monastic ideal of ascetism, and a more scientific knowledge of the natural world penetrated the shadows of medieval superstition. A clearer insight of the old world of the ancient Greeks and Romans stimulated a greater interest in their intellectual life. These new interests led to a study of the classical languages and literatures. Although Latin had been the language of the learned during the Middle Ages, Greek had been almost entirely neglected. The poet Petrarch represented the new spirit in Italy, as did Erasmus the Renaissance in Northern Europe. The content of the new education, called humanism, was largely made up of the study of the classics. Almost to our own day, it continued to be the accepted type of higher education and, with slight modification, represented the traditional idea of culture and of liberal education. The last century, however, witnessed the reaction. It must be remembered that the new learning was confined to the few, for the masses continued to live and labor in ignorance.

Until recent years, schools were regarded as private ventures, and a gentleman's education was regarded as a matter of concern only to himself and his parents. There were no national school systems at public expense. The pioneers of such a movement are to be found in various philanthropic institutions of education, such as the charity schools of England. The great progress of democracy in the last century had its effect upon education, which has come to be regarded as a civic necessity. The former aristocracy of learning is a thing of the past. The masses, whom the past regarded as mere " hewers of wood and drawers of water," are no longer content to remain in ignorance. The old medieval monarch may have wished merely a loyal peasantry, but modern democratic nations cannot continue to exist without educated citizenship. Thus, during the last century and a half, the leading nations of Europe have developed state systems of education. Prussia was one of the first to organize a scheme of universal education and to make the system compulsory. This was accomplished by the benevolent despot, Frederick the Great. A national system of education had its beginnings in France during the Revolutionary and Napoleonic periods. Louis Philippe, upon the advice of his minister Guizot, organized a scheme of elementary education, whereby

*Development of national school systems: In Europe.*

z

each commune was required to establish a primary school. Under the present Third Republic, elementary education has been made free to all and compulsory. The secularization of the school system from church control has also gradually taken place. The administration of schools in France is highly centralized under a Minister of Education. A national system of education was late in appearing in England, because the established Anglican church maintained a strong grip on educational institutions. In 1870, however, an important law was passed establishing elementary schools supported by government grants. Compulsory school laws have also been passed.

Our own early educational policy varied in the different colonies. The aristocratic ideal reflected itself in the *In the* famous dictum of Governor Berkeley of Virginia *United* condemning free schools. In New England, on *States.* the other hand, the schoolhouse, like the meetinghouse, was conspicuous in every township. As early as 1647, Massachusetts required each town of fifty families to have an elementary school, and each town of a hundred families a grammar school — an institution similar to the secondary school of to-day. That the fathers of our nation realized the importance of higher education was witnessed by the founding of such colleges as Harvard and William and Mary. The early part of the nineteenth century saw the rapid extension of the common school system throughout the United States. The " little red schoolhouse " dotted the western wilderness which had been so rapidly developed by our hardy pioneers. The public high school, a characteristic American educational institution, arose to take the place of the older Latin grammar schools and the private academies. Normal schools were also established for the training of teachers. Not only has the number of students increased but educational standards have risen.

There is no centralized administration of schools in the United States, for each commonwealth has its own independent system. These state systems, however, do not vary so widely as might be expected. Every state has a well-organized plan of elementary education, and nearly all have a secondary or high school system, providing instruction for three or four additional years. Many commonwealths have large and well-endowed state universities, so that free education from kindergarten to college is within the reach of all their citizens. Our American democracy, with its fundamental principle of the separation of church and state, has regarded education as the bulwark of free institutions. Unlike Europe, religious or sectarian schools have not been incorporated into our public educational system. Another difference between the school systems of Europe and those of America lies in our refusal to recognize class distinctions. In Germany, for example, there are separate schools for those who expect to prepare for the universities and for those who must leave school as soon as possible. The needed differentiation in preparation takes place in the elementary schools. In the United States, on the contrary, it is deferred to as late a date as possible. There is but one educational ladder for all classes. The system of separate schools for different groups may be more efficient in producing results, but it is distasteful to the ideals of American democracy.

**Recent Tendencies**. — The scientific experiments of Roger Bacon gleamed like a bright star in the dark sky of

medieval ignorance and superstition. The various proph-
ecies of his brilliant imagination have since become facts
of everyday experience. With the Renaissance,
began the dawn of a new era in physical
science. The theory of Copernicus shattered
the older astronomical ideas, while Galileo, peering through
his crude telescope, dared to assert that it was not the sun
but the earth which revolved. Scientific investigation
not only continued, but geographical discoveries widened
the field of knowledge. The movement gradually progressed until it culminated, in the nineteenth century,
in the development of the biological sciences. We have
already discussed the work of Darwin and Spencer, and
must here mention the name of Thomas Huxley. The
scientific movement also reflected itself, in a practical
manner, in a great series of mechanical inventions. The
steam engine, for example, revolutionized land and water
transportation as well as the methods of manufacturing.
Modern life has been transformed by the application of
steam and electricity to industry. As in the days of the
Renaissance, the human intellect has been reborn.

*The scientific movement.*

The scientific movement has affected not only industry
but also education. Through its influence, the content of
liberal education has begun to expand, and now numerous
new studies clamor for admission into the curriculum. In
his essay upon education, Herbert Spencer threw down
the gauntlet to conservatives and boldly asked the question,
" What knowledge is of most worth? " After discussing
various aims, he answers this question by declaring that
education should be a practical preparation for life. " How
to Live? — that is the essential question for us." In his
enumeration of the studies conducive to that end, the

sciences take a commanding position. The so-called cultural subjects are not entirely eliminated but are relegated to the leisure time of life and, therefore, of education. Thomas Huxley also advocated the value of the sciences in comparison with the traditional study of the classics. Not only is a knowledge of science valuable, but the training in scientific method is most important. Thus, science has found its way into an assured place in the curriculum, not only of the secondary schools, but also of the elementary schools. Physics and chemistry are, therefore, taught in the high schools in addition to mathematics and the classics. In the elementary schools, geography, physiology and nature study find a place beside the " three R's." Meanwhile, courses in the modern sciences had found their way into the colleges and universities. Great scientific and technical schools were founded for instruction in engineering, in chemistry and in industrial organization.

One other effect of the scientific movement in education must be mentioned. When the scientific method of observation and experimentation was directed toward education itself, great changes took place in the method of teaching and in school administration. Many accepted methods were found, in the light of scientific tests, to represent merely traditional ideas. With the development of psychology, education is becoming a science as well as a practical art. The popular cry for efficiency has been echoed from industry to education. The old-fashioned schoolmaster and the " little red schoolhouse " of our parents are passing into history. Changes are taking place so rapidly as to become bewildering. The " fad " evil is common to periods of transition, and mere radicalism must not be interpreted as progress. However, the new problems of a new age always require educational readjustment. In conclusion, we may state that the scientific movement of the nineteenth century has been characterized by a great increase in the content of education, by the addition of the natural sciences, and also by great changes in methods of school administration.

The sociological movement in education grew out of the scientific. It answers the question " What knowledge is of most worth? " by emphasizing the importance of that knowledge which fits the individual to meet the needs of his social and economic environment. The aim is social rather than individual. Upon its theoretical side, it would add to the curriculum the social, as well as the natural, sciences. Thus, in higher education, the social sciences have taken a most important place in the curriculum. Economics has found its way down into the secondary schools and civics into the elementary schools. Even sociology itself, in the form of a study of concrete social problems, is now being incorporated into the high school curriculum. On its practical side, the sociological view of education adds to the curriculum vocational training for those pupils who must soon join the ranks of wage earners. This ideal of education aims to prepare the individual for his economic and social environment by means of industrial education, or by commercial training, or by agricultural instruction.

**The sociological tendency.**

One of the most conspicuous educational movements of to-day is the development of vocational training. This may take three forms: (1) industrial, (2) commercial and (3) agricultural. Under the older system of industry, the individual passed through the stage of apprenticeship, wherein he was taught

**Vocational training:** *Industrial.*

by the master of the shop all phases of his future occupation. Following the Industrial Revolution and the development of the factory system, this method of " learning a trade " gradually declined. At present, the work of a factory employee is generally limited to a single process, and only occasionally does the employer attempt to broaden the knowledge of the workers. Hence the school, an outside agency, has been called upon to meet the demands of industrial education. Many states of Europe have had training of this sort for half a century. In Germany, continuation schools have been used for this purpose. A continuation school is so called because in it education is continued after the pupil has discontinued regular school sessions. The employee is permitted by his employer to return to school a certain number of hours each week. Many localities have made such attendance compulsory for all apprentices up to the age of eighteen and have required the employers to grant them time for such study. Not only is training provided for the lower grades of artisans, but instruction is given to foremen, superintendents and technical clerks. Similarly, girls are trained for numerous vocations, including housekeeping and motherhood.

The system of industrial training in Munich is well known. It provides a special elementary class devoted to instruction designed to link the school with the industrial world. It thus prepares for the higher and more technical classes of the continuation schools. The industrial development of Germany, before the World War, resulted partly from this and other allied types of education. Industrial education in our own country appeared later than in Europe. Real skill and technical knowledge were needed under the stress of international competition for industrial supremacy. The earliest industrial schools in America were founded by private philanthropy, or as a result of individual experiment. In the twentieth century, however, they appeared as an integral part of the public school system. Trade schools have been established in numerous cities, while continuation classes have sometimes been inaugurated in connection with compulsory education laws. Thus, the recent law of Pennsylvania requires partial school attendance for employees between fourteen and sixteen years of age. Manual training courses had already been established in secondary schools and have even appeared lately in the more elementary grades. The purpose of manual training instruction, as distinguished from that of trade schools, is to offer the student general industrial training rather than to prepare him for any particular occupation.

Vocational training has not been altogether industrial. With the great expansion of commerce, as well as of manu-
*Commercial schools.* facturing, came the demand for a thorough preparation for a business career. Only of recent years, in the United States, has this phase of education come to be regarded as a function of our public school system which, throughout the greater part of the nineteenth century, stressed the purely traditional side of education. At the present time, however, commercial courses have won a recognized place in our system of public education. In England, in spite of her dominating position in the markets of the world, commercial education has been but a recent development. In our own country, the early history of commercial education was the usual story of private enterprise fulfilling a public need.

Indeed, at the present time, business colleges and other such private institutions number about one-half of all students of commercial education. Finally, however, the insistent demand for a modern type of education won the recognition of public school authorities. Since the opening of the present century, great progress in this type of education has been made. Commercial courses, as well as the manual training, have been added to the older and more purely academic high school curriculum. By recognizing the divergent needs of the various students, who attend American public high schools, secondary education is no longer a merely traditional preparation for a classical college career. In fact, the universities themselves have long since recognized the need of practical education. Not only their splendid engineering schools, but also their widely attended courses in finance and commerce, bear eloquent witness to the great educational readjustment made by our American universities.

Another aspect of vocational education is the agricultural. In 1862 Congress appropriated lands in every state, amounting to millions of acres, for the promo- *Agricultural* tion of education. Because of the obvious *schools.* needs of national life, it was stipulated that agricultural education should be emphasized in the schools thus founded. Nearly all our states, therefore, have established colleges, which receive public support, and which provide means of agricultural instruction. The need for such training is great, because the United States is still primarily an agricultural nation and her present methods of farming are often wasteful and inadequate. In many rural communities, agricultural courses in high schools have been organized and, indeed, the movement is even taking root in the elementary school system. Not only has agricultural education resulted in more efficient methods of farming, but it has also stimulated an interest in country life and its opportunities. In many rural communities the school has become, for the surrounding farmers, a coöperative center where soils are tested, the results of experiments shown, and a general knowledge of scientific farming disseminated.

Vocational education is but one illustration of the increasing social service performed by the school. For those Social    who are too old to attend day sessions, the eleactivities.    mentary system provides night schools, where immigrants learn to read and write the English language and where the foundations of American citizenship are laid. High schools have their courses for the more advanced students, while the university extension movement and the evening college courses afford development for minds more matured. In fact, the educational opportunities of the present age are so great that no excuse exists for general ignorance. The functions of the school have increased in many ways. Playgrounds are now frequently operated in connection with the public school system and afford opportunities for recreation in the congested areas of the cities. School gardens have also been opened. Again, modern administrative school methods have provided special schools and classes for the mentally deficient. Many cities not only maintain open air classes for tubercular children, but also look after the education of the deaf and the blind. Free medical and dental service is provided for the poorer pupils, while many school systems even employ a special corps of trained nurses. School lunches are frequently served at cost to the pupils or furnished

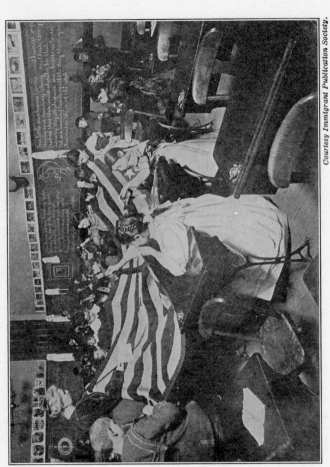

AMERICANS OF ANCIENT RACES MENDING OLD GLORY.

free to the poorer children in immigrant sections. Social service has become a department of the schools as well as of the hospitals. The attendance officers of the department of compulsory education coöperate with the probation officers of the juvenile courts to check the criminal careers of youthful lawbreakers.

Another educational development of social importance is what is known as the " Home and School Movement." It seeks not only to bring the parents of the children into closer touch with the work of the school, but also to acquaint the teacher with the social background of the pupil. In some communities the schoolhouse has become a social center. Here the people of the community gather to listen to lectures on present-day topics, or to enjoy some kind of dramatic or musical entertainment. While community singing is still new in America, it has nevertheless met with great success in social centers frequented by the music-loving immigrants. Athletic contests, classes in gymnastics, and even folk dancing have been held in these centers. In some sections, where the community spirit is strong, sociables and educational amusements have been planned. Since the school plant is public property, there is no good reason why it should not be used more frequently for community functions.

In addition to the public school, there are numerous other institutions of an educational character. Foremost among these is the public library. In this form of philanthropy, the late Mr. Carnegie excelled, having devoted a large part of his fortune to the building of public libraries. Here the leading magazines are on file and books of fiction, travel and scientific knowledge may be read. The newspaper has been a great means

*Other educational institutions.*

of popularizing education by the dissemination of information. The sensational journal, however, is more pernicious than valuable, for stories of scandal and details of harrowing crime exercise a most baneful influence upon the public mind. Museums and art galleries constitute another educational agency. Europe, however, is far ahead of America in art collections and in general appreciation of the artistic side of life. Since good pictures have great educational and moral value, many cities have established public museums and art galleries. Here are exhibited not only works of art, but scenes and products of far distant places. Industrial exhibits, showing the stages in the production of various commodities, have also been introduced. Zoölogical gardens and city aquariums must here be mentioned as containing specimens of animal life interesting and instructive to the general public.

**Education and Social Progress.** — One evidence of educational readjustment is the growing content of the curriculum. We have already mentioned the great development of the natural and social sciences. Since the sum total of human knowledge is constantly increasing, each age must decide for itself what knowledge is of most worth. Educational readjustment is one indication of intellectual progress, for static societies abhor educational changes. Again, methods of teaching and progress in school administration must keep pace with the growth of the science of education. A third factor in educational readjustment is the spread of the spirit of democracy. Education for all is the modern ideal, for education itself is both a cause and a result of democracy. The need of " the classes " is not

*Educational readjustment.*

that of "the masses"; the educational ideals of the
aristocracy of yesterday are not the democratic ideals of
to-day. Consequently, the curricula and the courses of
modern schools have expanded far beyond the straight
and narrow path of antiquity that lead to "culture" and a
"liberal education." We have seen that the enormous
commercial and industrial development of the past century
has reflected itself in educational changes. Industrial
society feels the need of intelligent workers, and the present
generation asks for that type of education which will best
prepare it for the practical duties of everyday life. Therefore, vocational courses are demanded by the many who
must soon leave school for the workaday world. Again,
the Industrial Revolution has largely cut down the educational function of the family, so that the school is now
forced to teach many things that were formerly learned
in the home. A final factor in educational readjustment
is the growth of the social ideal. The individualistic
education of the past must give way to the training for
group life and for democratic citizenship. The increasing
complexity of our social order and the growing interdependence of individualistic activities make coöperation and
social morality imperative.

Social maladjustments, like poverty, inefficiency and
backward traditions, are obstacles in the path of social
progress. Society may remove these by three **Methods of**
different methods. The first is the biological — **social**
that is, the improvement of the human stock **progress.**
through the process of selection whereby the unfit are
eliminated. The second plan of attack is to improve
social and economic conditions by a reorganization of
society and its institutions. There is still a third method

of approaching the problem. This emphasizes the importance of a sound education whereby every member of society is prepared for a life of usefulness in the community. The family, the school and the church must coöperate in instilling into the minds of the young such social ideals as the dignity of labor, subordination to authority, and respect for the rights of others. Education in its social sense is designed to fit the individual for his place in group life. It aims not merely to develop mental power and individual capacity, but also to strengthen moral character and to develop right habits of living. It seeks more than the mere transmission of culture from generation to generation. The schools of to-morrow, however, must not be content with merely producing skilled artisans or efficient business and professional men. They must strive to improve the quality of citizenship in the community. Hence the importance in the modern school of sound training in the social sciences, whereby the citizens of the Republic may learn to think and to act intelligently on the great civic questions of the day. A healthy public opinion is absolutely essential to the preservation of democracy.

## QUESTIONS FOR DISCUSSION

1. Discuss the methods of practical and religious training among primitive peoples.

2. Describe and give the significance of the ceremony of initiation.

3. How did Greek and Oriental education differ in ideals?

4. Discuss the monastic schools and the culture of the Middle Ages.

5. What do you understand by the "humanistic" education of the Renaissance?

6. Trace the development of national school systems in Europe.

7. Why has the progress of democracy stimulated this movement?

8. Compare the present school systems (elementary, secondary and higher) of England, France and Germany with our own.

9. Discuss education in colonial America.

10. Show our educational progress in the last century.

11. Give the effect upon education of the scientific movement.

12. Explain the sociological tendency in education.

13. Discuss the industrial education and the continuation schools of Germany.

14. What is the United States doing in this respect?

15. Discuss the progress of commercial education in the United States.

16. Discuss the value of agricultural schools.

17. Enumerate the social activities of the school.

18. What agencies for social betterment are now coöperating with the school?

19. Discuss the purpose and work of a social center.

20. Visit and describe a school used for this purpose.

21. Name some other agencies for popular education in addition to the school.

22. Describe in detail the possibilities of the one in which you are most interested.

23. Summarize the causes of educational readjustment.

24. Discuss three methods of social progress.

25. Explain the social ideal of the new education.

26. Defend or criticize the placing of this course in social problems in the curriculum of your school.

## TOPICS FOR SPECIAL REPORT

1. The old Chinese education and system of competitive examinations.

2. The liberal education of the Greeks.

3. The life of the students (and their studies) in the medieval universities (*e.g.* the University of Paris under Abelard).

4. The great humanists of the Renaissance (*e.g.* Petrarch and Erasmus).

5. Some famous public schools of England.

6. The educational institutions of Germany (*e.g.* the Gymnasia and Realschulen).

7. The secularization of the schools of Europe (*e.g.* in France).

8. The democratic ideals in American education.

9. Linking the schools with our industries.

10. Cultural ideals in education.

## REFERENCES

MONROE, P. "A Brief History of Education." Chapters I–VII, inclusive, and Chapters XII, XIII and XIV.

GRAVES, E. P. "A Student's History of Education."

GRAVES, E. P. "A History of Education in Modern Times." Chapters I, IV, VIII, IX, X, XI and XII.

KING, I. "Education for Social Efficiency."

GILLETTE, J. M. "Vocational Education."

DEWEY, J. "Democracy and Education."

DEWEY, J. "Schools of To-morrow."

BOONE, R. G. "Education in the United States."

WRIGHT, C. D. "A Practical Sociology." Chapter XI.

BURCH, H. R. "Economic and Social Side of the School Curriculum."

# CHAPTER XXIV

## MORAL PROGRESS

**Ideas of Primitive People**. — Primitive men imagine that the world about them is peopled with innumerable spirits. Their imagination attributes life to such inanimate objects as mountains, brooks and stones. The various phenomena of nature are explained, not as the result of natural causes, but as the work of these

Belief in spirits.

multitudinous spirits. To the primitive mind every act implies an actor and every effect a doer. The idea of abstract cause is beyond its comprehension. Thus the tree, swayed by the wind, is regarded as moved by the spirit either within itself or in the air. The scientific mind coldly analyzes echoes as sound waves, but the savage regards them as the voices of mocking spirits. Grottoes, strange bowlders or peculiarly shaped tree stumps are considered the abodes of such invisible creatures. To these spirits, the imagination of primitive people naturally gives human characteristics. Thus, there may be good and bad, or friendly and hostile, spirits. Primitive men live in constant fear of the supposedly evil spirits that people their environment of field and forest.

Such formal education as primitive man enjoyed was largely a study of how to placate the evil spirits and how

**Magic.**

to prevent them from harming him. Thus, the storm which destroyed his hut was regarded by our early ancestor as the work of an evil or hostile spirit which must be appeased. The search for spirit charmers led to a belief in various forms of magic. Many of our present-day superstitions are modern survivals of primitive belief in magic. For example, the drawing of a circle was supposed to keep the evil spirits within its circumference, and the horseshoe was imagined to hold within itself the friendly spirits of good luck. Fire has always been regarded as affording protection against evil spirits. Thus the sacred flame of the ancients gave protection against unseen terrors. Evil spirits were also regarded as incapable of crossing running water. Yelling and beating upon tom-toms was practiced by the medicine man of early days to drive the evil spirit from his sick patient.

The idea of mystery and the use of symbols produce fetishes and amulets, which were supposed to protect their wearers. Crops would not grow unless a certain ritual prescribed by the folkways was performed. The American Indians were amazed to see the white man's corn grow up, in spite of the fact that he had not appeased the spirits of the harvest.

Animate as well as inanimate objects were regarded as possessed by spirits. Certain animals were therefore held to be sacred, while others might be killed in the chase, provided an apologetic ritual was **Animism.** offered to the spirit thus dispossessed of its abode. In fact, the idea of the transmigration of the souls of departed men into the bodies of animals is still believed by some peoples. Man early came to regard himself as possessing a spirit or other self. This belief in a dual personality is called animism. The conjecture of primitive man concerning an other self was confirmed by seeing his own shadow follow him, or by observing his own image reflected in the clear water of some still pool. Again, the mental phenomena of dreams and sleep encouraged him in this belief. In his dream, primitive man travels afar or rides upon a venturesome chase, but upon awakening, he finds that he is in the same spot where he lay down to sleep. In spite of the vivid experiences of his dream, his friends tell him he has not been away from them. Consequently, he reasons that his other self must have been absent upon the adventures of his dream. In swoons or faints, the other self takes a similar temporary departure. Death he imagines must be a like experience, although the separation between spirit and body seems permanent. Consequently, the dead man's weapons are buried with him, for his spirit will need them in the "Happy Hunting Grounds."

The dead man's spirit is more to be feared than his actual living self. If powerful in life, how much more **Ancestor** powerful will be his unseen spirit? Thus, there **worship.** arises the need of appeasing these jealous vengeful spirits of the dead hovering about them. Often no one will dare appropriate the weapons or property of the deceased warrior. The survivors unite to chant his praises and procure mourners to continue the demonstration of their grief. Primitive man indeed feared to "speak ill of the dead." The departed spirit of a great chief might even be worshiped after his death. So also might be the deceased head of the patriarchal family, whose authority during life was so much feared. As the spirit was supposed to hover near the body it had just left, great care was taken in its burial. The graves and tombs of ancient people were therefore matters of the greatest importance. Offerings of food and wine were placed there at regular intervals, and the descendants of the dead ancestor met at his tomb to perform certain rites in his honor. Indeed, Herbert Spencer, in his "ghost theory," goes so far as to assert that graves were the first altars and tombs — the earliest temples of mankind.

**Religion and Group Life**. — Among primitive people religion is a matter of fear rather than of love and hope. **Higher de-** Nevertheless, the spirit of the dead ancestor **velopment.** would be apt to favor his own clansmen, if they did not neglect to do him honor. In this manner, the spirit of the departed chief was thought to become a tribal deity and to favor his chosen people. With the expansion of the patriarchal family into the tribe, the tribal deity in the explanation of the spiritual differences between the two religious philosophies of these civilizations. The desert associations of monotheism and the forest and hill environment of polytheism were also indicated. However, the social as well as the physical environment must be considered. For example, where backward social conditions prevail, the group may remain for a long time, or indeed permanently, in the stage of animism. Or, where cruel tribal wars of extermination persist, religion will be fettered by crude ideals. The god will be one of war who delights in blood and carnage. Dogma in religion is apt to flourish under a despotic government, while democracy encourages a more tolerant spirit. Again, commerce, resulting in intellectual expansion as well as in material development, frequently fosters the growth of higher ideals in religion. As the civilizations of different groups commingle, their religious beliefs frequently fuse. Thus, the conquests of Alexander the Great amalgamated not only the cultures, but the religious ideas, of the Greeks and Asiatics.

In exercising control over unfriendly or hostile spirits, certain individuals were supposed to have unusual power.

**A priestly class.** These became known as medicine men. They fasted occasionally, for it was conducive to sleeplessness and to the weird workings of their imaginations. Their dreams were often regarded as evidences of divine inspiration, and as the result of direct communication with the unseen spirits of the air. Mutilation of the body, or special dress, marked them off from other members of the tribe. Because of his supposed supernatural powers, the medicine man held a social position of great importance and veneration. His influence over the tribe was

becomes supreme over the various household gods. E
tribe has its own god to fight its battles against the peo]
and gods of other tribes. In the clash of conflict the
ligious, as well as the political organization, becomes stron
The successful tribal deity tends to become the one
over the ever-increasing group. Thus the way is pa
for monotheism. A polytheistic tendency, however, :
result in the formation of elaborate mythologies,
those of the Greeks and Romans. Existing institut
of the group are accredited to fabled ancestors, k
or leaders, while natural causes and origins are expla
in terms of a hierarchy of gods and goddesses. Freque
the lesser deities fade into obscurity and one god,
Jupiter, is recognized as supreme. Man's conceptio
his deity also changes as the group progresses in c
zation. The fear of the numerous spirits to be placat
succeeded by a feeling of awe and reverence toward
one great god. He is frequently regarded as a great
and the fountainhead of justice and power. Like
the bloody sacrifices and the offerings of food chan
higher and more symbolic forms of ritual. Only b
sacrifice of a pure heart and an upright spirit can civ
man come into communication with the Deity. In ge
the higher the civilization of the group, the higher the
standards of its religion. Thus, all the truly great rel
of the world have emphasized ethics and moral rel
ships.

The influence of the physical environment upo
religious ideas of a people has already been disc
Greece with its gentle, varied landscape was con-    Influ
of en
trasted with the awe-inspiring aspects of nature    men
in India. This physical difference is probably one el

frequently greater than that of the chief. His methods of social control were often despotic, but resulted in greater group unity or solidarity. As the tribe grew in size, the number of medicine men increased, until gradually a so-called priestly class arose in society. They alone were learned in the group traditions and in the secrets of magic art. The ritual and sacrifice had especial value when performed by them. At a very early stage in the history of human society, they sought to have their knowledge regarded as a sacred secret. Only the select few were admitted within the inner circle, while the masses were kept in dark ignorance. A great burden of ritual and of sacrificial ceremony was built up in order to make necessary the public support of this leisure class. Frequently, however, the priests were the earliest students, scientists, philosophers and teachers. Thus they aided the cultural advancement, not only of their own group, but of the civilized world. The learned priests of ancient Egypt were supported by the income from the land especially set aside for that purpose. Both the mathematical science and the astrological magic of the priests of Chaldea were bequeathed to later European civilization.

The church is the social institution of the group consecrated to religious purposes. Primitive society is homogeneous and shows little tendency toward differentiation into separate institutions. One of the earliest developments of group activities, however, is found in the separation of a ruling class from the masses. The evolution of the state has already been traced. Another early class distinction is found in the formation of a priestly class, who as we have seen developed from the men of supposed supernatural power in

*The church as an institution.*

primitive society. The church, as an institution separate from the state, is rarely found in early society. Indeed, the complete separation of church and state has been accomplished only in modern times. In former days, heretics were tried by the church courts and executed by the secular authorities of the state. The city of Geneva, under John Calvin, was a theocracy and maintained a close union of church and state. The organization of the church, like that of the state, is determined by the ideals of the times — monarchical, aristocratic or democratic. Despotism is willing to vest in some central authority power over men's consciences and to enforce moral and religious conformity. Democracies favor toleration and the separation of church from state, as well as civil and political liberty.

Religion has always been a powerful social force tending toward group solidarity. Indeed, in many primitive **Effect on group life.** societies, it was the main bulwark of the social order, long before law and government were established. Since men cling to the faith of the fathers, religion is naturally a most conservative force. The church, therefore, has been one of the most static of all social institutions. A heretic in the Middle Ages was regarded as antagonistic and dangerous to the social order. Nonconformity to church teachings was a politcal offense in many Protestant countries. One of the saddest pages of history is the long story of the bloody persecutions and religious wars waged by the Established Church against those who disagreed with its teachings. Thus, men have drawn the sword to enforce or defend their own interpretation of the Gospel of Peace. The aim, however, was to develop group solidarity in belief.

**Evolution of Morality**. — Religion is concerned with man's relations to the Supreme Being, while morality deals with the code of conduct governing the Social relations between men themselves. The origin origins. of this code of conduct stretches far back into the vista of the past. Indeed, there may have been a time in the history of primitive society when man was unmoral, that is, neither moral nor immoral. His mentality may not have been sufficiently developed to have formulated standards of conduct. In fact, some very uncivilized tribes of to-day are not far above this level. Such is also the condition of the young child who has not yet formed any conceptions of right and wrong. On the other hand, lower animals sometimes appear to have very admirable qualities, such as devotion and mother love, but these are based largely upon mere biological instinct. Indeed, the instinctive basis of human nature must not be underestimated even in the morality of civilized man. Evolution has made the human reason a factor in guiding blind instinct. Progress has been marked by a greater use of the intellect in making ethical distinctions between right and wrong. The beginnings of a crude morality resulted from the necessities of group life. Where men lived together there grew up certain customs, or methods of action, prescribed by usage. Whatever, by experience or coincidence, seemed harmful to the group was frowned upon and became " taboo." Certain other actions, of instinctive or chance origin, proved themselves by the process of natural selection to be of value to group survival. Frequently, however, irrational ideas based upon mere superstition unconsciously became part of the social tradition.

Standards of conduct vary among different peoples. The *mores* of the group determine what is right and what
Group standards.
is wrong. Thus, cannibalism is a sacred rite in the moral code of certain savage tribes; while the sacrifice to the gods of youths and maidens was a religious duty among such an otherwise advanced people as the Aztecs. Christian ethics commands " love your enemies," but vengeance is the solemn duty of the heathen savage. On the other hand, the moral code of primitive communistic societies would not tolerate our ethics of individual property rights. Thus we see that morality is a social, rather than an individual, valuation. From this point of view, an individual should be called good or bad only in the light of his social environment. He is considered the most moral who best lives up to the ethical standards of his group — whatever they may be. Even the greatest moral philosophers of antiquity, like Confucius and Socrates, must be considered in the light of their age and civilization. Individual morality is a greater or less variation from the standards of the group. Moreover, another social characteristic of morality lies in the fact that there may be two separate standards of conduct, — one applicable to members of the group and another applicable to outsiders. Thus, the savage might indiscriminately scalp those outside the group, but not his fellow tribesmen. Again, the colonists of America often regarded the Indian as an inferior creature who might be robbed of his lands, but they were most scrupulous in their ethical relations toward each other.

When primitive man develops beyond the stage of mere physical pleasure, he enters upon a period of morality more restrictive in character. In early civilizations, certain prohibitions thus come to be placed upon man's conduct, and obedience is secured through fear of punishment. But a civilization founded upon mere prohibition, like the " taboo " of the savage, is necessarily backward and unreasoning. It assumes that men are too wicked or ignorant to act positively for the attainment of definite objects. Primitive man was restrained from committing certain actions, inimical to group interests, through fear of punishment or social ostracism. In fact, our own recent and, perhaps, present method of suppressing crime by intimidation is the natural outgrowth of this theory of morality. The next stage of moral development is an advance over that of mere prohibition. When a certain social custom was seen to be partly good and partly bad, some scheme of discrimination was devised by the growing intelligence. This power of intellectual consideration showed that the group had advanced in its attitude toward human conduct. It may well be illustrated by Roman civilization in which the spirit of compromise was developed and handed down to later generations. The problem was. looked at from the social point of view, and an attempt was made to arrive at a course of conduct best suited to the general interest. The third stage in the development of morality represents a protest against this predominance of group interests. The individual begins to weigh his own importance and to set his interests against those of society. This view is well illustrated, to-day, by the attitude of the " conscientious objector," who really represents a survival of the older individualistic attitude toward conduct. Although well meaning, he is usually antagonistic to group interests. He does not seem to realize that the world is entering

*Four stages of progress.*

upon the threshold of a fourth stage of morality, — a morality of the world order. This is the international aspect of social morality. This morality is not only positive, striving for the attainment of definite ideals, but humanitarian, endeavoring to embrace within its operation all lands and peoples.

The great problem of morality, therefore, is that of reconciling the interests of the individual with those of society. The clash of selfish personal desires with social interests has been an agelong conflict. Early civilizations in their attempts to develop group morality frequently followed irrational folkways which, nevertheless, were rigidly enforced by law and religion. When primitive society was communistic, the conflict between individual and group interests was not so keen. With the growth of social classes, however, the few have claimed the right to decide what was best for the social interest. It thus happened that frequently their own ideas and interests colored the social fabric of human institutions. Against the formalism of the dominant classes, reformers and prophets have arisen to preach the falsity of current beliefs and practices. Thus, Socrates taught a nobler code of ethics than that of the Sophists, and the Founder of Christianity rebuked the Pharisees who followed the letter rather than the spirit of the law. Individuals, in advance of their age, have suffered martyrdom for insisting upon the right to follow the dictates of their own consciences when these came into conflict with the accepted ideas of society. Subsequent history discloses whether or not they have succeeded in their attempt to bring about a readjustment of the group morality to a higher level. However, those who

*Society and the individual.*

refuse to conform to the current morality may not only be those who rise above it, but also those who fall below it. Each age has not only its reformers but those who are egoistic, or even vicious enough, to insist upon the acceptance of their own point of view, irrespective of society's mandates. In the treatment of nonconformists, society must choose between a policy of toleration and one of repression. An inflexible civilization deals out the same fate, alike, to the misguided idealist and to the criminal; for the offense in both cases is one of nonconformity. A higher civilization strives to work out the problem of how an individual may obey the moral code of the group and at the same time follow the dictates of his conscience. In this manner, the group ethics becomes less rigid and more elastic. A constant moral readjustment must go on in a progressive society, the ideals of which are constantly advancing.

The origin of altruism may be traced to the biological fact of parenthood, and to the increasing length of the period of infancy. Its value in group survival **The rôle of** has been discussed in an earlier chapter. Co- **altruism.** operation, as well as conflict, has been a favorable element in the process of natural selection at work in human societies. The importance of this element has been ideally expressed in the thought that " the meek shall inherit the earth." But it is, nevertheless, true that man has had to struggle not only against his physical environment but also against his fellow men. Strong instincts of self-assertion still remain in the human breast. Along with the struggle for his own existence, however, went man's struggle for the lives of his fellows. Altruism and self-interest have clashed at times, but the former has steadily increased in importance. It has become more purposive in modern society, because it is directed by the growing human intelligence. Thus, slavery has disappeared in civilized lands. Modern altruism is content not merely with temporary alleviation of distress, but it seeks to banish the very causes of human misery. Again, the social circle within which altruism operates has constantly widened. Thus, sympathy is felt not only toward members of the family and clan, but toward fellow tribesmen and, finally, toward all members of the nation. Indeed, sympathy to-day, like culture and commerce, is international in its manifestations. Christianity is evolving a new world order. Generous help is extended to distressed Belgians and Armenians, as well as to those within our own national boundaries. Patriotism or love of country is an intensely national aspect of altruism and coöperation. The fires of war may bring to light the more primitive instincts of men and nations, but from the ashes, phœnix-like, will rise a humanitarianism greater than the world has ever before experienced.

**Moral Adjustment**. — If civilization is not to remain static, moral ideas must become more rational with every period of historical evolution. Constant readjustments are therefore necessary if higher levels of morality are to be attained. Viewed in this light, the moral systems of the past represented the attempts of their founders to bring the group morality up to the standard of the new social ideals. The process of adjustment was sometimes evolutionary and sometimes revolutionary. At the present time, through the development of Christian ideals, society is attempting to evolve a positive system of world morality. Repression must give

*The aim of adjustment.*

way to expression. The primitive "taboo" of early society may be well enough for ignorant savagery, but it is essentially antagonistic to the new world order. The morality of freedom should supersede that of compulsion without danger to the social order. This development is rendered difficult, however, by the growing complexity of society and by the multiplicity of human relationships. The individual must exercise an intelligent discrimination against those acts harmful to the social welfare. He must seek not merely to avoid a penalty, but rather to attain the happiness which lies in social well-being. This ideal is becoming the new basis of world morality. Professor Patten has shown that, not the avoidance of pain, but the attainment of pleasure is the need of modern society. Human nature is not so depraved that men will seek the evil rather than the good. It is the duty of society, therefore, to eliminate as far as possible social and economic ills in order that man may attain highest happiness. This objective method may be known as the moralization of man's environment. From the subjective side, the highest social ideals should be impressed upon the heart and mind of the growing individual.

Thus, a social morality of an ever-widening scope is the great need of the present age. In earlier times it was thought proper for the individual to flee from Social the wickedness of the world in order to save his morality. own soul. In monastic isolation, apart from his fellows, the ascetic of the Middle Ages sought to work out his own salvation. In the twentieth century, however, such conduct would be regarded as purely negative in the social good accomplished. The change of ideal is expressed in the poetic "Vision of Sir Launfal" who, in a burst of sympathetic altruism, saw at last the Holy Grail. Social morality does not underestimate individual goodness. Virtue is personal and a society can be only as moral as the individuals composing it. The modern view of morality does, however, evaluate the goodness or badness of an act by its social, rather than by its individual, consequences. Thus, a crime against society is of deeper significance than an individual vice; although society does not, for a single instant, condone the act of vice. When men lived in comparative isolation, a social morality was not so imperative. The modern age, however, is as social as our civilization is cosmopolitan. Books and newspapers disseminate all kinds of knowledge, while foreign commerce reaches to all parts of the globe. Although division of labor in modern industrial society makes individuals mutually dependent upon each other, this interdependence is remote and indirect. We have, for example, little direct communication with those who manufacture our foods, build our houses and make our laws. Who indeed, to-day, is our neighbor? He is invisible but effective. Hence the need of a wider and more far-reaching social morality. Men may hesitate to-day to rob orphans and widows, but they unblushingly sell goods of an inferior quality to the general public. The long-range crimes of the present century make necessary, therefore, a similar long-range morality. In conclusion, let us state that social morality insists that man is his brother's keeper and interprets in the widest possible sense the term " brother."

The Great Teacher, in defining the greatest law, added the corollary " Love thy neighbor as thyself." We are at present still far removed from this exalted ideal of humanitarianism; nor have we yet attained the new world order. The church, however, has always been an altruistic institution. Let us not forget that **The church** the medieval monks, whose asceticism we have **and social** mentioned, performed pioneer social work. By **reform.** practical example, they taught the dignity of manual labor as well as the art of philanthropy. Monasteries were retreats for the sick of body as well as for the sick of heart. Here were received the weary traveler, the orphan and the pauper. With the Renaissance and the breaking up of the medieval system, the spirit of individualism wrought changes in religious ideals. At present, too, it would seem that the church is going through another period of readjustment, for character rather than creed is being emphasized. Sectarianism declines with the rise of the ideal of social service. Thus, the twentieth century will witness the church fulfilling the mission of its Founder, spreading its altruistic spirit throughout society, and cementing once more the broken fabric of civilization. To accomplish this end, it will become the stanch ally of the family, the school and the state in their attack upon the obstacles that lie in the path of human progress. Such an alliance will be mutually helpful and the church itself will instill into the work of regeneration the vital spirit of hope and human sympathy.

## QUESTIONS FOR DISCUSSION

1. Do you think the belief of the savage in spirits is natural?
2. What was the purpose of magic? Illustrate.
3. Explain animism and the factors in its development.
4. Explain the existence of ancestor worship among many peoples.
5. What effect has the expansion of the group upon religion?

2 B

6. What does polytheism seek to explain? Illustrate from Greek history and mythology.

7. Contrast the religious conceptions of backward and advanced civilizations.

8. Explain the influence upon religion of the physical and social environment.

9. Explain the authority of the medicine man.

10. Discuss the historical importance and social position of the priests of ancient Egypt and Babylon.

11. Discuss the historical connection between church and state.

12. How was religion a factor in favor of group solidarity?

13. Trace the social origins and evolution of morality.

14. What is the effect of the *mores* of the group upon the conduct of the individual?

15. Explain four stages in moral progress.

16. Discuss two different classes of individual nonconformists to the current morality approved by the group.

17. What policies toward them may society follow?

18. In what way does modern altruism differ from the earlier altruism?

19. Why does progress necessitate a constant moral readjustment?

20. Why is a social morality especially necessary for the present age?

21. How do you think that it can best be taught?

22. Discuss the past philanthropic work of the church.

23. How do you explain the present readjustment of the church?

24. What is the church now doing for social welfare?

25. What is your church doing? What else can it do?

26. How may the church aid in teaching a social morality?

## TOPICS FOR SPECIAL REPORT

1. The medicine man among the American Indians.

2. The ancestor worship of the Romans and Chinese.

3. The social ethics of some great religious teachers (*e.g.* Buddha and Confucius).

4. The heretic of the Middle Ages.

5. The separation of church and state (*e.g.* in France, England and Italy).

6. The church as a factor in social progress.

## REFERENCES

Ross, E. A.  "Sin and Society."

Ross, E. A.  "Social Control."

Patten, S. N.  "New Basis of Civilization."

Patten, S. N.  "The Social Basis of Religion."

Thompson, R. E.  "Divine Order of Human Society."

Stelzle, C.  "American Social and Religious Conditions."  Chapter XI.

Spencer, H.  "Principles of Sociology."

Dealey, J. Q.  "Sociology."  Chapter VII.

Hayes, E. C.  "Introduction to a Study of Sociology."  Morality — pp. 541 to 550; Religion — Chapter XXX.

Blackmar, F. W., and Gillin.  "Outlines of Sociology."  Chapters XI, XII, XIII.

Wright, C. D.  "A Practical Sociology."  The Church, pp. 72–76.

The separation of Church and state (e.g. in France, England and
Spain)

e. The Church as a factor in social progress.

## REFERENCES

Ross, E. A. Sin and Society.
Ross, E. A. Social Control.
Patten, S. N. New Basis of Civilization.
Patten, S. N. The Social Basis of Religion.
Thompson, R. L. Divine Order of Human Society.
............... America, Social and Religious Conditions. Chapter
XI.
Stuckenberg, H. Sociologie etc.
Bradley, J. O. Sociology. Chapter VII.
Blackmar, L. C. Introduction to a Study of Sociology. Morality
pp. 37-46 etc. Religion. Chapter XXXI.
Blackmar, F. W. and Gillin, J. C. Outlines of Sociology. Chapters
XLVII, XLII.
Wright, C. D. Practical Sociology. The Church etc. p. 276.

# INDEX

objections        in reld.

(1) With greater scurity methods the same land can produce several

(2) New lands have been open

(3) With the advance of civilization have a lower birth rate

Padrone system — number of persons under leadership of one master

Asiatic immigration
(1) biological ( Mongolian )
(2) social
(3) economic reason
(4) entirely of different culture

a state is a union of people inhabiting a definate area of land and self protection and unto the group.

1802 - The health & moral acts was Past in England. Children under 9 can not work in cotton factories and can not be bound. They were limited to 12 hr day. 1833 the working p̄ those under 13 ys old was 9 hr da or 48 hrs week. They were given the average two hours school day. Prevented into work p̄ those under 18. 1847 Provided the 10 hour day for women & young persons

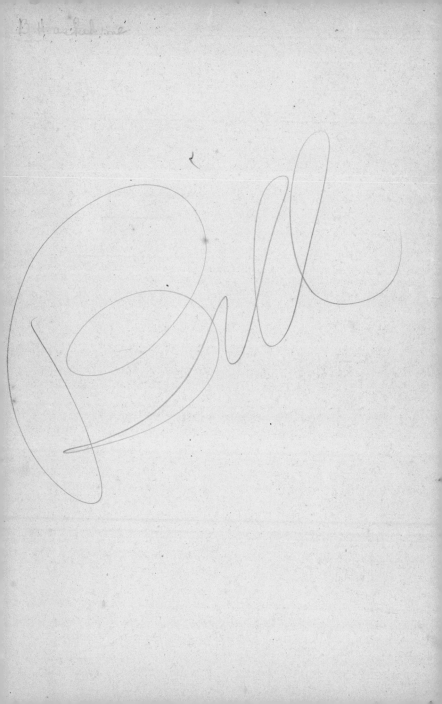

**Date Due**